THE READER'S GUIDE
TO
INTELLIGENCE PERIODICALS

THE READER'S GUIDE

TO

INTELLIGENCE PERIODICALS

HAYDEN B. PEAKE

NIBC PRESS

National Intelligence Book Center

Washington DC

6-17-93

20

Library of Congress Cataloging-in-Publication Data
Peake, Hayden B., 1932-
The reader's guide to intelligence periodicals / by Hayden B. Peake
p. cm.
Includes bibliographical references and index.
ISBN: 1-878292-01-3 (lib. bdg.) : $29.95 (est.).
— ISBN: 1-878292-00-5 (pbk.) : $19.95 (est.)
1. Intelligence service—Periodicals—Handbooks, manuals, etc.
I. Title.
JF1525.I6P43 1992
016.32712'05—dc20   91-42046
                                          CIP

Manufactured in the United States of America
January 1992

10 9 8 7 6 5 4 3 2 1

FIRST EDITION

For Joan, Leslie, Graham, and Kelly

TABLE OF CONTENTS

PERIODIC BIBLIOGRAPHIES
OF INTELLIGENCE LITERATURE

FOREWORD

In 1955, Sherman Kent, long time head of the CIA's Office of National Estimates and a leading writer on the craft of intelligence, wrote a trenchant monograph entitled *The Need for an Intelligence Literature*. In it he noted that, since World War II, intelligence had become "not merely a profession, but like most professions it had taken on the aspects of a discipline:... What it lacks is a literature." What Kent could not have imagined was the plethora of books on intelligence which was to come; a small number of these books are excellent; some are good to fair; and some are just dreadful or inaccurate. So it has continued to this day.

Then something unexpected happened. Many of the intelligence veterans of World War II began to retire, and as they did, they formed "alumni" organizations, such as the Association of Former Intelligence Officers (AFIO), and the Central Intelligence Retirees' Association (CIRA). Similar organizations, like the Naval Intelligence Professionals, were formed by retired military intelligence personnel. These groups complemented existing associations of former counterintelligence, and communications intelligence. In nearly all cases these organizations spawned periodic house organs which carry historical articles on some phase of intelligence, plus the usual "chapter notes" on their activities. But, more importantly, these house organs also carry reviews of recent intelligence books so that their readership may be aware of the current works in their profession, whether good, bad or indifferent. Many of the reviews are written by experts in the fields covered by these volumes, and they bring particular importance to these periodic publications.

In addition to the above, a new category of intelligence periodicals began to appear — those published by groups not affiliated with former government agencies and edited by persons who, with some notable exceptions, had not been involved formally with the profession. Among these publications are newsletters and scholarly journals that contain articles of historical and current intelligence interest, and, above all, often knowledgeable reviews of the current intelligence literature. Also included in this category are periodicals with a new-left anti-intelligence slant, where the articles and other contributions reveal a distinct bias against the Intelligence Community — even strong urgings toward the Community's abolition.

The interest in intelligence matters has even spread to learned journals outside the profession where articles had seldom appeared before. Consequently, there are now (would Sherman Kent ever have believed it!) about one hundred and fifty such publications, pro, con, and neutral — from well-known to obscure. Aside from the difficulty of learning about them, one important point to remember is that the quality of the articles and reviews tends to be uneven. How does one wade through this minefield?

Until now the readers and researchers have been left to their own devices in sorting out these matters. Fortunately, we have here *The Reader's Guide to Intelligence Periodicals* by Hayden B. Peake, a thorough-going professional in the field, which will ease their burden substantially. In this unique and painstaking work, Peake has produced a guide to each of the roughly one hundred and fifty publications setting forth what it is that each of them tells us, and in most cases describing the origins of the publication, identifying the editors and indicating how it can be obtained. His book divides the publications into categories of intelligence periodicals, intelligence-related periodicals, those no longer in print but still of interest, and those that more than occasionally contain intelligence articles. His annotations for each entry are particularly important as a guide.

One can but imagine the long hours that have been spent in producing so meticulous a volume. As the writer of this Foreword, I am lost in admiration of the care and patience which produced this most necessary aid. Without it, one could well be lost in the morass of all these works. Now, at least, we have some guide-posts in this field. No intelligence professional's library should be without it; nor can university libraries afford not to have it on their reference shelves. It is an indispensable tool, especially for those ever growing numbers of faculty members who are teaching courses and seminars on Intelligence.

It is now several decades ago that a famous American rare book collector wrote in the preface to his library's catalogue:

"Let him who has any conceit as to his accuracy attempt to write a catalogue." Here the word conceit means pride. It is not pride as to his accuracy alone that has led Hayden Peake to produce so exacting a guide for us. It is also his willingness to take the time to dig out the titles and facts which make this a valuable contribution to one corner of the literature of intelligence, its strengths and short comings, as revealed in the entries in this *Reader's Guide*.

I think Sherman Kent would have been very pleased indeed.

Walter L. Pforzheimer
Washington, D.C.

ACKNOWLEDGMENTS

The task of finding and describing the intelligence and intelligence-related periodicals included below was both immensely enjoyable and agreeably frustrating. Enjoyable because of the learning and new people encountered, and frustrating because change in the intelligence periodical field is frequent and not always widely announced. To spread the joy and ease the burden, considerable help was sought and forthcoming — it contributed greatly to the final product.

Special thanks go to the editors and staff members with whom I spoke or corresponded for giving their time and comments. They are identified in the sections on their periodical.

A number of colleagues contributed comments and assistance in identifying and procuring little known and hard to find periodicals. Thus my thanks and appreciation to Marjorie Cline, Todd Leventhal, Daniel Mulvenna, Herbert Romerstein, and Thomas F. Troy.

The task of reading and commenting on the manuscript was accomplished by Russell J. Bowen, Samuel Halpern, David Kahn, George Constantinides, Nigel West and Walter Pforzheimer (who also contributed the Foreword). Merely acknowledging these contributions doesn't adequately express my gratitude.

Elizabeth Bancroft merits singular recognition not only because she carefully edited the final draft, or because she was so helpful in finding copies of the periodicals themselves. More than that, she has seen fit to make this volume her first venture into the world of book publishing. For each of these reasons I am deeply grateful to her.

All the assistance notwithstanding, I, of course, bear full responsibility for the results.

PREFACE

The need for an annotated reader's guide to intelligence and intelligence related periodicals became apparent while teaching at the Defense Intelligence College. Knowing what information is in the public domain, the open literature, is an important function of both intelligence and scholarship even when the subject is intelligence itself. The function of the *Reader's Guide to Intelligence Periodicals (RGIP)* is to identify and briefly describe periodical sources of intelligence-related information.[1]

Toward that end, the *RGIP* provides background and comments on the perspective, content, and authority of the publications. In all cases the *RGIP* includes basic publication and subscription data. Only those periodicals printed in English have been mentioned. In a few cases periodicals have been included, like *Intelligence* (see page 201), which at first glance appear to be related to the intelligence profession, but which on examination are devoted to other pursuits. They are mentioned just to make this point.

The table of contents lists the titles alphabetically by category to speed selection. The general content of each category is described in the **Periodical Categories** section of the Introduction. Specific comments on each category are made at the beginning of each section.

The source of the publication information presented in the *RGIP* is the periodical concerned. Comments, sometimes in quotation marks, on publication history, policy, future plans,

---

1. As used in the RGIP, the term **intelligence** is context dependent and refers as appropriate to the usually secret process or practice of information collection and analysis, and the resultant reports and their dissemination to the authorized consumer for national security purposes. It also includes those practices of counterintelligence, security, etc., by which one protects secrets and prevents adversaries from obtaining them. Finally, intelligence also encompasses covert action, a complex process of secret assistance and/or influence given to or exerted on another government or movement in which the the role of the sponsoring agency is not acknowledged. In most cases, to avoid confusion, the various forms of intelligence are specifically identified.

etc., come from the editor or staff concerned unless otherwise identified. Owing to the vicissitudes of the market economy, prices and other publication details may change from those mentioned herein.

During the writing of the *RGIP* the question arose as to how to handle periodicals which at various times echo pre-coup Soviet policy, political views, historical explanations, and disinformation themes. I decided that the analysis of articles and editorials inside a magazine or newsletter was outside the scope of the *RGIP*. In three instances (*LOBSTER, Top Secret* and *Intelligence Newsletter*), however, the possibility of some form of Soviet-related support came up during discussions with the editors involved. All vigorously maintained their total independence. In *LOBSTER's* case, an allegation in the British press that Soviet support, or *Moscow Gold*, was involved, was explicitly denied.

One of the most surprising headlines found during the preparation of this work read: "KGB Officially Abolished." The announcement went on to say that in place of the KGB three new and separate organs are created: (1) "the USSR central intelligence service," formerly the KGB's First Chief Directorate, (2) "the interrepublican security service," formerly the KGB's Second Chief Directorate, (3) the "committee for guarding the USSR state border...," formerly the KGB Border Guards Directorate. Since the events mentioned in the periodicals described herein occurred while the KGB, or one of its predecessors existed, none of the new titles are used.

There are very likely other publications which have escaped my attention that deserve mention. Any suggestions will be gratefully received as will comments on other aspects of the *RGIP*, including errors.

HBP
Alexandria, Virginia
December, 1991

INTRODUCTION

Most current periodicals devoted to intelligence are a product of the late 1960s and 1970s when they began supplementing newspapers and television as sources of information about this increasingly controversial government activity. One of the earliest in America was the now defunct magazine called, *CounterSpy*. According to Philip Agee, *"CounterSpy* was the quarterly magazine of... The Organizing Committee for a Fifth Estate. Norman Mailer... started the magazine in 1973...."[2] It was this anti-establishment quarterly that helped define what intelligence bibliographer George C. Constantinides has called the "literature of discontent."[3] *CounterSpy* was also the first to publish a list of alleged "CIA officers," including the one that named Richard Welch (shown serving in Lima, Peru), who was later assassinated in Athens in December 1975.[4]

In that same year, the late David Atlee Phillips and some of his colleagues founded what became the Association of Former Intelligence Officers (AFIO).[5] Their purpose was to help create

2. Philip Agee, *On The Run* (Lyle Stuart, 1987), p. 100. The *CounterSpy* masthead contradicts Agee on some points. The magazine was originally published (March 1973, Vol 1, #1) as a monthly by the *Committee for Action/Research on the Intelligence Community (CARIC)*. A 19 July 1973 *Village Voice* article by Nat Hentoff mentions trying to contact Mailer for support without success. Issues 2 (May 73) & 3 (Fall 73), were also published by *CARIC*. A combined issue (Vol 1, #s 4 & 5) copyrighted in 1974 but undated, listed *CounterSpy* as the *Journal of the Organizing Committee for the Fifth Estate,* though Mailer is not mentioned. Issues #1 & 2, Vol 2, indicated the magazine was published by the *Fifth Estate Security Education, Inc.* Variations of these publisher names were used subsequently.
3. Mr. Constantinides used the term "literature of discontent" in a paper, discussing books on the WWII Office of Strategic Services (OSS), given at the National Archives, Washington, DC, on 12 July 1991.
4. According to Agee, op. cit., p. 100-101, *CounterSpy* compiled their lists based on instructions found in John Marks's article, "How to Spot a Spook," published in the November 1974 issue of the *Washington Monthly*. Richard Welch's name had previously appeared in Julius Mader's, *Who's Who in CIA*, in 1968, but it was the mention in *CounterSpy* (Vol. 2, #2, Winter 1975, pp. 23-27) that got the credit, deserved or not, for drawing attention to him in Greece.
5. AFIO began as the Association of Retired Intelligence Officers (ARIO)

an informed public on intelligence matters, and one step toward this end was the AFIO newsletter, *PERISCOPE*, which began publication in August 1975. Since then over 75 other intelligence and intelligence-related newsletters, magazines, journals and several digital intelligence-related databases have emerged, although a few included in the *RGIP* were started before WWII.

During this period a number of other periodicals devoted to related subjects began to publish articles on intelligence and these too are included in the *RGIP*, bringing the total number of entries to 155. They have been grouped into categories which are described below.

The question of content reliability is an important factor and I have found no hard and fast rule to apply to the periodicals discussed herein that will rate them is this regard. Some provide no indication of sources and stake reliability on reputation. Others give complete citations or short title sources with name and date of publication. Still others use a mix of the two and some offer source details upon request. And although I have commented on this point in most of the principal entries, if the article or issue concerned is important to your argument, then as a matter of prudence, verify it by checking the reference or find an independent source, no matter who wrote it.

While most of the periodicals herein do not presuppose expertise in a particular profession, an interest in national security, international relations, history and some aspect of intelligence (pro or con) is assumed. Some cryptologic publications, those dealing with electronic warfare and other technical matters do assume specialty knowledge, but most also have articles of interest to beginners. It is hoped that the *RGIP* will help newcomers and the more experienced in the field to become familiar with what is available and where to find it.

The problem of getting your hands on a particular periodical is for the most part straightforward, but a few can be difficult. Some come only with employment or membership in an organization. Others are available by subscription (or 'donations'), from selected newsstands, and some mainly in libraries. Fortunately, nearly all are in the Library of Congress

and changed its name in 1977.

(exceptions are noted). Each entry provides an address to which the reader may write for details on this question. Where paid subscriptions are available, costs range from $5.00 to $6000.00 per year (corporate); most are less than $50.00. Three, the *NATIONAL SECURITY LAW REPORT (NSLR)* of the ABA (see page 161), the *PROPAGANDA - DISINFORMATION - PERSUASION (PDP)* series from Boston University (see page 112), and the CIA *FACT BOOK ON INTELLIGENCE* are available at no cost (see page 176).

Publication frequency for magazines and newsletters varies from weekly to annually. A few, mostly bibliographies, are published less frequently or even irregularly. Further details are given in each description and may also be obtained from the publications directly.

PERIODICAL CATEGORIES IN THE *RGIP*

Eight types or categories of periodical are included in the *RGIP*. The first covers 50 publications that deal primarily with intelligence writings, history, and practice in any of its forms. The second category contains 25 periodicals whose primary focus is topically related to intelligence and which frequently include articles on the subject. Example topics in this category are national security, international relations, and military history.

The third group lists four periodicals whose distribution is limited in some fashion, though unclassified issues can be obtained and are worth knowing more about. Excluded from this category (or any other category) are those available only to former members of the retirement organizations of the CIA, FBI, Secret Service, NSA, and the like.

The fourth category includes comments on 13 periodicals no longer published. Each dealt with some aspect of the intelligence practice. The introduction to the section also mentions several series of intelligence articles which appeared in now defunct general reader magazines. In both cases, magazine or article, the reader may wish to consider these sources for reference or research.

The fifth division is a list of 50 periodicals, exclusive of the popular news weeklies, which publish worthwhile articles of intelligence interest from time to time, but not at a frequency that warrants inclusion in category two.

The sixth section of the *RGIP* presents 4 periodic bibliographies of books and articles on intelligence. Three are softbound books. The fourth is in digital form and is available for use on a personal computer (PC) with a hard disk.

The seventh category first discusses four intelligence databases and one bulletin board, in digital form, that can be accessed and used on a PC. Each is changed or updated at varying times and is thus considered a periodical in the broad sense of the term. A section of the electronic bulletin board concerns espionage and related topics. Two of the paper newsletters described elsewhere in the **RGIP** can also be accessed on a PC monitor with this system (see **NEWSNET** page 246). The other two "periodicals" are intelligence databases called **NAMEBASE** and **CIABASE** (see pages 230 and 225), the computer based members of the "literature of discontent."

The eighth category of the **RGIP** is concerned with five commercial computer databases that offer ways, outside a visit to the library, to access the many newspapers, journals, dissertations, and magazines that mention books and contain articles and papers concerning various domestic and foreign intelligence activities. Some periodicals, like *The New York Times* and *The Washington Post*, publish indexes and are mentioned in the computer databases described. Five items in this category also index some of the weekly news magazines and offer a variety of services to make articles available to subscribers with personal computers and a modem. Several predictions about these databases can be made with near certainty. First, they are updated and expanded regularly. Second, the costs associated with using them change frequently but in small increments, so the figures given here must be taken as starting points. Finally, they are the wave of the furture — becoming familiar with their use will enhance research efficiency — and they are fun.

INTELLIGENCE PERIODICALS

The 50 periodicals (11 foreign) in this category include newsletters, magazines and journals concerned with various aspects of the practice of intelligence. Some are widely known, the existence of others may be a surprise. They are published by private, commercial, and government organizations that span much of the political spectrum. Their physical and editorial quality varies widely, but no fixed correlation with content quality has been observed. They range from the well written, glossy, multi-color publications like *Jane's Intelligence Review* (see page 83) to the newsprint of *UNCLASSIFIED* (see page 131) and *CRYPTOLOG* (see page 37) to the xeroxed single spaced communication like the *Covert Intel Letter* (see page 36). Each has its message and the editors and staff are dedicated to getting it to the public, often under difficult conditions.

Where possible the *RGIP* annotations provide some historical background on the periodical, comment on the nature and reliability of the material presented, and then describe the general format, length, layout and subscription details of the publication. In cases where the political viewpoint or perspective is a factor in its very existence, that is made clear. Where errors of fact or omission have been noted examples may be mentioned if they follow a pattern or reflect a policy. Where comments, analysis or criticisms about periodicals in the *RGIP* are not footnoted, the views expressed reflect the author's judgments.

A few words on periodical content reliability (as distinct from analyses and conclusions) are warranted. As a rule, estimates of material or data reliability were reached by weighing the nature (primary, secondary, etc.) and application of the sources provided. The absence of sources is not necessarily construed as an indicator of unreliability and where this is standard practice for the periodical, some indication of track record is provided if available. But regardless of reputation or what is said herein, if a particular point is important to an argument the reader is advised to compare alternate sources.

AMERICAN INTELLIGENCE JOURNAL (AIJ)

The *AIJ* is a quarterly publication of the National Military Intelligence Association (NMIA), a non-government organization. Although described as a "magazine for intelligence professionals," its articles will be of interest to those concerned with national security. Contributions run the gamut of think pieces, first hand accounts, book reviews and expert analysis. Articles are generally attributed and documented; in some cases source citations are not printed but are available on request. Topics range from the problems of analyzing African military capabilities to dealing with Soviet espionage. The column on "Upcoming Topics" notes that the Winter 91/92 issue will focus on "Women In Intelligence."

A 1988 special issue on "Intelligence Leaks," contained comments by journalists William Burrows and Bob Woodward; Congressmen Henry Hyde, Louis Stokes and George Brown; Robert Gates, then Deputy Director of Central Intelligence, plus the views of a number of senior military officers.

Certain basic themes recur in order to keep the professional up-to-date. To meet this requirement issues regularly include articles on counterintelligence (CI), HUMINT, SIGINT, and imagery intelligence. A 1989 special issue on CI as seen from the top contained articles by the chiefs of the various intelligence services and agencies. The Spring 1990 topics were espionage and treason with contributions by academics and intelligence officers. The article on the problem of "Prosecuting Spies: An Uneasy Alliance of Security, Ethics and Law," by Navy Captain M.E. Bowman is particularly timely and interesting. The principal theme of the Winter 1991 issue was "Intelligence Deception," and it contained 11 articles and 10 book reviews on the subject. Examples include expert historical contributions like the "Revolutionary War Deception," by MGEN (Ret) Edmund R. Thompson, Natalie Grant's account of "The Trust," and Col. David Glantz's article on "Soviet Military Deception in WWII." There were also post war overviews like "Deception & Special Operations," by Capt. Edward R. McClesky, USAF, and "Warning and Deception," by Cynthia M. Grabo. A look at the future of deception studies is found in "Studying Strategic Deception" by CMDR George Witt, USN.

While the tone of *AIJ* is definitely pro-intelligence, opposing views are included. For example, pro-leakers advocate, Bob Woodward, argues in an interview that the journalist can and should make the decision on what is classified and what should be printed in the open press, though he graciously agrees to consider the source's views on the matter.

AIJ has an 8 1/2 x 11" format, usually contains from 50-70 pages and is printed in B & W with photos, charts etc. as appropriate. Copies can be found in most military and industrial, but few public, libraries. Submission of articles is encouraged and in this respect it serves as an excellent forum for professionals and beginners. Subscriptions come with NMIA membership which is open to active and retired military, reservists, industry, academics and others interested in the subject. Membership rates vary with category from $11.00 to $25.00 per year. For further information write NMIA, Pentagon Station, P.O. Box 46583, Washington, D.C. 20050-6583, or call the Journal Editor, Roy K. Jonkers, Col. USA (Ret), 301-294-8500.

BACK CHANNELS
A Journal of Espionage, Assassinations and Conspiracy

BACK CHANNELS was one of the projects on Editor Peter Kross's "someday I'll do it" list — and now he's done it. The premier issue of this new quarterly appeared in November 1991. Mr. Kross is a free-lance author who has published in the *IJIC* (see page 78) in addition to newspapers and magazines. His intent with *BACK CHANNELS* is to provide a source of articles for the layman, and laywomen, interested in the topics.

Working toward this goal, Mr. Kross has carefully carved out a slice of the intelligence literature domain which for the most part is not being attended to elsewhere. *BACK CHANNELS* is distinguished from intelligence newsletters and other journals by the inclusion of 10 relatively short nonfiction articles in each 30 page issue. Maximum length is about 1200 words (4 double spaced pages), no footnotes. Sources, if identified, are mentioned in the text. Further individual research will be necessary if more detail or verification is required.[6]

The principal subject categories are intelligence, in all its contexts (collection, analysis, espionage, counterespionage, etc.), conspiracies and assassinations. Articles will range over

---

6. This approach is found in several of the periodicals mentioned in the *RGIP*. A good place to start for additional detail on American intelligence subjects is George O'Toole's *The Encyclopedia of American Intelligence and Espionage: From The Revolutionary War to the Present* (New York: Facts On File, 1988). There is no foreign equivalent of O'Toole's book (in English), but a reasonable starting point would be Vincent and Nan Buranelli's *Spy/Counter-Spy: An Encyclopedia of Espionage* (New York: McGraw-Hill Book Company, 1982), and the more recent though less comprehensive *SPYCLOPAEDIA* by Richard Deacon (New York: Morrow, 1987). Each of these books has additional references, mostly secondary.

the entire temporal and geographical spectrum in an effort to inform readers about the historical and contemporary role of intelligence and related fields. The first issue has articles on "FDR's Spies," "JFK and the French Connection," and "The Las Vegas Skimming Conspiracy."

BACK CHANNELS will also contain short reviews of both fiction and nonfiction books. The inclusion of works of fiction provides review-writers with a forum not available in most *RGIP* entries. The nonfiction reviews, of course, will compete with the other periodicals described in the *RGIP*. Book reviewers will receive a complimentary copy of the book and $10.00.

The name *BACK CHANNELS* was chosen by Kross from a list of intelligence terms. It is meant to suggest an alternative channel for learning about the subjects and has no political or other connotations.

Organizationally, *BACK CHANNELS* is a "mom and pop" production, with Mrs. Kross serving as the production manager. It is lettersize, three column black on white with photos when appropriate. Topic related advertising is planned.

BACK CHANNELS is available only by subscription ($13.00/year, 4 issues), with no single or complimentary introductory copy option. Authors interested in contributing articles or reviews are encouraged to write for guidelines and details on compensation rates. For subscriptions and further information write *BACK CHANNELS*, P.O. Box 9, Franklin Park, NJ 08823-0009, or call 908-297-7923.

BRITISH STUDY GROUP ON INTELLIGENCE (BSGI)
(NEWSLETTER)

When a copy of this newsletter arrived I promptly examined all twelve pages for the masthead, editorial credits and subscription data box looking for the statement of purpose, organizational sponsor, and publication data. After completing the task, the conclusion was inescapable; there is no masthead, list of editorial credits or subscription information — these topics are totally ignored. The emphasis is on information. There is a reference to the editor and as it turned out, his name is mentioned (Dr. Richard Aldrich, University of Salford), but not with that title (or any other). Leave it to the British to think of such a clever cover.

After a few phone calls the logical explanation here too was forthcoming; no need for these administrative details, those for whom the newsletter was initially intended are quite aware of the particulars. When an expression of interest from abroad was made clear, the blanks were filled in.

The British Study Group on Intelligence was formed in the mid 1980s and modeled after an American organization called the Consortium for the Study of Intelligence (CSI) [see page 21]. Both groups seek to advance the study of intelligence as a component of government, international relations and history. The *BSGI*, unlike its American forerunner, publishes a newsletter whose proper name is, *STUDY GROUP ON INTELLIGENCE (SGOI)*. It is aimed at students and scholars in the UK who teach, or are considering teaching, courses in intelligence. But it will be of interest to scholars and students of intelligence everywhere.

The *SGOI* newsletter provides information not available elsewhere in one place. This includes comments on courses in intelligence in UK universities; descriptions of archival materials (in the UK and USA); a bibliography of recently published books, articles, and theses (world wide selection), and announcements on forthcoming conferences and seminars.

Each of the issues to date of *SGOI* contributes to a "directory of the teaching of intelligence in the United Kingdom either as a full course or as a component." In the former category there is a masters level degree program in Intelligence and International Relations at the University of Salford. Unfortunately, there is no comparable private program in the United States, but for those interested, this is a good model. Examples of senior undergraduate courses include those taught by Dr. R. Jeffreys-Jones at the University of Edinburgh on American Secret Intelligence and American Espionage. British Intelligence Operations and Organizations are covered in courses given at Cambridge and Dublin City University.

A feature of the newsletter of interest to American scholars is the detailed descriptions of intelligence archives. For example, the Archives Centre at Churchill College, Cambridge, contains materials on Montgomery Hyde, Admiral Sir Reginald Hall, A.G. Denniston, and Room 40, to name just a few. The Liddell Collection at the University of Leeds contains material on World War I intelligence including first hand accounts of MI5 "counter-espionage" activities.

The list of published and upcoming books and theses includes, Samir al-Khalil's, *Republic Of Fear: The Politics Of Modern Iraq* (Berkeley, CA: University of California Press, 1989), 300 pp., which is concerned with Iraqi internal security. A thesis by R.J. Saver, "The KGB's German Surrogate: Active Measures," Boston College, 1984, is also worth attention.

The *SGOI* newsletter is published about twice yearly. It is austere, black and white, double column (8 1/4" x 12"), and informative. Subscriptions are available for £4.00 from Dr. Kenneth Robertson, University of Reading, Whiteknights, P.O. Box 218, Reading RG6 2AA, England.

CAMPUS WATCH (CW)

In its February 1989 premier issue, *CW* states that it "seeks to raise the awareness of intelligence activities concerning the academic community." Despite this general purpose, every article and the editorial in its 12 (8 1/2 x 11) pages is devoted to opposing the CIA and only the CIA, in its campus recruiting program. Any possible confusion on this point was clarified in a July 15, 1989 letter to subscribers from co-editor Vernon Elliot who stated that *CW* is "a newsletter on the specialized and obscure topic of 'CIA in Academia'."

Nevertheless, for those concerned with the role of intelligence in society, *CW* provides a definite viewpoint that must be considered on its merits. In the first issue, the signed articles are all by one of the co-editors, Mr. Elliot and Philip Agee, Jr; none are sourced. Topics covered include campus anti-CIA demonstrations and the CIA Officer-In-Residence Program. Opposing views, from the CIA, are presented and the Agency telephone contact is given.

The signed editorial by co-editor, Philip Agee, Jr., has many of the right ideas, as when he writes of the "obligation to strive for the truth and defend it from falsehood." But these noble words should be read in the context of other articles that applaud, among other extracurricular activities, the use of "stink bombs" and that characterize the CIA as "Murder Incorporated." A more accurate indication of *CW*'s agenda is found in the four page interview with CIA defector, Philip Agee, Sr.

Unlike many of the other periodicals reviewed herein, the credentials of the authors, despite Agee Jr.'s derivative celebrity, are not immediately apparent and *CW* does not enlighten the reader on this point. On the basis of the content, however, one might reasonably surmise that Philip Agee, Sr. plays a silent partner authority role.

CW may also prove to be a source for learning of relatively obscure left wing books on intelligence or intelligence related subjects. Philip H. Melanson's *The Murkin Conspiracy: An Investigation into the Assassination of Dr. Martin Luther King, Jr.*, is reviewed in the Spring 1990 issue. It examines the "possibility of Intelligence involvement" in the King assassination. The same issue contains an excerpt from the *CIA Off-Campus Handbook*, a guide to anti CIA civil disobedience on campus.[7]

Upcoming issues, says *CW*, will contain articles on "Project MKULTRA: The CIA and Mind Control Research," and more contemporary subjects such as "Harvard Discusses it Officer-in-Residence Program" (see Vol II, No. 2.), and "College Courses in Intelligence."

CW was initially planned to be published four times during the academic year. But in the letter mentioned above, the editors reveal that publication frequency has been changed to once a semester to provide "a substantial improvement in the quantity and quality of information in each issue." This will not, however, affect the number of issues received per subscription, four for those who initially subscribed. Students and faculty are encouraged to "submit articles or opinion pieces concerning intelligence related activities on their campus."

Current subscription rates are $6.00 per year (2 issues), or $10.00 for 2 years (4 issues). Institutions add $6.00. Requests for more information on subscriptions and other submissions should be sent to: *Campus Watch*, P.O. Box 9623, Warwick, RI 02889. **NOTE**: the telephone number [212-569-0069] given on the masthead of *Campus Watch* is incorrect. The correct number as of September 1991, is 312-939-0675; ask for Deborah Crawford.

---

7.   Philip H. Melanson's *The Murkin Conspiracy: An Investigation into the Assassination of Dr. Martin Luther King, Jr.* (New York: Praeger, 1989); Ami Chen Mills, *CIA Off-Campus Handbook*, (Chicago Il: Chicago Bill of Rights Foundation, 1989), 126 pp., Introduction by Philip Agee.

CASIS NEWSLETTER

The Canadian Association for Security and Intelligence (CASIS) is an organization of academics, intelligence professionals and interested members of the public, committed to the study of the intelligence services." It traces its inspiration to Georgetown professor Roy Godson's Consortium for the Study of Intelligence (CSI), and its genesis to a 1984 conference at Glendon College in Toronto, co-sponsored by the CSI and the York University strategic studies program. The first issue of *CASIS Newsletter* appeared the same year.[8]

An issue typically includes a selection from items like "The Canadian Intelligence Scene," notes on teaching intelligence, notices of upcoming intelligence conferences, a summary of on-going research, a bibliography of intelligence books and papers, and feature articles. The bibliographic items frequently include books not always picked up in American newsletters or journals, such as the book by Andre Gerolymatos, *Espionage and Treason: A Study of the Proxima in Political and Military Intelligence Gathering in Classical Greece* (Amsterdam, Holland: Gieben, 1986).[9]

Typical of the feature articles is the contribution by Jean-Jacques Blais, "The Political Accountability of Intelligence Agencies — Canada."[10] Counter-terrorism is a frequent subject of the *CASIS Newsletter*, probably because of the

8. *CASIS Newsletter*, combined issues #s 6 & 7, Feb. 1987, page 1. The Consortium for the Study of Intelligence does not publish a newsletter, but it has published a series of books on intelligence. For further details write, CSI, 1730 Rhode Island Ave., NM, Washington, D.C. 20036 (202) 429-0129).

9. *CASIS Newsletter*, No. 6 & 7, Feb 1987, p. 18.

10. Ibid., No. 11, November 1988.

responsibilities of the Canadian Security and Intelligence Service (CSIS). CSIS, a relatively new service still evolving, also gets attention as it comes to grips with its mission and parliamentary oversight.[11] In this vein "The Role of the Inspector General of CSIS" (December 1990) will be of interest. The same issue presents views on the controversial topic, "Does Canada Need A Secret Intelligence Service to Operate Abroad?" The articles are usually but not always signed and some appear without sources. In either case, the reliability track record is good.

The current editor of the *Newsletter*, Professor Jean-Paul Brodeur of the University of Montreal, succeeded Professor Wesley Wark, University of Toronto. The first issue under Professor Brodeur contains a review of the CSIS Act and the Security Offenses Act, with extracts of testimony on, inter alia, "the parliamentary role in the system of accountability." Oversight may be coming to Ottawa. The issue also contains an article by CIA officer Arthur Hulnick on the CIA experience with a Public Affairs Office.

Submission of articles by members is encouraged. Subscriptions (three issues) come with annual membership: Canadians $17.00, those outside Canada must add $5.00. The *CASIS Newsletter* provides an excellent way for Americans to keep informed about intelligence activities up north. For membership details write to CASIS, Professor Geoffrey R. Weller, University of Northern British Columbia, Box 1050, Station A, Prince George, British Columbia, Canada V5L 5E3: tel (604) 564-4844, FAX (604) 564-3777.

---

11. *CASIS Newsletter*, Spero Meliora, "The Right Stuff," No. 11, November 1988, pp. 20-21.

CIA OFF CAMPUS
National Clearinghouse

In March 1991 a copy of *CIA Off Campus* was distributed to subscribers of *Campus Watch*. It is described as the "First Annual Update From The CIA Off Campus Clearinghouse." A letter to "Dear Activists and Supporters," notes that the organization's goal is to "put an end to covert operations as an instrument of U.S. foreign policy." Students are encouraged to lead the fight.

This issue of *CIA Off Campus* contains 11 pages of articles (plus one for the address), advertisements, notices, campus activity reports, and news items. Most but not all the items, despite the title, are about the ways to struggle against the CIA. There are also several directed at the FBI.

The first article, "The CIA and the US Role in the Gulf War," argues that "Philip Agee believes there is mounting evidence that 'George Bush and his entourage wanted the Iraqi invasion of Kuwait, encouraged it, and the refused to prevent it when they could have." It goes on to defend Iraq's invasion while stating that Iraq was given no warning that "the U.S. would oppose an Iraqi  takeover." "Why would the U.S. seek a world crisis?" asks author Deborah Crawford. She replies, "To know the full story of how Agee answers this question you will have to read [his] article, order his video taped speech or bring him to your city to speak." Some hints are provided which include the "S&L scandal" and the "peace dividend."

A column called "TIP SHEET for staff organizers," contains a piece by Sheila O'Donnell, titled "Common Sense Security." Ms. O'Donnell is described as a "Maryland based investigator with more than a decade's experience on civil liberties cases, [and] a co-founder of the *Public Eye* Magazine. Her advice is mainly a list of steps to be taken to assure personal security. They include, "Don't talk to the FBI (or any government investigator) without your lawyer present," Don't hire a strange messenger," Don't gossip on the phone," "Debrief yourself after each incident," and "Brief your membership on known or suspected surveillance."

One advertisement mentions that "The Clearinghouse database includes all schools doing anti-CIA work. Types of CIA presence and student actions on each campus are regularly updated. Useful reports and statistics can be generated. (For security reasons the database is not for sale.)" Other items mentioned include "panels, speakers, and workshops," an "educational package," a "Do It Yourself Handbook," and a hotline: 312-427-4559. Another ads offers a 45 minute "Philip Agee Video" (profits to the Agee defense committee).

Recently published books and periodicals are listed along with ordering information. The periodicals are all described in the *RGIP (Campus Watch, Unclassified, and Covert Action Information Bulletin)*. One of the books, John Stockwell's latest *The Praetorian Guard*, is mentioned in more glowing terms here than in *Unclassified*.

Listed under the title "Real Human Effects of U.S. Covert Actions (Total thousands of death, injuries and economic catastrophe impossible to estimate)" one finds country names and dates and various categories, but no data or other specifics about covert actions or deaths etc. This lack of specifics and sources is typical of the entire publication.

CIA Off Campus is "a project of The Bill of Rights Foundation" 523 S. Plymouth Court, Suite 800, Chicago, IL 60605. The newsletter is lettersize with purple ink on white stock. Subscriptions and requests for information should be sent to that address, or call 312-939-0675.

CLANDESTINE CONFIDENTIAL (CC)

CC is an "in" newsletter for radio operators and others interested in clandestine radio broadcasts whatever their source. It reports frequencies, language and time of broadcasts where available. *CC* is organized alphabetically by country, starting with Afghanistan and ending with Suriname. Fake transmissions are identified. Examples of coverage include broadcasts from Iran, the Nicaraguan resistance, and various communist programs (look for a decline here?) in all parts of the world.

If you are not already acquainted with radio terminology, you will need some help with the technical terms used in *CC*. Acronyms are not explained, sources of data are not always cited, and knowledge of technical jargon and station identifiers is assumed.

Editor, Gerry L. Dexter, has monitored short wave broadcasts for 30 years. He began *CC* in 1984 after writing a book on the subject.[12] For those who wish to find out for themselves what various clandestine movements, real and fake, are saying on the air, the information on how to do it is available here.

Radio broadcasts are not the only thing clandestine about *CC*. Publication frequency also falls in that category although it appears to be about four times a year. Issues are four pages (8 1/2 x 11"), typed and xeroxed. Subscriptions are $10.00 per year. For further information write, Gary L. Dexter, RR 4, Box 110, Lake Geneva, Wisconsin 53147.

---

12. Gerry L. Dexter, *Clandestine Confidential* (Columbus, OH: Universal Electronics, 1984).

COLLOQUY

COLLOQUY is the newsletter of The Security Affairs Support Association (SASA), an organization with the objective of "enhancing relationships and understanding among all those who support the national intelligence endeavor." In the eleven years of its existence SASA "has become a useful force in the Intelligence Community."

This is an unusual statement for a nongovernment organization, but its basis becomes clear with a glance at the board of directors and the program content. SASA president, E.C. "Pete" Aldridge, Jr. (Pres. McDonnell Douglas Electronic Systems Co.), serves a Board of Directors that includes Douglas Gow (serving FBI), The Honorable Richard J. Kerr (serving, Deputy Director of Central Intelligence), and Clarence E. Smith, Space Applications Corporation. Over the years the board positions have been filled by John N. McMahon (former CIA/DDCI), Robert Gates (former CIA/DDCI, currently NSC), LTG Harry E. Soyster, USA (Dir/DIA), VADM William O. Studeman, USN (DIRNSA), MGEN John Kulpa, USAF (Ret.), ADM. Bobby Inman, USN (Ret.), Robert Singel (former CIA) and Robert Kohler (former CIA, currently a TRW V.P.).

The major SASA programs include an annual award for contributions to the field of intelligence, symposia on intelligence and security issues, and the Security Support Program (considers industrial security problems). The 1989 symposium was held at NSA and devoted to "Treaty Monitoring and Verification." Previous symposia topics include, "Tactical Intelligence and Related Activities (TIARA)," "Software Trends in the Intelligence Community," and "Intelligence in Support of NATO."

COLLOQUY not only reports these program activities, it reprints talks by participants that often do not receive wide attention in the national media. One might be excused for suspecting that speeches in any public forum, by current and former members of the intelligence community, would lack a certain depth, critical analysis, or just plain substance, and could therefore be ignored. There is a degree of truth in this. Occasional speeches and reports in *COLLOQUY* ooze bureaucratic natural gas with familiar phrases like, "authority and responsibility will be pushed down through the management chain..." or "we're making a concerted effort too...," or we "will ensure that complex systems reflect the proper combination of cost, schedule and performance parameters" (without giving a clue as to how the proper combination would be recognized if it were achieved).

On the other hand, the norm for comments in *COLLOQUY* is just the opposite. Recent examples include remarks by General Colin Powell, USA, Chairman, JCS, on his "Vision of the Future," an article by former DCI James Schlesinger on "Energy and Geopolitics in the 21st Century," and "Protecting Secrets in the Changing Environment," by Maynard Anderson, Assistant Secretary of Defense, for Counterintelligence and Security.[13] Secretary Maynard's comments are a mixture of common sense, subtlety and wit which should be read by all concerned with the topic.

COLLOQUY averages about 20 pages. It is printed on glossy stock (white & brown, 8 1/2 x 11"). Currently in its 12th volume, some back issues are available. Subscriptions come with annual membership in SASA; candidates require sponsorship by a board member or two regular members. Rates vary with category. Individual government members, $40.00, individual non-government members $75.00; group memberships vary from $150.00 to $1500.00. For further details, write SASA, One National Business Park, Suite 110, Annapolis Junction, MD 20701, or call (301) 470-4445, (301) 470-4446, FAX (301) 604-6413.

---

13. *Colloquy*, February 1990.

NEW COUNTERPOINT

The original *COUNTERPOINT* began publication in April 1985 under the editorship of Stanislav Levchenko and Peter Deriabin, both former officers in the KGB and now American citizens. Their objective was to expose Soviet disinformation and active measures efforts using the truth.

One of the feature articles in the first issue described a KGB operation aimed at influencing world opinion that the there was substance to the argument that United States was responsible for the KAL-007 shootdown. The technique employed was an old but effective one. Working under KGB guidance, the Novosti News Agency published a translation of a book, *The Crime of the President* by an unknown Japanese author, which argued that the plane was on an espionage mission for the United States. Subsequent events have shown that this story was accepted by many in both the West and the Third World and it serves as an exemplar of the disinformation operations *COUNTERPOINT* explained to its readers in later issues.

Although little known at first, and largely ignored by publications and analysts implicitly supporting the Soviet Union, *COUNTERPOINT* has gradually became a respected source of current information on the worldwide "Soviet Active Measures" program. That this reputation was not diminished by Deriabin's retirement in early 1990, is a credit to his successor, himself a well known expert in Soviet active measures, Herbert Romerstein.

COUNTERPOINT'S topical coverage sometimes overlaps with *POLITICAL WARFARE*[14] (see page 108). The result, how-

---

14. Most recently called *Soviet Intelligence & Active Measures*, and before that it was known as *DISINFORMATION*; the publisher has

ever, is greater information, not redundancy, because of the range of subjects and the diversity of expertise available to both publications. Furthermore, *COUNTERPOINT'S* current editors' have expanded emphasis on active measures history, espionage case studies and the role of Soviet players, which sharpens the distinction between the two. Where comprehensive coverage is desired, reading both is recommended. If currency, depth and breadth are the prime factors, start with the monthly *COUNTERPOINT*.

The principal themes of a *COUNTERPOINT* issue are divided between discussions of current and historical examples of Soviet active measures and analysis of their role in more recent KGB operations (e.g., Markov and the Bulgarian Umbrella, Vol. 6, #12). In addition, most issues include valuable profiles of key personnel. These are complimented with evaluations of organization and policy changes in the Soviet bureaucracy which impact the overt propaganda program of the government, and the covert active measures programs of the KGB. Recent changes in all these areas, in what is now called the Commonwealth of Independent States (CIS), should provide ample material for upcoming issues.

An example of the expanded scope of coverage in the *NEW COUNTERPOINT*, is Romerstein's article, *"More On Stalin's Secret Past,"* that analyzes the documentary evidence supporting the thesis that Stalin had been an Ochrana agent. There is also more consideration of current problems like the disintegration of the Soviet Union, with emphasis on the KGB. A guest commentary by Maurice Tugwell examines the effect of the loss of the Bloc countries on Soviet industry. Another by Alexandra Costa, written before the coup, looks at hardliner efforts to "suffocate" glasnost. Other topics include environmental difficulties, internal political pluralism, computer spying, a series on industrial espionage, problems in the nuclear industry, the Vlaslov attack on the KGB, and the problem of former KGB General Oleg Kalugin.[15] Although *COUNTERPOINT* didn't predict the recent coup, it did provide a compelling case that the survival of the Party and the government was dependent on KGB support.

---

remained the same only the Soviet world has changed.

15. *COUNTERPOINT*, vol. 5, #s 1 & 12; vol. 6, #1. For Costa article, see vol. 6 #12, pp. 5-6.

Until 1991, each February issue contained what became Levchenko's annual forecast of Soviet Active Measures for the coming year. The succeeding January issue reviewed and critiqued the previous years activity. Levchenko's track-record is quite good when discussing direction and policy. Reader's concerned with specific topics, will have to make their own assessment. Overall, this is a valuable feature which deserves to be continued. It serves as a quick summary of trends, levels of activity, and a good comparison of what the CIS nations say with what they do.

COUNTERPOINT is of real value to the reader who wants substantive background comment on events treated in less depth or neglected by the world press from an active measures viewpoint. An example of this was its report on the sacking of Vitaly Fedorchuk, Head of the MVD. Similarly, the abolition of the International Information Department (IID) and the assumption of its overt propaganda responsibilities by the International and Propaganda Departments of the Central Committee, was examined in depth before other publications[16].

An active measures topic that has received extensive treatment is the KGB forgery campaign. One example presented includes a copy of a forged letter to Senator Durenburger, then Chairman of the Senate Select Committee on Intelligence, putatively from Herb Romerstein.

Despite Gorbachev's assurances that active measures would cease, many remain unconvinced and *COUNTERPOINT* provides the evidence to demonstrate they were correct. In one instance, this amounted to an article documenting continued Soviet attempts to convince the world that the United States developed the AIDS virus as part of its experiments with biological weapons. Another example involves the refutation of the outrageous charges that the United States promoted the sale of "baby parts" from third world countries.

In sum, *COUNTERPOINT* is an informative well written tutorial on active measures and a source of insight from that perspective into domestic political, social and economic problems facing the CIS. Sources are usually cited in the text,

---

16. *COUNTERPOINT*, vol. 2, issues 1, 5, & 8.

however, in some cases the reader must either rely on the editors' experience and research, or write for details.

Starting with issue No., 12, Vol. 6 (May 1991) when Levchenko and Romerstein assumed publication responsibilities, the name was changed to *NEW COUNTERPOINT*. It remains a no frills but professional periodical; photographs and diagrams are frequently included. The characteristic logo of inverted red and black equilateral triangles touching at their apexes has been retained.[17] The format is 8 1/2 x 11", black ink on white background. Publication frequency has been reduced from 12 to 11 issues per year.

Submissions by other authors are encouraged, though compensation is not paid. *COUNTERPOINT* is available by subscription only ($25.00/year, 11 issues, for USA subscribers) from *NEW COUNTERPOINT*, P.O. Box 23751, Washington, D.C. 20026-3751, U.S.A. Photocopies of back issues are available for $2.00 each.

---

17. The first 4 volumes of *COUNTERPOINT* were printed on yellow stock. Volumes 5 and most of 6 were on gray stock. Both used black ink on 21 x 30 cm paper.

COVERT ACTION INFORMATION BULLETIN (CAIB)

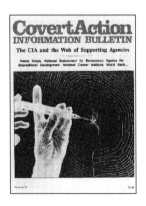

CAIB, the ideological successor to *CounterSpy* (see page 183), began publication with a 24 page issue in 1978 and the modest objective of making the publication "a permanent weapon in the fight against the CIA, the FBI, military intelligence, and all the other instruments of U.S. imperialist oppression throughout the world."[18] Or, to quote Philip Agee, one of *CAIB'S* founders, *CAIB* seeks to help "the progressive forces around the world" in their "campaign to destabilize the CIA through exposure of its operations and personnel."[19] Agee was once a member of the editorial board and though his name no longer appears on the masthead, he is an occasional contributor. In a recent issue he named his co-founders "Ellen Ray, filmmaker and journalist...," her husband "William Schaap, a lawyer," and Louis Wolf, "journalist and conscientious objector." Each along with some new additions, remains on the *CAIB* staff.[20]

The anti CIA and covert action[21] thrust of *CAIB* hasn't changed in its more than 10 year history, but the editors are not quite right when they say its issues have always been "filled with information on the CIA and the right wing **not found elsewhere**." (emphasis added). The contents of magazines like

---

18. Editorial, *CAIB*, Tenth Anniversary Issue, No. 32, Summer 1989, p. 3. Of the 29 articles and commentaries in the issue, only one is designated as original (by Philip Agee), one is left unclear. The balance are partial reprints from earlier issues. This provides a good way to get a historical overview of *CAIB* and its views.

19. Philip Agee, *On The Run* (Secaucus, NJ: Lyle Stuart, 1989), p. 280.

20. Philip Agee, "*CAIB* - Eleven Years in Retrospect," *CAIB*, Number 32, Summer 1989, p. 4.

21. Espionage and analysis are seldom mentioned directly by *CAIB*. Whatever their view, the attempts to wreck the CIA, would, if successful, have the same effect on espionage as on covert action.

CounterSpy, Top Secret (see page 125), and the old *Intelligence and Parapolitics* (see page 65), often cover much the same ground, with a North-South political bent, if not precisely the same incidents.[22] Curiously, the now defunct *Pravda International* (see page 194) was less strident, if not more objective. A discussion of *CAIB* in a recent article by Todd Leventhal noted a "well established track record.... It has published anti-U.S. disinformation and propaganda in tandem with the Soviet active measures apparatus from its founding."[23]

CAIB has gradually acquired a very glossy professional look and increased its length, now about 70 pages. At least one change was not voluntary. Because of the Intelligence Identities Protection Act of 1982, *CAIB* is no longer able to pursue one of its self-imposed missions, the publishing of "CIA agents [sic] names." This is now the agenda of *Top Secret* (see page 125).

A hint of the standard tone and substance of *CAIB* articles is provided in an issue on "U.S. sponsorship of terrorism," with its lead article on the then U.S. Ambassador to the UN, Vernon Walters, entitled in part, "Crypto-diplomat and Terrorist."[24] For another example read "Origin and Spread of AIDS: Is the West Responsible?," by Robert Lederer,[25] who concludes, "Western institutions - military, government, corporate and especially medical- played a major role in the origin and spread of AIDS." He allows that this was probably due to normal

---

22. *CAIB*, Number 32, 1989, Editor's note, p. 3.
23. Todd Leventhal, "Soviet Active Measures and Disinformation in the Gorbachev Ear," presented at the Athens conference of the Consortium for the Study of Intelligence, October 1991.
24. Ellen Ray and William Schaap, "The Modern Mithridates: Vernon Walters: Crypto-diplomat and Terrorist," *CAIB*, Number 26, (Summer 1986), pp. 3-8. This unfortunately typical *CAIB* article is a strident, ad hominem attack. Footnote content does not document or factually support the items at issue.
25. *CAIB*, Number 29, Winter 1988, pp. 52-65. Lederer is described by the editors as a "New York free-lance journalist, gay activist, and Puerto Rico solidarity activist." There are many other examples of *CAIB* anti-American viewpoints such as when it blasted the CIA, without any documentation, for "accusing the Soviet Union of disseminating the phoney documents it [CIA] has itself produced." William Preston, Jr. and Ellen Ray, "Disinformation and Mass Deception: Democracy as a Cover Story," *CAIB*, Number 19, Spring-Summer 1983, p. 7.

functioning rather "than by a specific CBW 'conspiracy,' though that cannot be ruled out."

The extent of misinformation typical of *CAIB* is evident in its comments about President Reagan's Executive Order 12333 which it claimed, "unleashes the CIA within the United States, subjecting people here to the same surveillance, infiltration, manipulation, and dirty tricks which have plagued the rest of the world... for the last 35 years."[26] No evidence of these charges is presented and they do not identify any portion of the executive order where such authorization appears. An article in the Summer 1991 issue titled "Disinformation and Covert Operations," based on "considerable and convincing speculation," accuses the U.S. of "sandbagging Iraq into invading Kuwait." The authors, Ellen Ray and William H. Schaap, go on to cast doubt on the "very questionable allegations" against Iraq which include the charges that "Iraq used chemical agents against its indigenous Kurds," and that "Hussein may be on the verge of acquiring an atomic weapon."

A sense of the *CAIB* editorial evenness and rhetorical hyperbole is expressed in an issue devoted to domestic [US] surveillance, where the editorial begins, "After supplying crack to the ghettos at considerable profit for the contra war against Nicaragua, the Reagan administration...."[27] While the CIA gets its usual treatment ("The CIA has a long and sordid history of activity on U.S. university campuses."[28]), and is joined in the radical spotlight by the FBI, only one key player in this domestic intelligence drama goes unmentioned throughout the issue, the KGB.

Viewed as an information source, *CAIB* provides a clear window to the thinking and actions of the "progressive movement" or radical left. This is a serious publication with a dedicated staff; most articles are signed. It makes no attempt to hide its viewpoint, and sources are cited, though most often secondary, not always germane and frequently unverifiable, a problem not unique to *CAIB*.

CAIB has changed issue identifiers several times over the years, sometimes using months, sometimes seasons, leaving

---

26. Editorial, *CAIB*, Number 16, March 1982, p. 2.
27. Editorial, *CAIB*, Number 31 (Winter) 1989, p. 2.
28. ibid., p. 25.

the actual date of publication in doubt and complicating citations. It uses photographs well, sometimes has a "New Notes" column, and often contains a book review. Issues are printed in black on white 8 1/2 x 11" format, with a two-color cover where the title spelled out in red. The back copies still available are listed on the inside rear cover with purchase and overseas subscription data. Subscriptions may be obtained from Covert Action Publications, P.O. Box 50272, Washington, D.C. 20004, (202-331-9763), for $17.00 per year, U.S. Individual issues are sold at some newsstands.

COVERT INTEL LETTER (CIL)

This monthly, uncopyrighted, non-government publication is marked "**RESTRICTED**" at the bottom, and "YOUR EYES ONLY NOT FOR QUOTATION OR REPRODUCTION" at the top. Typical topics include domestic terrorism problems, political-military issues, the Vietnam War POW controversy, the JFK assassination 'conspiracy' and FBI cases.

The originator and editor, identified only as Walt, is quite willing to talk about *CIL*. He says, in brief, that it is a "stream of consciousness about the problems the nation is likely to experience if we do not deal with the drug and terrorist issues." Walt "takes a dim view of most clandestine activity" and suggests that readers write congressmen and insist they take some action. Walt describes his conception of the alternatives in gruesome detail.

CIL is a source of opinion and doesn't pretend otherwise. One issue, in 1986, begins by stating that what followed was not "entirely verifiable" and then continued with some items which were admittedly based on rumor. Likewise the June-July 1991 issue has a paragraph titled: "Speculative Intel." Clearly, caution is indicated.

It is not clear why all the restrictions are included in the masthead, since subscribers are desired. In any case, for those desiring a different perspective on some of today's international difficulties, *CIL* may be of interest.

CIL is typed, single spaced, about 2 pages per issue, and not well edited. It is available for "$2.00 per copy, or 12 issues $13.00 (USA), $17.00 12 issues overseas mail." For further information, write *Covert Intel Letter* Horizone, Box 67, St. Charles MO. 63302, or call (314) 731-0993 "Nightly 9-11:PM local time."

CRYPTOLOG

One of cardinal rules of intelligence bibliographer George C. Constantinides,[29] is to avoid the use of the word "unique," because, he argues, it almost never applies. *CRYPTOLOG* is an exception to that rule. It began in 1979 as a standard social events oriented newsletter of the Naval Cryptologic Veterans Association (NCVA). Then, on the initiative of its current editor, cryptographer Graydon Lewis, it was expanded in 1980, into a forum for cryptologic history that was not being recorded in other periodicals or books. As a bonus, they also republish articles on cryptology and related issues.

The result of this policy has been a number of first hand accounts and documented historical contributions well worth the attention of those concerned with this field. Only a few examples can be noted here. The analysis by Louis W. Tordella, former Deputy Director of NSA, of four previous *CRYPTOLOG* articles on the "Winds Execute Intercept," particularly the "destruction thesis," takes a practical look at elements of the controversy.[30] The articles on COMINT in WWI and WWII which include Captain L.F. Safford's, "The Undeclared War: 'History of R.I.' [radio interception]" are all first hand accounts with pictures.[31] The entire Winter 1989 issue looks at Naval intelligence in the Pacific War "Through

---

29. George C. Constantinides, *Intelligence and Espionage: An Analytical Bibliography* (Boulder, Colorado: Westview Press, 1983). Although Constantinides would never himself apply the term "unique" to his precedent setting work, it genuinely deserves the description. One can only hope that it will someday be updated periodically.

30. Louis. W. Tordella, "The 'Winds' Execute 'Intercept'," *CRYPTOLOG*, Vol. 8, #4, Summer 1987, pp. 1,6.

31. Captain L.F. Safford, "The Undeclared War: 'History of R.I.'" *CRYPTOLOG*, Vol. 8, #4, Special Supplement, Summer 1987, pp. 8-16.

the Eyes of Forrest R. 'Tex' Biard."[32] A July 1984 special issue was devoted to an abridgement of the recently declassified official report on the attack on the U.S.S. Liberty.[33] Finally, there is the original paper by Navy Lt. Susan M. Lujan, USNR, on the little known 41 year career in cryptology of Agnes Meyer Driscoll.[34]

CRYPTOLOG is published in tabloid format, on newsprint, with issues varying in length from 16 - 30 pages. It sometimes has four-color pictures, but most often black and white. It can be found in the Library of Congress (ISSN 0740-7602), may be obtained on an exchange basis with related publications, and is available to NCVA members. Under certain not entirely clear circumstances, it can also be acquired by others. Perhaps CRYPTOLOG'S most surprising unique feature is that it does not solicit subscribers and the issues contain no information on that subject. For further details, write Editor Graydon A. Lewis, 3421 Stark Street, Eugene, Oregon 97404.

---

32. Forest R. "Tex" Biard, "Through the Eyes of Forest R. "Tex" Biard," CRYPTOLOG, Vol. 10, #2, Winter 1989, pp. 1-27.
33. Graydon Lewis, "U.S.S. Liberty," CRYPTOLOG, Vol. 5, #5., July, 1984, pp. 1-11.
34. Susan M. Lujan, "Agnes Meyer Driscoll," CRYPTOLOG, Vol. 9, #5, August, 1988, pp. 4-6.

CRYPTOLOGIA
A Quarterly Journal Devoted To Cryptology

CRYPTOLOGIA is a professional journal that is as intriguing and interesting as its enigmatic name. "What does the name mean?," is often the first question asked by students and readers when discussing *CRYPTOLOGIA*. The second is, "Is 'Cipher' the real name" of one of the editors, Cipher A. Deavours.

The answer to the first question goes back to the summer of 1975 when three cryptologists and editors-to-be, Brian Winkel and David Kahn and Cipher Deavours, were meeting in Deavours's New Jersey home.  Winkel and Deavours had been planning a journal of cryptology, which they intended to call *POLYGRAPHIA*, a word taken from the title of a sixteenth century book, the first printed on cryptology.[35]. In fact, a bank account had been opened in that name. After explaining this to Kahn he countered with *CRYPTOLOGIA*; until that moment there was no such word. After some discussion and further meetings, the bank account was changed and the first issue of *CRYPTOLOGIA* appeared in January 1977.

Yes, Cipher is his real name; he goes by Ci. The precise circumstances for the selection remain unclear even to Professor Deavours. It may, he suggests, be a variation of the custom of naming off-spring after admirable qualities, as in,

---

35. The full title of the printed version was, *Polygraphiae libri sex, Ioannis Trithemii abbatis Peapolitani, quondam Spanheimensis, ad Maximiianum Caesarem (Six Books of Polygraphy, by Johannes Trithemius, Abbot at Wurzburg, formerly at Spanheim, for the Emperor Maximilian)*, July 1518, 540 pages. See: David Kahn, *CODEBREAKERS* (NY: The Macmillan Company, 1967), p. 133.

Purity, Chastity, Hope, Grace, etc. Certainly the practice of naming them after an element of one's occupation is more unusual, if not precedent setting. Mr. Deavours's father was a Navy cryptologist. If there is more to it than that, it is no doubt classified.[36]

CRYPTOLOGIA now has five editors, Louis Kruh and Greg Mellen completing the team. Each one contributes frequently and is a distinguished cryptologic expert.[37]

While its principal focus is on "mathematics and computer related aspects of cryptography," CRYPTOLOGIA also contains original refereed, well documented articles on historical topics of cryptanalysis. For example, it was the first to print RADM. Dundas P. Tucker's, Rhapsody in Purple, which gives a first hand account of "Purple Magic" in WWII.[38] It also reviews intelligence related books, non-fiction and fiction. In the former category, Ralph Erskine's review of Alan Turing: The Enigma presents an expert's assessment of this controversial biography by Andrew Hodges.[39] When fiction is reviewed, it is often the "thinly disguised" variety, to reduce the burden of the security review board. Ted Wildman's, The Expendables (Clearwater, FL: T.W. Pub., 1983) is such a case. According to CRYPTOLOGIA, it is really the story of the author's career in the Naval Cryptologic Organization.[40]

One of the articles most useful to those interested in the intelligence aspects of cryptology is David Kahn's, "The Annotated The American Black Chamber."[41] After noting that

---

36. The author thanks David Kahn and Cipher Deavours for their assistance in clearing up this vital matter.

37. The first three included, David Kahn, cryptologic book collector, author of, inter alia, The CODEBREAKERS (a classic in its field), and Hitler's Spies; Cipher A. Deavours, a mathematics professor, author, consultant and teacher of cryptography and cryptanalysis at Kean College of New Jersey; and Brian J. Winkel, an expert in microcomputers, teaches mathematics at the Rose-Hulman Institute of Technology, Terre Haute, IN. They were later joined by Louis Kruh, cryptologist for 40 years, collector of crypto material and machines, author and lawyer; and Gregg Mellen, a cipher expert with Sperry Univac, in Bloomington, MN.

38. RADM. Dundas P. Tucker, "Rhapsody in Purple: A New History of Pearl Harbor," CRYPTOLOGIA, Vol 6 #3, July 1982, pp. 193-228.

39. Andrew Hodges, Alan Turing: The Enigma (New York: Simon and Schuster, 1983).

40. CRYPTOLOGIA, volume 10, #1, January 1986, p. 45.

41. David Kahn, "The Annotated The American Black Chamber,"

Yardley's book "provides more detail, more color, more specifics than any other book" on the "activities and personalities of the cryptanalytic bureau," Kahn points out that for several reasons, "sometimes Yardley erred, sometimes exaggerated, sometimes fictionalized." Then, with the help of William Friedman's annotated copy of the book, Kahn spends the next 37 pages clarifying, commenting and correcting. All students of the subject owe Kahn thanks.

In January 1982, *CRYPTOLOGIA* devoted an issue to ENIGMA, which is essential reading for those interested in WWII intelligence. And, more recently, the lead article in the July 1989 issue, "Anguish Under Siege: High-Grade Japanese Signal Intelligence and the Fall of Berlin," examines a seldom looked at topic of interest to many.

In its fascinating and precedent setting column called, "From The Archives," *CRYPTOLOGIA* publishes material discovered by scholars and researchers in the course of their work which might not otherwise find its way into print. The editors actively solicit items recently declassified, and material discovered "in private collections, libraries, and archives which are not widely known." These are often published and attributed to the donor.[42] The October 1983 issue contains a declassified document, "Examples of Intelligence Obtained from Cryptanalysis, 1 August 1946,"[43] that looks at the results of cryptanalysis of enemy messages and where possible the action taken and results achieved. Finally, the July 1989 issue contains such an item of intelligence interest, a memorandum obtained by one of editors, Louis Kruh, through the FOIA, "Subject: Staff Study on OSS Cryptographic Plan."[44]

CRYPTOLOGIA'S approach is strictly professional. There is no editorializing about the politics of cryptology or intelligence, in fact there are no editorials. It is the premier source in

---

CRYPTOLOGIA, January 1985, Vol. 9, #1. The title of the article refers to Herbert O. Yardley, *The American Black Chamber* (Indianapolis, IN: Bobbs Merrill, 1931).

42. *CRYPTOLOGIA*, July 1989, p. 283. Those finding such material should contact editor, David Kahn, 120 Wooleys Lane, Great Neck, NY 11023.

43. National Archives, Record Group 457, Item SRH-066.

44. An eight year FOIA action by Louis Kruh secured the declassification of most of the 1952 Truman memorandum that established the NSA. See, *CRYPTOLOGIA*, April 1986, volume 10, #2, pp. 65-74.

its field and is recommended for all those seriously interested in SIGINT history and cryptology.

CRYPTOLOGIA welcomes articles on all aspects of cryptology." The journal also sponsors an undergraduate competition of papers on cryptography. Submission requirements are given in each copy. Currently each *CRYPTOLOGIA* issue is about 100 pages (7"x10"), well illustrated with photos, diagrams, and there is an occasional advertisement. Volume indices are printed each year in issue #4. Subscriptions are $34.00 per year. Most back issues are available for $9.00 a copy. For further information write *CRYPTOLOGIA*, Rose-Hulman Institute of Technology, Terre Haute, IN 47803.

THE DEFENSE INTELLIGENCE JOURNAL (DIJ)

The Defense Intelligence College (DIC) has announced the April 1992 inaugural issue of its new *Defense Intelligence Journal (DIJ)*. It will be "published by the Defense Intelligence College Foundation (DICF)," a non-profit organization established to assist the College by sponsoring lectures series, publishing monographs and conducting award programs for student papers.

The new journal "will be designed to publish important substantive articles on issues related to defense intelligence... provide current information of the defense intelligence community," and will contain book reviews as well as a section

on teaching intelligence. The theme of the first issue will be *"The Defense Intelligence Community: Organizing for A Changing World."*

The *DIJ* will be the first government publication of its kind since the CIA began *Studies in Intelligence* (see page 178), in 1955. It will provide a forum for the faculty and students who serve a community of more than 10,000 professionals.

The editors, Dr. Robert O. Slater and Dr. Mark Weisenbloom, are from the DIC, as is the managing editor, Lt. Neysa Slater (no relation to Robert), USN. The editorial board includes John F. Blake of the DIC, Dr. Ernest May of Harvard, Dr. Linda Brady from West Point, LTG James A. Williams, USA (Ret), Ambassador Rozanne Ridgway, Mr. William Grace, Dr. Adda Bozeman, Mr. Craig L. Wilson (OASD C^3I/I), and the DIC Commandant, LTG Charles J. Cunningham, Jr.

The *DIJ* will be published twice a year (Spring & Fall) in a 6" x 9" format with about 128 pages. Copies will be available through DICF membership ($35.00/year) and individual subscriptions ($25.00/year). For more information contact the Defense Intelligence College, c/o DIA/DIC-R, Washington DC 20340-5485.

DIC NEWSLETTER

The *DIC Newsletter* has the traditional columns found in in-house publications — Commandant's Corner, Alumni News, calendar of events, faculty comments, notes on distinguished graduates, etc. This is normal considering it is oriented toward the *Defense Intelligence College (DIC)* faculty, staff and students. But at the same time, the **DIC Newsletter** provides the outsider with a glimpse of activities and intelligence programs not easily available elsewhere. It was the Summer 1991 issue that announced the publication of the **Defense Intelligence Journal** and the establishment of a new undergraduate program in intelligence leading to a Bachelor of Science in Inteligence (BSI).

DIC Newsletter is published twice a year by the Defense Intelligence College. Issues have 8 pages, lettersize with College crest on the masthead. Text is black on white, often accompanied by photos. Articles and other contributions are signed. Comments are encouraged. For copies and other information, write the Editor, Lt. Neysa M. Slater, USN, DIC Newsletter, Washington, D.C. 20340-5485

FOREIGN INTELLIGENCE LITERARY SCENE (FILS)
A Bimonthly Newsletter/Book Review

FILS, (pronounced "fills"), is not exactly what it claims to be. Contrary to its title, it gives full attention to the domestic as well as "foreign intelligence," and its topics are not all literary in nature. Issues present professional commentary, analysis, bibliographic material, and reader comment on various aspects of intelligence with emphasis on its literature. *FILS* was the first of its kind and no other current newsletter reviews as many books in as great a depth.

In its first issue in 1982, *FILS* creator, author and intelligence historian Thomas F. Troy (also its first editor), said its "Most important" purpose is "to serve those who enjoy books on intelligence." *FILS*, he continued, is intended to act as a "literary vehicle" or forum "for the devotees of intelligence."[45] It has worked persistently toward those goals. In 1986, with *FILS* firmly established, Mr. Troy decided to devote full time to research and writing. Publication of *FILS* was then taken over by the National Intelligence Study Center (NISC) under the editorship of Marjorie Cline. Although clearly somewhat different in tone, it still aspires to the same goals while seeking to advance public awareness of important intelligence matters.

In its current configuration, about half of each issue is devoted to reviews of recently published books on intelligence written mainly in English, but including some in French and German. Examples include Tom Polgar's critical assessment of the controversial *WIDOWS: Four American spies, the wives they left behind, and the KGB's crippling of American intelligence*; Adrian Hillary's review of Desmond Ball's, *Soviet*

---

45. *FILS*, vol. 1, no. 1, p. 4.

Signals Intelligence (SIGINT); Ralph Briggs's account of *America's Secret Army: The Untold Story of the Counter Intelligence Corps*, by Ian Sayer & Douglas Botting; Hal Feinstein's review of *The Cuckoo's Egg: Tracking a Spy Through the Maze of Computer Espionage*, by Clifford Stoll; Peter Unsinger's commentary on *Oyster: The Story Of The Australian Secret Intelligence Service*, by Brian Toohey and William Pinwill and Tennent H. Bagley's perceptive analysis of *KGB: The Inside Story of its Foreign Operations* by Christopher Andrew and Oleg Gordievsky.[46]

In the area of foreign language books there is Warren Frank's synopsis of a 771 page 1978 work by Albrecht Charisius and Julius Mader [of *Who's Who In CIA?* fame], *Nicht Länger Geheim* (No Longer Secret), never translated into English; and Russell B. Holmes on *The Chinese Secret Service* by Roger Faligot and Rémi Kauffer and *Les Visiteurs de l'Ombre* [Visitors From The Twilight Zone], by Marcel Chalet and Thierry Wolton.[47]

About 100 books (in English) on or related to intelligence are currently published annually. Thus, some selectivity is required and only about half are reviewed. Thirty or so receive lengthy treatment, the balance are "Briefly Noted." The long reviews are signed, written by former intelligence officers or scholars from all over the world and are generally a pleasure to read. Where appropriate, footnotes are included, though many rely on the expertise of the reviewer. In general, they attempt to separate fact from fiction, outline the story, and take a position on the general merits of the work.

Reviews are not the entire story, however. The lead article is often an essay on contemporary events with intelligence implications or a piece on the background of an important book. In the former category is Constantine Melnik's, "The Collapse of the Third Rome," which looks at the implications of the changes in Eastern Europe for the Soviet Union. He

46. ibid., Polgar review of *WIDOWS: Four American spies, the wives they left behind, and the KGB's crippling of American intelligence*, by William R. Corson, Susan B. Trento and Joseph J. Trento, vol. 8, #5, pp. 4-5, ; Hillary, vol. 9, #1, pp. 3-5; Briggs, vol. 9, #1, pp. 6-8; Feinstein, vol. 8, #6, pp. 9-10; Unsinger, vol. 9, #2, pp. 5-6; Bagley, vol. 10, #1, 1991, pp. 3-6.

47. ibid., Frank, vol. 8, #4, pp. 6-7; Holmes, vol. 8, #5, p. 6, and vol. 10, #2, pp. 3-4.

didn't predict the timing, but he clearly foresaw the demise of Communism.[48]

Another article "Notes On History," by Edward E. Thomas, discusses the little known background of the writing of the four volumes of *British Intelligence in the Second World War: Its Influence on Strategy and Operations*, of which he was one of four authors. Among other things, he reveals that the original government intent was for one volume but authors felt there should be five; they settled for four.[49]

In addition to the articles and reviews, some issues contain a column of intelligence trivia "called Clandestine Pursuits," by George O'Toole, author of the The Encyclopedia of American Intelligence and Espionage. Most issues also have a column called "NISC-INT" that contains odd bins items of interest. There are also letters from readers, and a popular feature called "Periodicals and Documents" which lists recently published intelligence related articles, monographs and theses.

FILS assumes no particular political position; but it is, in principle, pro, not anti, intelligence. This does not mean, however, that it gives a blanket uncritical endorsement to all forms of intelligence activity. Whether discussing the intelligence community, covert action, analysis, espionage, congressional support (or micromangement), it attempts a balanced assessment and will gladly consider opposing views.

Submissions in any category are encouraged and will be considered by an experienced editorial review board comprised of Walter Pforzheimer, Samuel Halpern, and Warren Franks. Unfortunately, there is as yet no published index of previous issues, although one has been prepared and is due in 1992.

FILS issues are 12 pages (8 1/2 x 11"), three color (red and blue on white) with occasional photos, cartoons, and charts.

---

48. ibid., Melnik, vol. 9, #2, pp. 1-2, 6-8.
49. Writing in Britain, with its penchant for official secrecy and reluctance to open official records, Thomas and his British colleagues (led by F. H. Hinsley, with C.F.G. Ransom, R.C. Knight and C.A.G. Simkins) managed to overcome both hurdles. While they have yet to receive any formal British recognition, they have received an award from the National Intelligence Study Center.

Subscriptions come with membership in NISC, $50.00 annually; international mailings, add $10.00. Further information can be obtained by calling (202) 466-6029, or writing NISC, 1800 K Street, Suite 1102, Washington, D.C. 20006.

GOLDEN SPHINX
The Voice of Intelligence

Probably the best known (from old movies) and least written about American WWII military intelligence organization was the Army's Counterintelligence Corps, usually referred to as the CIC. Members included some very recognizable names like Henry A. Kissinger, J.D. Salinger, and Leroy Anderson. Less well known, but more effective in their way were Richard Sakakida and Arthur Komori, the first CIC agents of Japanese decent. Both worked against the Japanese, prior to the war, in Manila. One former agent, Erhard Dabringhaus caught the public eye only in the 1980s when he realized while watching TV that the real name of one of his agents was Klaus Barbie, and to his credit, informed authorities.[50]

After the war, veteran CIC agents formed the National Counterintelligence Corps Association (NCICA) which soon began publishing the Golden Sphinx. While the focus is primarily on NCICA events and activities, Golden Sphinx also offers articles and other items of interest to intelligence historians who are searching for leads to primary source material. The upcoming series of articles based on Ann Bray's 30 volume CIC history falls in this category. Those who also like exciting stories with a personal point of view not likely to appear elsewhere will not be disappointed.

Most issues include first hand accounts of intelligence experiences like those of agents Vincent Matasavage and Nils Euki, who, disguised as local nationals, passed the U.S.S. Missouri during the peace signing ceremony in Tokyo Bay on their way to assess Japanese reaction to the surrender. In the

---

50. Ian K.T. Sayer and Douglas Botting, America's Secret Army: The Untold Story of the Counterintelligence Corps, (London: Grafton Books, 1989) [NY: Franklin Watts, 1989], pp. 79-97.

Fall 1989 issue, former agent Vince Hughes tells of his "day with Churchill." The Spring 1990 issue tells of a German agent named "GRETA" with a remarkable record, who was persuaded to help the CIC before being returned to her native Belgium.

Another feature worth following is the occasional review of related out-of-print books like the one on Col. Boris T. Pash's, *The Alsos Mission*, which revealed the little known CIC role in that operation, which was itself an outgrowth of their participation in the Manhattan Project.[51]

There are also comments on upcoming books. A recent article had to do with member contributions to a book on the CIC itself, *America's Secret Army: The Untold Story of the Counterintelligence Corps,* by two British authors, Ian K.T. Sayer and Douglas Botting.[52]

Golden Sphinx is published quarterly. Until 1990 issues were printed in tabloid format of newspaper quality. The current format is 8 1/2 x 11"and varies in length from 8 - 16 pages. Subscriptions are $10.00 annually and come with NCICA membership which is open to active and former military members, and others with interests in intelligence. For more information write/call: Duval Edwards, Editor *Golden Sphinx*, 1524 NE 140th, Seattle WA 98125, (206) 368-0209; or VP for Public Relations, James Calogero, 982 Summer St., Lynnfield, MA 01940, (617) 334-6450.

---

51. See: Duvall A. Edwards, "ALSOS Mission gains goal with the help of CIC agents," GOLDEN SPHINX, Summer 1989, p. 3. Col. Boris T. Pash (AUS Ret.), The Alsos Mission (NY: Award House, 1969).
52. *GOLDEN SPHINX*, Winter 1988.

INSCOM JOURNAL

INSCOM is an acronym for the Intelligence and Security Command of the U.S. Army. Like the *Naval Intelligence Bulletin* (see page 96) the *INSCOM Journal* contains practical matters of concern to Army intelligence professionals in the pursuit career goals. It provides a glimpse of what the military aintelligence professional must know and deal with during a career.

Typical topics vary from income tax requirements, field training, security issues, personnel vignettes, and the result of a felony conviction (say for espionage) on retirement pay — you don't get any.

The Journal will not then be a source of current intelligence techniques for students of the profession. It does give a view of the practical side of life as an MI professional which should be of interest to anyone looking toward that career or studying military intelligence as a profession.

The *INSCOM Journal* is an "unofficial Command Information publication" with a circulation of 6000. It encourages contributions from the field which should be sent to HQ USA INSCOM, ATTN: IAPA, INSCOM Journal, Building 2444, Fort Belvoir, VA 22060-5370. For information on acquiring copies write that address or call 703-706-1469.

INTELLIGENCE BRIEFS (IBs)
SPECIAL REPORT
NIGHTWATCH

The first two of these publications are new, there are plans to revive the third. They are not getting off to a good start.

The first issue of the monthly *IB* is out but the second is not and questions as to its future remain unanswered. Two issues of *Special Report* have been published, but *Nightwatch* remains in its two year, so far, suspension. Their publisher, the Center for Intelligence Studies (CIS) is working to put things right.

CIS is the successor to the Security and Intelligence Foundation (SIF) founded by James Angleton, Ambassador Eldridge Durbrow, Senator George L. Murphy, and James R. Murphy (former Chief of OSS Counterintelligence), among others.[53]

There is an unambiguous right of center political perspective in the CIS agenda, which includes the imposing

---

53. The Foundation was "a lineal descendent of the Security and Intelligence Fund which was formed in 1977." The Fund itself was apparently a spin off of a group called the American Cause, Inc., of which Senator George Murphy was director. *The American Cause* was also the name of the organization's newsletter which featured articles signed by Angleton and Charles Murphy, one of the few places where one can find signed articles by Angleton. The original Fund was established to provide financial support for members of the intelligence community accused of crimes. The name was changed to Foundation in 1985. The shield in its logo was initially broken into quadrants with each one containing the initials of one of the principal members of the intelligence community (FBI, CIA, NSA and DIA). Above the shield were the words, "To Defend and Strengthen." In early 1988 the agency identifiers were removed, and by 1989 the inscription was also gone. *NIGHTWATCH* publication was suspended in 1989.

objective of "educating the American people — and their elected representatives — as to the need for a strong and responsible national intelligence community." The Center publications, particularly the *Intelligence Briefs*, convey these views directly to members and help accomplish the public education. The Congressional part of the task falls to the Center staff with support from members and a group of distinguished Senior Fellows and Policy Advisors.[54]

The *Special Reports* are short single topic papers which have so far been more private analysis of national security issues, than reports on intelligence matters. Not all have footnotes. The first issue contained a viewpoint article by Martin C. Miler, a New Orleans banker, "Hey Amerikanskii, Can You Spare A Billion?." The second issue is an extract from an upcoming book by Dr. Jerome P. Gideon, legislative assistant to Congressman Robert K. Dornan, "Beyond Glasnost: Soviet Space and Strategic Programs for the 1990s."[55]

Under the SIF, *NIGHTWATCH* was a key element in the program to enhance public awareness of intelligence issues and build an "educated constituency for the Intelligence Community."[56] At the outset it presented interesting and provocative, often footnoted though mostly unsigned, articles.

---

54. The Senior Fellows are: Professor Adda Bozeman; National Security Consultants Joseph D. Douglass Jr. & Jerome P. Gideon; LTG Daniel O. Graham USA, (Ret.); Stanislav Levchenko, AMB. Charles M. Lichenstein; Francis J. McNamara; Sebastian S. Mignosa, former FBI Counterterrorism section chief, and S. Scott Powell, political affairs specialist. Raymond Rocca, former Deputy Chief Counterintelligence, CIA and N. Scott Miler, former Deputy Chief Counterintelligence, CIA, serve as Policy Advisors.

55. Martin C. Miler, "Hey Amerikanskii, Can You Spare A Billion?," SPECIAL REPORT, vol. 1, #1. Dr. Jerome P. Gideon, "Beyond Glasnost: Soviet Space and Strategic Programs for the 1990s," SPECIAL REPORT, vol. 2, #2.

56. *NIGHTWATCH* was the successor to SIF's original quarterly *Situation Report* (SR) which commenced publication March 1978 and became *NIGHTWATCH* in the 1980s. SR chronicled the treatment of the Intelligence Community by the Congress and the Executive Department, from the point of viewpoint of former professionals. It assessed the practical results of the Church and Pike committees, the "innovations" of the Carter years, the new oversight committees and the attempts to pass charter legislation. The final issues looked at the beginnings of the Reagan administration and the steps to put intelligence back on its feet. Ambassador Durbrow and Charles Murphy wrote several attributed contributions.

Its later issues, though the subject matter was topical, *NIGHTWATCH* adopted the disconcerting practice of augmenting the author's footnotes with what is termed an "Editor's Note," that either "explains" or expands the point discussed. No doubt intending to be helpful, the practice tends to impugn the reader's intellectual gifts while creating doubt about the ability of the author to express his/her views.

In the event, in terms of substance, the articles get good marks. They provide both analysis and viewpoint focusing mainly on the intelligence aspects of the contemporary foreign and domestic policy debate. Typical topics include verification, terrorism, active measures and SDI, the contribution of Congress, and the KGB. On occasion, articles from other publications are reprinted. For example, the April 1987 issue reproduced, in full, an executive branch report on Foreign Espionage in the United States. What portion of this function will be assumed by Intelligence Briefs remains to be seen.

From time to time the CIS also publishes monographs (20-30 pages by well known experts). Herbert Romerstein's, *The KGB Enters The 1990s*, is a recent example. Another, by former FBI Assistant Director, W. Raymond Wannall, published in December 1988, analyzes *A Subtle Anti-Intelligence Proposal: Welcome Communist Immigrants*, with all accompanying implications.

The *IBs* will contain book reviews as did their predecessor *NIGHTWATCH*. The more recent were of mixed quality and uniform style.[57] On occasion, when a book is of special interest, a comprehensive assessment in a *Situation Report* is published; a review of Golitsyn's *New Lies For Old* was issued in this manner; it can be obtained now only in xerox form.[58]

---

57. For example, see the very positive review of a book by two University of Texas (Dallas) professors, H. Cooper and L. Redlinger, *Making Spies* (Boulder: Paladin Press), in *NIGHTWATCH*, March 1989, Vol. 4, No. 2, pp. 17-19. Others, especially this author, see this book as professionally misleading as it strives for mediocrity without success.

58. Anatoliy GOLITSYN, *New Lies For Old: An Ex KGB Officer warns how communist deception threatens survival of the West* (NY: Dodd, Mead & Company, 1984), 412 pages, with chapter notes, index & glossary. *Situation Report*, Vol 4, # 4, parts 1-3. SIF also published a *Special Report*, when circumstances warranted. The most recent issue, entitled *"Disinformation At Work,"* by Amb. Eldridge Durbrow (Dec 1986, 10 pages), is a comparison of the US and Soviet societies and the problems resulting when government truth is not a

Overall, *NIGHTWATCH* and the periodicals of the old SIF are still a valuable research source. Issues were printed in an impressive two color design (8 1/2 x 11", length 16 - 28 pages); the format of the new *Special Report* follows this tradition. The *IB*s are expected to be similar. Subscriptions to the CIS publications come with membership which is open to all; minimum $50.00, on a sliding scale, up. For information regarding membership, subscriptions to the new periodicals and back issues of the old ones, write to the Center for Intelligence Studies, 301 South Columbus Street, Alexandria, VA, 22314, or call 703 684-0625, FAX 703 836-8329.

INTELLIGENCE AND NATIONAL SECURITY (INS)

As the number of university and college courses on intelligence increased in the 1970s and early 1980s, the need for a professional journal of intelligence became ever more apparent. But it was only after Professor Michael Handel then at the Army War College took the initiative in 1985 and contacted Dr. Christopher Andrew of Cambridge University, that the idea took form and gained momentum. They created and became the editors of *Intelligence and National Security (INS)*. And in an amazingly short time, considering the high quality achieved and the bureaucracies involved, the first issue was published in January 1986.

From the editors' perspective, *INS* set out to be a scholarly "interdisciplinary journal devoted to the past history of intelligence work, to the analysis of its contemporary functions and problems, and to the assessment of its influence on foreign policy and national security." They have succeeded. In the nearly six volumes completed to date, *INS* has produced an impressive record of original refereed articles on current and historical topics by a distinguished international array of practitioners, former professionals and academics.

A few examples will illustrate the range of subjects covered. In the special issue on codebreaking and signals intelligence, the late Gordon Welchman's article, "From Polish Bomba to British Bombe: The Birth of Ultra,"[59] identified and corrected misconceptions related to the Polish role in "breaking" the Enigma cipher. Professor Handel's, "The Politics of Intelligence," is a provocative look at the intelligence community in a democracy which deserves the attention of students of political science and intelligence.[60] In "Appeasement and In-

---

59. Gordon Welchman, "From Polish Bomba to British Bombe: The Birth of Ultra," *Intelligence and National Security*, vol 1, #1, pp. 71-110.

60. Michael Handel, "The Politics of Intelligence," *Intelligence and*

telligence," Williamson Murray looks at the quality of analysis as a function of politics and worldview, and is forced to pessimistic conclusions.[61] The world of espionage and counterintelligence is represented in Professor Cameron Watt's article, "Francis Herbert King: A Soviet Source in the Foreign Office."[62] Military intelligence and deception are analyzed by David M. Glantz in his, "The Red Mask: The Nature and Legacy of Soviet Military Deception in the Second World War."[63] The impact of intelligence on foreign policy is the subject of Sir Reginald Hibbert's fascinating article, "Intelligence and Policy,"[64] and Peter S. Usiwski's "Intelligence Estimates and US Policy Toward Laos, 1960-63," shows that timely accurate estimates can be ignored when they do not agree with Presidential policy desires.[65]

Readers will find the treatment of military intelligence satisfying in all its respects. In addition to regular articles on the subject, three special issues edited by Professor Handel, make a substantial contribution in this area. The first is on strategic deception, the second looks at leaders and intelligence, and the third examines "Intelligence and Military Operations (vol. 5, No. 2). The latter volume also contains an especially interesting article by Patrick Beesly, "Convoy PQ 17: A Study of Intelligence and Decision Making."

The views advanced in *INS* have not been without controversy and an article in the October 1989 issue, by John Ferris, analyzes a crisp debate on the relationship between intelligence and deception as formulated by, inter alios, Michael Handel and Klaus-Jürgen Müller in a series of articles. The same issue deals with two topics which have not heretofore received adequate attention. The first is by Isaac Ben-Israel who makes a challenging contribution to the theory of intelligence in "Philosophy and Methodology of Intelligence." The second is by Michael Herman who examines

National Security, vol 2, #4, pp. 5-46.

61. *INS*, vol. 2, #4, pp. 47-66.
62. D. Cameron Watt, "Francis Herbert King: A Soviet Source in the Foreign Office," *Intelligence and National Security*, vol. 3, #4, pp. 62-82.
63. David M. Glantz, "The Red Mask: The Nature and Legacy of Soviet Military Deception in the Second World War," *Intelligence and National Security*, vol. 2, #3, pp. 175-259.
64. *INS*, vol. 5, #1, pp. 110-128.
65. *INS*, vol. 6, #2, pp. 367-394.

analysis of military capabilities in, "Intelligence and the Assessment of Military Capabilities: Reasonable Sufficiency or the Worst Case?"

Espionage and counterintelligence appear occasionally in *INS*. This may be a reflection of editorial interest, a matter of access to documentation, or some combination of these factors.[66]

In addition to the U.S. and the U.K., *INS* authors come from a variety of countries, including Israel, Yugoslavia, West Germany, Canada, Ireland, Norway, New Zealand, and Australia. And with the recent changes in the Soviet Union, one should not be surprised to see contributions from Russia and the other new nations of the old Soviet Union. China may take somewhat longer.

Readers can rely on well documented material in all categories, including book reviews. The latter, done by experts, are to the point, valuable and sometimes controversial. Worthwhile examples include, Robert Cecil's review of, Anthony Glees's, *The Secrets of the Service: British Intelligence and Communist Subversion* and Reg Whitaker's balanced treatment of, *In The Sleep Room*, by Anne Collins, winner of the Canadian Governor General's Award. David Sinclair, in his assessment of Wolf Blitzer's *Territory of Lies*, suggests what really motivated Jonathan Pollard was money, Blitzer notwithstanding.[67] The letters to the editor are particularly worthwhile. They provide expert comment, note important errors and clarify positions where disagreements have arisen.

---

66. The *INS* has an impressive editorial advisory board: Professor Sir F. H. Hinsley, Lord Dacre of Glanton, M.R.D. Foot; Professors Lawrence Freedman, Robert Jervis, Harry Howe Ransom, Samuel P. Huntington, Ernest May, Klaus Jürgen-Müller, Jürgen Rohwer, Richard Betts, Ralph Bennett, Harvey Barnett, David Kahn, David Stafford, D. Cameron Watt, and Professor R.V. Jones, among them. Except for Mr. Barnett, few of these distinguished gentlemen have experience in clandestine operations.

67. Robert Cecil, *Intelligence and National Security*, vol. 3, #2, pp. 342-343, review of Anthony Glees, *The Secrets of the Service: British Intelligence and Communist Subversion* (London, Jonathan Cape, 1987). Reg Whitaker, *INS*, vol. 5, #1, pp. 202-203 review of, Anne Collins's, *In The Sleep Room: The Story of the CIA Brainwashing Experiments in Canada* (Toronto: Lester Orpen & Dennys, 1988). David Sinclair, *INS*, vol. 6, #2, pp. 494-496.

INS is a quarterly, although the first volume has only three issues. Manuscripts are encouraged, format requirements are included in each issue. Subscriptions are $39.00 (£30.00) annually. Some bookstores in the U.S. do get copies, but they charge $15.00 each. On the other hand, single copies from the publisher are $24.00. For subscriptions or further details write, Frank Cass & Co, Ltd, Gainsborough House, 11 Gainsborough Road, London E11 1RS.

INTELLIGENCE DIGEST - U.K. (ID-UK)
A Review Of World Affairs

The addition of the "UK" to the title is an arbitrary act by this author in order to discriminate between the British and American periodicals of the same name. *Intelligence Digest -*

UK is the one active periodical in this survey that began long before the '70s. It was founded by Kenneth de Courcy, after he established "the Imperial Policy Group (IPG) in 1935." The IPG produced reports "widely read in government circles, and a particularly close relationship was established with Chamberlain and Sir Stewart Menzies." *The Digest*, with its conservative viewpoint, grew out of the IPG reports in 1938.[68]

By the post war period, Kenneth de Courcy was something of an intelligence authority because of his publication, and he later became one of few people with whom George Blake discussed his spying activities. Ironically, his "intelligence authority status" had nothing to do with meeting Blake; they were in prison together. De Courcy was convicted of fraud in December 1963 and sent to Wormwood Scrubs; Blake had arrived in April. Blake knew of de Courcy, he [Blake] had sent copies of *Intelligence Digest* to Moscow. De Courcy set an example for Blake by escaping, but was soon caught. Blake was more successful and now lives in Moscow where he recently published his memoirs. Rumors that he would be returned to

---

68. Letter to the author, dated 8 August 1989, from the current editor of *Intelligence Digest*, Joe de Courcy, the founder's son. Mr. de Courcy quotes Lord Home, from his book, *The Way The Wind Blows* (p. 243), about the quality of the *Digest*'s reports; " The intelligence gathered by Kenneth de Courcy was a great deal nearer the true state of morale in the French Army than that distributed by our service attaches in Paris."

England as a traitor have been denied by the KGB public affairs office.[69]

The *Digest* is currently headed by de Courcy's son Joe. Its political perspective is still conservative, and, in its own words, *ID* "has, since 1938, been the leading authority on international political and strategic intelligence and in exposing the aims of world communism," to which it now adds international terrorism, drug trafficking and Islamic fanaticism.

The focus of *ID-UK* however, is not primarily intelligence agencies or operations,[70] but rather the results of its own political analysis of information collected by its sources (unnamed) about activities around the world that threaten democracy. Typical topics include Soviet policy towards South Africa, gun-running in Latin America, Cuban clandestine warfare, Gorbachev and Baltic dissent, and freedom of the press in Algeria. Intelligence agencies are mentioned when appropriate; the 4 August 1989 issue noted the CIA's role in the exposure of Cuba's drug links in the Caribbean. In intelligence jargon, *ID-UK* is a private current intelligence periodical.

But whether an intelligence analyst, or interested layman who links reliability of information with source veracity, the reader who turns to *ID-UK* will find largely undocumented reports. Instead of dates, there are references to "recent visits," and instead of by-lines there are "our highly placed intelligence sources." Then there are claims like "there's recently been evidence of more united opposition to Moscow rule" (8

---

69. See, H. Montgomery Hyde, *George Blake Superspy* (London: Constable and Company, 1987), p. 55. De Courcy wrote a long memorandum (never published, but smuggled out of prison) about Blake. Among other things, he describes Blake's contacts with another Soviet agent, John Vassall, also a Wormwood Scrubs lodger, and then discusses Blake's psychological attributes, concluding he was not suitable for SIS employment. De Courcy, who claimed he had been framed and wrongly convicted, gave his papers concerning Blake, including the memo, to the Hoover Institution at Stanford University, California, in 1983. Ibid., pp. 10, 60-63, 97. For the Blake rumor see Reuter dispatch, London, 27 August 1991.

70. The *Intelligence Digest (UK)* publishes what was once termed *Special Studies*, now called *Special Briefs*. In 1967 it published a very interesting *Special Study*, No. 10, a detailed 32 page single spaced description and analysis of what it called "The Soviet Intelligence System," by an anonymous author. No sources were provided and as with the current *Digest*, the reliability assessment is left to the reader.

March 1989, p. 3) that do not mention the evidence. *ID-UK* apparently trades off source protection for results, which if publishing longevity is an indicator, must be good.

In retrospect, *ID-UK*'s 29 March 1989 (p. 3) discussion of the Chinese clash with Tibet had prophetic overtones in light of the June 1989 violence in Beijing. *ID-UK* reported that the "recent behavior... in Tibet, where many unarmed people were shot dead... is a sharp reminder of the underlying evil of a communist state which had recently confused many observers by its professed liberalism and humanity." In principle, reports like this taken over a period of time should provide a sound basis for decision, though each situation will be different and user analysts must make the judgment themselves.

An issue of the *Intelligence Digest* is about eight letter-size pages, printed on off-white stock with black ink. It is published in 48 weekly issues for about $200.00. Six *Special Briefs* are also available each year and in some cases they are included as a subscription bonus. For subscriptions and further information write, Intelligence International Limited, 17 Rodney Road, Cheltenham, Glos GL50 1HX, U.K. (telephone 44-242 517774).

INTELLIGENCE MUSEUM FOUNDATION NEWSLETTER (IMFN)

The Intelligence Museum Foundation exists "to promote Army Intelligence History and build a museum at the [U.S. Army] Intelligence Center and School" on Ft. Huachuca, Arizona. Many Foundation members are former intelligence officers, all the staff are volunteers.

The *IMFN* is used to apprise members of the fund-raising efforts for the new museum building and the current exhibitions in the temporary facility. The first three volumes have been devoted, for the most part, to describing membership categories, funding requirements, sources of revenue, and the need for intelligence artifacts such as photographs, flags, maps, charts, and appropriate items of espionage equipment. In the latter category, recent donations include a "Soviet built R-105M FM field radio" once used by Red Army infantry and armor units, and several sections of the Berlin wall.

Besides membership fees, the Foundation has provided a number of other ways to raise money for the museum. The Spring 1991 issue of *IMFN* includes a list of T-shirts, sweatshirts, belt buckles, stationery, tie clasps, crests and associated items with various military intelligence insignia and limited edition prints, which may be purchased. Profits go toward the museum.

The *IMFN* plans to expand from its 6 pages length as circumstances permit. In this connection articles are being sought on MI topics ranging from items of historical interest to personal anecdotes.

There is no masthead on the *IMFN*, nor is there mention of an editor. It is printed in two columns, on letter-size blue stock. Subscriptions come with membership in the Foundation which starts at $10.00 for one year and is open to anyone interested in the profession and the museum. Correspondence should be addressed to the President and Executive Director of the Foundation, Don Blascak, Col. (R) U.S. Army, P.O. Box

595, Sierra Vista, Arizona 85636. Make checks payable to the Intelligence Museum Foundation.

INTELLIGENCE NEWSLETTER (IN)

If you are looking for timely news about a wide variety of national intelligence organizations of the world, this is the right newsletter, no other comes close.[71] *Intelligence Newsletter: Le Monde Du Renseignement (The World of Intelligence)*, has been published in Paris since 1988. In its current biweekly format, *IN* is a completely new publication compared with its predecessor Intelligence Parapolitics, (a monthly) begun in 1984.[72]

Each issue begins with a lead feature or "Spotlight" article, perhaps one and one half pages. Typical leads stories include "France: Intelligence Politics & Press;" the "DGSE industrial network" in the United States, euphemistically titled "Intelligence and Business;" "GERMANY: No Options for the Stasi," and "U.S.A.: The DIA Takes Over."[73]

---

71. The term parapolitics is employed to mean "a discipline or activity that deals with the investigation of political phenomena." The quote is from the masthead on issue No. 87, March 1987.

72. *Intelligence Parapolitics (I/P)* is itself the 1984 offspring of two publications, *Parapolitics* (started in 1980) and *Intelligence*, the latter an English edition of *Le Monde du Renseignement (The World of Intelligence)*, started in 1983 when it dropped its old name *Bulletin d'Information sur les Interventions Clandestines*, started in 1980 and modeled on *CAIB* (see page 32). *I/P* was "published monthly by Association pour le droit à l'information, (ADI)," or the Association for the Right to Information. ADI is a non-profit organization founded in about 1982, "whose honorary president is Sean McBride." Initially, ADI (which appeared on the masthead) also published the *IN*, from its 16 rue des Ecoles, 75005, Paris address, with a correspondence and subscription address at 39 rue du Sentier, 75002 Paris, France. Starting with the 30 November 1988 issue, ADI was dropped from the masthead, and replaced with Indigo Publications. At the same time, the rue des Ecoles address was dropped, and publisher, Marie-Pierre Tezier, was replaced with Maurice Botbol. Issues of *I/P* are generally anti-American and CIA. They provided the student of intelligence politics with a view from the left. For a more detailed discussion of the provenance of these periodicals, which followed closely the start of *CAIB* in the USA, see the December 1987-January 1988 issue of *I/P*. For an analysis of their content as disinformation, see "Soviet Active Measures and Disinformation in the Gorbachev Ear," by Todd Leventhal, presented at the Athens conference of the Consortium for the Study of Intelligence, October 1991.

Another regular column is called "People." It has interesting items about intelligence officials from various nations. The June 21, 1989 issue included comments of Qiao Shi, head of China's Ministry of Public Security, a service seldom heard about in the publications summarized here. Another item mentioned the retirement of Hungarian Ambassador to

Moscow, Sandor Rajnai, a "high official of Hungarian intelligence and KGB 'correspondent' [who] was responsible for the arrest in 1956 of Imre Nagy. East Germany's former HVA (foreign intelligence service) head, Markus Wolf, also receives frequent attention. Even Lloyd Bucher, (former captain of the U.S.S. Pueblo) was mentioned (6 June 1990) when he and his crew received POW medals after much Pentagon - Congressional controversy.

In 1990 and again in 1991, the *IN* (Scope) carried an item claiming Dr. Julius Mader, author of Who's Who In CIA, was "in reality Major Thomas Bergner, an Offizier in besonderen Einsatz (OibE) assigned to the ZAIG (Central Evaluation and Information Group) of the former... MfS or Stasi." *IN* did not mention that a former Stasi officer says this story is incorrect and that Mader was just an author who wrote from files provided him by the MfS. Nor does *IN* report that the both the Czech and East German intelligence services identified the book in 1980 as a disinformation operation.[74] *IN* does acknowledge (Issue #176, p. 3) that Mader denies being Bergner.[75] Omissions such as these leave *IN* open to charges of being a vehicle, willing or not, for Soviet disinformation.

In a column called "Techniques," one finds stories like the one on the new biometric "Eye-Dentify system," adopted by the Bundesamt für Verfassungsschutz (BfV), the West German

73. *Intelligence Newsletter*, 9 May 1990, N. 145, p. 1., 23 May 1990, N. 146, p. 1, and 31 July 1991, No. 175.
74. Leventhal, op. cit., p. 6. The name of the former Stasi officer has not been released.
75. *Intelligence Newsletter*, # 162, January 31, 1991, p. 2.

security service, for use in identifying individuals. The September 11, 1991 issue tells of a new 'spy proof' glass developed in England that prevents electronic transmissions from escaping the area. In a lighter vein, readers were informed about the U.S. Army "Military Intelligence Language Olympics" in West Germany. Czech and Dutch programs to develop anti-stealth technology were the main subjects in a recent column.[76]

Aside from announcements of upcoming books and short comments on books recently published, the remainder of each issue is a comprehensive geographical survey of intelligence related matters in various regions and countries of the world, allowing the reader to focus quickly on his/her interests. The coverage is broad as expressed in both articles and short items. Institutional, documentary and periodical sources like *Janes's Defense Weekly* are sometimes mentioned, but author sources are seldom identified. Typical topics include, Pakistan's intelligence reorganization, Algerian intelligence, West Germany's BfV catching KGB computer spies, the "Kennebunk Intelligence Nest,"[77] a "scandal concerning the head of Shin Bet counter-intelligence" in Israel, and 15 former intelligence officers in Great Britain who are writing books. There was no indication of Mrs. Thatcher's response, it probably wasn't printable.

As might be expected considerable attention has been given to the crumbling of the Eastern European intelligence services and the consequent impact on the West. One result in the then West Germany, according to *IN*, was BfV's recognition that its security was "considered laughable" by the East German foreign intelligence service (HVA) which thoroughly penetrated the BfV and listened to its communications.[78] In a related item, *IN* reveals "the existence of a KGB secret intelligence database located in Moscow, called the 1179 System," supported by nine other countries. With the recent upheaval, access requirements are being renegotiated.[79]

---

76. Intelligence Newsletter, No. 124, 21 June 1989, p. 2; No. 123, 7 June 1989, p. 2; No. 126, 19 July 1989, p. 2; and No. 175, 31 July 1991, p. 2.
77. Lest the reader be mislead, this had nothing to do with the President, and everything to do with a meeting of the David Atlee Phillips Chapter of AFIO.
78. *Intelligence Newsletter*, 25 April 1990, N. 144, p. 4.
79. Ibid., p. 7.

A review of *IN* coverage of intelligence organization reveals a somewhat uneven treatment when considering Western, "Eastern bloc," and Soviet services. During 1990 and 1991 to July, the front page SPOTLIGHT column did not feature the KGB or GRU, while the CIA and other Western or former bloc services are frequent subjects. This is especially curious in view of the recent turmoil in the Soviet Union. Items concerning the KGB do appear in most issues but they tend to report on organizational, budget and personnel matters. When it comes to criticism, the Western services get the bulk of the attention. When the KGB is criticized, it is mild compared to what even the Soviets are publishing (see *FBIS* entry, page 150). I did not find a single case where the KGB was attacked by *IN* in the same way it blisters the Western services like the Mossad, MI5, MI6, and especially the CIA.

For example, *IN*'s unsubstantiated statements like "the CIA's bloody and unsuccessful assassination attempt against Sheik Fadlallah," only misinform, especially when they give no indication that this charge has been officially denied by the United States. Furthermore, misleading and provocative headlines like, "CIA Back Into Drugs?" (issue No. 124), will only be effective where truth is not an issue.[80] An equally crude ploy, or disinformation attack, was *IN*'s attempt convince readers that the United States government wants to legalize assassination for "duly authorized personnel of the CIA or the Pentagon."[81] Sometimes the attacks get personal as when *IN* stated that Paul Hentze, former "CIA station chief in Ankara where he is attributed with supporting the development of the Gray Wolves extreme-right terrorist organization via CIA agent Rudi Nazar." This echoes an old Soviet disinformation story that, together with the awkward syntax, castes suspicion on *IN* and its sources which are not cited. These are but a few instances which raise legitimate doubts about *IN*'s objectivity and the reader should take them into account.

The versatile *IN* editor Olivier Schmidt, better known to readers of *Dirty Work 2: The CIA in Africa* as one of its editors, Karl Van Meter, and under the same name, to readers of *On The Run* as a Philip Agee confidant,[82] has been at the helm of

80. Ibid., 10 May 1989, p. 7.

81. Ibid., No. 123, 7 June 1989, p. 3; and No. 124, 21 June 1989, p. 1.

82. Philip Agee describes Karl van Meter as "my friend" and an "American journalist and mathematician," with whom he once

both *Intelligence Parapolitics (I/P)* and *IN* from the beginning. He has observed the striking metamorphosis of the low budget monthly *I/P* to the polished, carefully edited professional biweekly *IN*, with its impressive new two color layout (red and black on yellow stock, 21 x 30cm pages). Indices are published annually (as they were in *I/P*). The *IN* stories, says Mr. Schmidt, come from a "network of specialized journalists and scholars" most of whom "prefer to remain anonymous for professional reasons and because their name is usually associated with a commercial media organization."[83]

Finally, perhaps the most noticeable of the changes in *IN* is its subscription rate which has increased from $25.00 to $500.00 per year (24 issues). All the changes, the background of its editor, and the subtle inclusion of disinformation stories, have led to speculation that *IN* found a vein of Moscow Gold.

Further information and subscriptions (English or French) may be obtained by writing *Intelligence Newsletter*, 39 rue du Sentier 75002 PARIS, France, or calling, (1) 45.08.14.80; Fax (1) 45.08.59.83.

---

stayed in Paris. Sources: Philip Agee, *On The Run* (Secaucus, NJ: 1987), p. 105. During a conversation with Olivier Schmidt on January 17, 1989 between 1314-1325 hours, EST. I asked him if it were true and he said it was. It was later independently confirmed by Daniel Brandt, author of *NAMEBASE* (see page 230) and mentioned in "Agee At It Again," Laughlin Campbell, *FILS*, vol. 8, #2, 1989, p. 4.

83. For a detailed analysis of *IN* as a source of sophisticated disinformation and the coincidence of the upgrading of *I/P* with a change in Soviet disinformation policy, see Leventhal, op. cit.

THE INTELLIGENCE PROFESSION SERIES (IPS)

The *IPS* is a group of monographs by authorities in their fields and published (about one a year) by the Association of Former Intelligence Officers (AFIO). Each monograph presents an excellent short (25-60 pages) summary of a subject of general interest. The late Hans Moses, a retired CIA operations officer, wrote the first one, *The Clandestine Service of the Central Intelligence Agency*, which was published in

The Intelligence Profession Series
Number SEVEN

INTELLIGENCE:
What It Is And How To Use It
by
John Macartney

The seventh of a series of monographs published by
the Association of Former Intelligence Officers

6723 Whittier Avenue, Suite 303A
McLean, Virginia 22101
(703) 790-0320

1983. The second was *Warning Intelligence*, by Cynthia M. Grabo a former strategic warning analyst with DIA. Then came *The KGB* by Tom Polgar, a former CIA chief of station. Number four, *National Security and the First Amendment* is by John S. Warner, former CIA General Counsel. *The Role of Women in Intelligence* by Elizabeth P. McIntosh, former OSS officer and author, is number five. Number six, *The Central Intelligence Agency: An Overview*, by soldier and retired senior CIA officer Lewis Sorley, appeared in 1989. Number 7, *Intelligence: What It Is And How To Use It*, by John Macartney, discusses the functioning of the U.S. Intelligence Community.[84]

With the exception of the Warner monograph, each one provides a list of suggested reading. Dr. Sorley also includes a useful and succinct glossary of common intelligence terms, endnotes and helpful organization charts. Similarly, Professor Macartney also uses end notes and some charts.

---

84. John Warner, former CIA General Counsel, *National Security and the First Amendment*, No. 2, (McLean, VA: AFIO, ND), 33 pp; Thomas Polgar, *The KGB* (McLean, VA: AFIO, ND), No. 3, 25 pp; Cynthia M. Grabo, *Warning Intelligence* (McLean, VA: AFIO, 1987), No. 4, 42 pp; Elizabeth P. McIntosh, *The Role of Women in Intelligence* (McLean, VA: AFIO, 1989), No. 5, 44 pp; Lewis Sorley, *The Central Intelligence Agency: An Overview* (McLean, VA: AFIO, 1990), No. 6, 66pp; John Macartney, *Intelligence: What It Is And How To Use It* (McLean, VA: AFIO, 1990), No. 7, 42 pp.

AFIO plans to continue the series but the next topic has not been announced. The *IPS* monographs are paper bound, 5" x 7", with a pale blue cover and black letters. They vary in cost from $1.25 to $5.00 and may be obtained by writing AFIO Headquarters, 6723 Whittier Ave., Suite 303A, McLean, VA 22101; tel: 703-790-0320.

INTELLIGENCE QUARTERLY (UK)
INTERNATIONAL INTELLIGENCE QUARTERLY (IIQ)

In the early 1980s, British author Nigel West was seeking out-of-print books on intelligence for his collection when he encountered American Michael Speers, seller of out-of-print intelligence books. The outcome of their book transactions is lost to history. The outgrowth of their common fascination in the subject of intelligence is not — the first issue of the *Intelligence Quarterly (IQ)* appeared in April 1985.

Originally co-edited by West and Speers, *IQ* appeared simultaneously in the United States and the United Kingdom until August 1989 when publication was suspended after issue Number 3, Volume 4, due to editorial difficulties which were manifest in bouts of publication irregularity. So far as can be determined, there are no plans to resume publication of the US edition of *IQ*; however, should this happen it would be as an independent periodical with no connection to the UK edition.

The UK edition, however, does plan to resume publication using the same name *(IQ-UK)* sometime in 1992, with West continuing as the UK editor. There will also be an international edition, *(IIQ)*, available outside the UK, which West will co-editor with Dr. Lee Houchins, a former DIA intelligence officer. With the exception of the paper stock in the U.K. edition and perhaps some advertisements included only in the US version, the editions will be essentially the same. Articles and commentary will contain a mix of intelligence news and book reviews from authors worldwide.

The content precedent for *IQ-UK* & *IIQ* is demanding, assuming the early versions of *IQ-UK* serve as a benchmark. In fact, they included somewhat more than was claimed in the masthead which read: "A journal devoted to the review of books and events in the intelligence field." Historical articles, generally by experts in the field, make the point. The two by former CIA analyst, Earnest Oney, "The Eyes and Ears of the Shah," and "Drach Nach Islam: Germany in Iran 1914-1918,"[85] and E. R. Thompson's "Sleuthing the Trail of Nathan Hale,"[86] are particularly good. In the area of counterintelligence, Arthur S. Hurlburt's firsthand account of his CIC experience is a valuable contribution.[87] Finally, Etienne Huygens's original articles on defectors, a subject which deserves more serious analysis, are still worthy of attention.[88]

In the book commentary and review category, West's criticism-with-class and reviews by professionals like Bill Hood, John Waller and Winn Taplin provided substance with wit and were a pleasure to read.

Issues of the former *IQ* vary in length from 8 (V1, #1) to 16 lettersize pages, black on white. *IQ-UK* used glossy stock, was printed in two colors (color in the title only) and cost £30.00 per year. Current plans for *IQ-UK* indicate it will retain the same format, size (about 8" x 12") and cost. *IIQ* is expected to be 16 pages and subscriptions will be $30.00 annually. The printing details for *IIQ* have not been announced but indications are, despite the same size, it will be easily distinguishable from its predecessor. Photos will be included as appropriate.

Notification of publication resumption for *IQ-UK* and start-up for *IIQ*, will be made by mail using an entirely new list. Notices will also appear in *SURVEILLANT* (see page 122) and *FILS* (see page 46). In the interim additional information can be obtained from *IQ-UK* Commonwealth Editor, Nigel West, 310 Fulham Road, London, SW10 9UG, tel: 011-44-71-352-1110, FAX 011-44-71-352-1111, or the American editor of *IIQ*, Lee Houchins, 5049 Garfield Street, N.W., Washington, D.C. 20016; tel: 202-966-7788, FAX: 202-966-6116.

---

85. See: *IQ* vol. 1 #4, p. 1; and vol 2 #4, p. 1 respectively.
86. See: *IQ*, vol. 2, #3, Oct 1986, p. 1.
87. Arthur S. Hurlburt, "What Ever Happened to Counter Intelligence?," *IQ* vol. 2, No. 1, April 1986, pp. 1-3.
88. Etienne Huygens, "What is a Defector," *IQ* vol. 1, #3, May 1987, pp. 10-12; and "Defectors From The Tropics," *IQ* vol. 3, #4, pp. 10-14.

INTELLIGENCE STUDIES NEWSLETTER (ISN)

ISN has been published twice a year since 1987 by the Intelligence Section of the International Studies Association (ISA). Its initial purpose was to inform section members about upcoming activities including conferences, teaching faculty seminars, and calls for papers. Since then *ISN* editor, Professor Jefferson Adams, Sarah Lawrence College, has expanded its scope by starting a series of articles called "Intelligence in the Classroom." These are written by professors telling about the intelligence courses they teach. Most discuss their approaches, texts, reference materials, reading requirements, and how the courses originated.

The series began with an essay by Professor Bradford Westerfield, Yale University, where he teaches "Intelligence and Covert Operations," a demanding course carefully crafted over five years. Professor Robert D'A Henderson, University of Western Ontario, contributed a summary of his course, "Intelligence, Subversion and Terrorism," which looks at subversion and terrorism in society and examines the roles of intelligence and covert action to bring them under control.

Probably one of the most familiar course titles is that of the third article, "Intelligence and National Security." But Professors Gregory Gleason and Peter Lupsha have teamed up to give it an unusual twist by using guest speakers with experience in intelligence.

Although most of the professors report that intelligence is still a controversial subject in universities, they agree that the courses are continually oversubscribed.

Other items in *ISN* include suggestions for getting material from the intelligence agencies directly, and comments on book stores specializing in books on intelligence.

ISN is 4-6 (8 1/2 x 11") xeroxed pages. Contributions are encouraged. A subscription costs $5.00 per year, but that is for members of the parent organization, the ISA. For details about ISA membership write the Executive Officer, International Studies Association, University of South Carolina, Columbia, SC 29208. For further details about the newsletter, contact Professor Adams, Sarah Lawrence College, Department of History, Bronxville, NY 10708.

INTELLIGENCER

The AFIO Academic Exchange Program
Newsletter for Intelligence Scholars

The Academic Exchange Program (AEP) of the Association of Former Intelligence Officers (AFIO) was established to help academics teaching, or desiring to teach, college and university courses on intelligence. *The Intelligencer* is one of the links established by AFIO to meet its goal. Issues typically include AEP and AFIO announcements, an event calendar, book reviews, notices of forthcoming books, letters, and a "Perquisites" column which lists intelligence books available to qualified academics with AFIO compliments.

The Spring 1990 issue is a good exemplar. First, it contains a content-outline and syllabus for a course in "Espionage and History" taught by Professor Douglas L. Wheeler at the University of New Hampshire, which should be of value to anyone thinking of teaching on this topic. There are also two reviews of the book *WIDOWS*, by William R. Corson, Susan B. Trento and Joseph J. Trento (New York: Crown, 1989). Both cast doubt (perhaps demolish would be more accurate) on the its veracity. Reviews like this should be of real help to those trying to assess the validity of intelligence books which are not, and often cannot, be thoroughly documented.

The most recent issue, Spring 1991, announces another in AFIO's *Intelligence Profession Series, Intelligence: What is It and How To Use It, and it* discusses consideration of a computer-based bulletin board for the AE. The latter item could speed transmission of notices and stimulate greater interaction of the participants. And those following the *WIDOWS* controversy should read Tom Polgar's response to Joe Trento's letter (*Intelligencer*, Fall 1990) to get an idea of why *WIDOWS* is so lowly regarded.

The AEP Coordinator, J. E. Naftzinger, encourages input and feedback from *Intelligencer* readers. The categories of comment sought include: teaching an intelligence course, current projects and research, and other professional activities such as notice of intelligence papers published in professional journals.

Intelligencer, published twice yearly, uses a 8 1/2 x 11" black and white format, with 12 pages per issue. Copies are sent to on-campus AEP participants and are also a bonus of AFIO membership. Send you comments or requests for more details to, AFIO Headquarters, 6723 Whittier Ave., Suite 303A, McLean, VA 22101; or phone 703/790-0320,

INTERNATIONAL JOURNAL OF INTELLIGENCE AND COUNTERINTELLIGENCE (IJIC)

The origins of the *IJIC* can be traced back to World War II and editor F. Reese Brown's service in the Office of Naval Intelligence. Although he later turned to the world of finance, he never lost his interest in his wartime specialty and frequently spoke of the need for an intelligence journal with his publisher friend, Milo Dowden. The talk became serious in the early 1980s and though unaware of similar plans by Professor Michael Handel and Dr. Christopher Andrew (*INS*, page 56), Brown and Dowden decided the time was right to implement their idea. In 1985 they set about soliciting contributions and the other essential assets. The first issue appeared a notably short time later, in the spring of 1986, and it has been published, roughly quarterly, since then.

In terms of content, the *IJIC* is narrowly distinctive when compared to its British counterpart, *INS*. *IJIC* seeks to present articles that analyze and explain the practice of intelligence, the methods, techniques, processes, and obstacles of intelligence work, and the organizations that comprise the worldwide community, while examining the bureaucracies, policies and legal parameters which bound daily functioning and operations.[89]

Unlike *INS*, the terms "history" and "interdisciplinary journal" have not been used in this expression of purpose. But the difference is more one of semantics than substance. The first *IJIC* article was about intelligence history and the topic has, of necessity been a recurrent one as "Knifing the OSS," by Thomas F. Troy, and Rose Mary Sheldon's, "Hannibal's Spies,"

---

89. Conversation with F. Reese Brown, Editor In Chief, *IJIC*, 12 August 1989.

make clear.[90]. Similarly, the "interdisciplinary" concept is reflected in Journal articles like Edward S. Barkin's "COMINT and Pearl Harbor: FDR's Mistake" (V2, #4), John Horton's "Reflections on Covert Action and Its Anxieties" (V4, #1), Arthur Hulnick's " Managing Analysis Strategies for Playing the End Game" (V2, #3), and Anthony R. Moriarty's "Abating Military Espionage Problems" (V4, #4).

In practice *IJIC* contains more articles on contemporary issues, perhaps because of the relatively greater access to materials in the US, the government's formal review policies, and the statutory basis of the intelligence community agencies. A recent example of this kind of article is, "Understanding CIA's Role in Intelligence," by Michael A. Turner, CIA's coordinator for Academic Affairs.[91] One consequence of this policy is that somewhat greater reliance is placed on secondary sources and personal interviews than the authors might like. Overall, however, the scholarship standards are high and the articles well written. As one contributor put it, there is a conscious policy of avoiding authors who "utilize dubious material serenely and reviewers [who] commend their work uncritically."[92] Where controversial views are expressed by an author, the policy is to publish, when possible, an article with opposing viewpoints.

Another distinction is the composition of the editorial board. With the exception of Steven Dedijer, University of Lund, Sweden, and Dr. Kenneth G. Robertson, University of Reading, it is an all American cast. And unlike the *INS*, which is dominated by historians, most members of the *IJIC* editorial board are former intelligence professionals or historians and political scientists who have had varying amounts of extended contact with the elements of the intelligence community. The latter category includes several now in academia, like Richard Pipes (Harvard), Richard Jervis (Columbia), and Loch Johnson (University of Georgia).[93] And although the *IJIC* does not have

---

90. See respectively, *IJIC*, volume 1, #3, pp. 95-108 and pp. 53-70.

91. *IJIC*, vol. 4, No. 3, pp. 295-305.

92. As quoted from William R. Harris, by Edward F. Sayle in, "Setting The Record Straight," *IJIC*, vol. 1, #1, p. 126.

93. Other editors and board members are: John F. Blake, Former Deputy Director for Administration, CIA; Douglas Blaufarb, William Hood, William R, Johnson, Joseph C. Evans, and George J. A. O'Toole, all former CIA officers; Robert Jervis and David W. Miller of Columbia University; David Kahn; BG James W. Lucas, and Hayden B. Peake,

a formal anonymous referee policy, articles are reviewed by selected members of the editorial board prior to acceptance.

IJIC has one publication policy sure to get authors attention: it pays for articles published. As a general rule, authors receive $500.00 for 6000 words or more, and less for shorter papers. Book reviewers receive $50.00 plus a copy of the book.[94]

The *IJIC* attempts to remain apolitical and is generally successful, notwithstanding a basic premise that a first rate intelligence capability in government, is essential. Authors come from within and without the international intelligence community and the range of topics is equally eclectic. There appears to be no pattern of dominance of tradecraft over analysis, or policy over organizational aspects.

Some examples from American authors include Ed Sayle's "The Historical Underpinnings of the U.S. Intelligence Community;"[95] Jefferson Adams, "Crisis and Resurgence: East German State Security," v2, #4, pp. 487-512, Winn Taplin's "Six General Principles of Intelligence, v3, #4, and "The Legitimacy of Covert Action: Sorting Out the Moral Responsibilities," by Lincoln P. Bloomfield, Jr.

One article deserves special mention. In his tales of the more dedicated than adept agents and services of the world, George Constantinides's, "Tradecraft: Follies and Foibles,"[96] provides

---

Defense Intelligence College; Fredric Mitchell, Arizona State University; Douglas Porch, The Citadel; Rose Mary Sheldon, Norwich Academy; Major J. Thompson Strong, USAF; Richard R. Valcourt, City University of New York; Edwin C. Fishel, formerly of NSA, and Daniel O'Neal Vona, III, John Jay College of Criminal Justice. The Hon. Richard Helms serves as Advisory Editor.

94. In fairness, most other periodicals mentioned in the *RGIP* that review books, also provide complimentary copies of the book to reviewers, though each one should be contacted independently to determine the particular policy.

95. *IJIC*, vol. 1, #1. Be sure to contact the publisher for a copy of the errata sheet that goes with this article if it is not with the copy of the journal available.

96. For an excellent article on the West German intelligence services see: Tom Polgar, "Intelligence Services of West Germany," v1, #4, pp. 79-96. For comment on the ever provocative covert action, see Senator William Cohen, "Congressional Oversight of Covert Actions," v2, #2 and Hugh Tovar, "Thoughts on Running a Small War," v1, #3. On the intelligence process itself, see: Loch Johnson, "Making the Intelligence Process Work," v1, #4; Robert Jervis, "What's Wrong

anecdotes for lecturers, students and after dinner speakers, while establishing a baseline of bumbledom for would be case officers. It is also good reading.

Foreign author contributions include Tel Aviv University professor Gideon Doron's, "Israeli Intelligence: Tactics, Strategy, and Prediction;" Lakehead University (Canada) professor Geoffrey R. Weller's, "Accountability in Canadian Intelligence Service;" and a paper by Argentinean, Enrique H. J. Cavalini, a student at the Monterey Institute of International Studies, "The Malvinas - Falkland Affair: A New Look."[97]

Book reviews are an important part of *IJIC*'s content. They are often short articles in themselves and include books with peripheral but substantial relevance to intelligence like, *The Soviet Union and Revolutionary Warfare*, by Richard Shultz Jr., reviewed by Richard Valcourt. Another example is the review of Ronald Kessler's *Moscow Station* by Joseph Culver Evans. Mr. Evans documents the major problems with the book and provides a critical basis on which readers can assess veracity.

IJIC also reviews books not yet published in English, a good example is, *GRU — Le plus secret des services sovietiques, 1918-1988* [*GRU — Top of the Soviet Secret Services*] (Stock, Paris, 1988), commentary by Ewa Rurarz-Huygens.[98]

A reader's forum serves the purpose of a letters to the editor column and often contains lively worthwhile exchanges. Articles are encouraged and authors should send two copies of their manuscripts to the Editor-In-Chief, F. Reese Brown, Editorial Department, *I.J.I.C.*, P.O. Box 411, New York, NY 10021. Style and format details are provided in each issue.

The *IJIC* is published by Albert Milo Dowden. It usually contains about 150 pages (7 1/2 x 10 1/2"). The pages are tan with black print, the cover is two tone brown. Annual subscriptions are available for $35.00 (personal), $55.00 (institutional), plus $7.00 for overseas subscribers. They may

with the Intelligence Process?," v1, #1; and Pedro Loureiro, "The Imperial Japanese Navy and Espionage: The Itaru Tachibana Case," vol 3, #1, pp. 105-121.

97. See respectively, *IJIC*, volume 2, #3, pp. 305-319; volume 2, #3, pp. 415-441; volume 2, #2, pp. 203-216.

98. See respectively, *IJIC*, volume 3, #1, pp. 129-136; pp. 137-139.

be obtained by writing to, *IJIC*, P.O. Box 188, Stroudsburg, PA 18360.

JANE'S INTELLIGENCE REVIEW (JIR)

The *JIR* (formerly, *Jane's Soviet Intelligence Review*) is not a review of secret espionage operations. Nor is it mainly a review of intelligence services, although there is some of that. What it does provide is the results of Jane's analysis, Jane's intelligence so to speak, with a heavy concentration on order of battle (OB) — equipment, organizations, force structure, capabilities, key personnel. Or, as Jane's puts it, *JIR* "brings you the latest unbiased factual information, intelligence and photographic evidence" on the Soviet Union and "other parts of the world, in particular the Middle East and China... every month." The product meets Jane's usual high standards and makes a singular and valuable contribution to the field of national security studies.

Implicit in these comments is the assumption that the data and analysis are accurate; but how does one know? As for the data, sources are usually given and analysis is augmented by photos, whether or not the source can be identified. In some cases, an assessment of analytic reliability must be based on Jane's reputation, supplementary data and the reader's own knowledge; Jane's track record is excellent.

There is usually one intelligence related article in each issue. For example, a three part series on the nature of what *JIR* terms "intelligence art," concluded in July 1989 with an article entitled "Soviet Space Weapons: The Greatest Challenge to Intelligence Art." The same issue also contained an article on Soviet defectors which summarizes this often intractable problem, and its converse, redefection, from the position of the receiving government and the defector.

The May 1990 issue contains an unusual, perhaps a first, 7 page interview (with pictures) by British researcher Carey Schofield, of Col. Gen. Vladlen Mikhailovich Mikhailov, (Kim

Philby's neighbor until the latter's death), the head of the Red Army military intelligence (the Glavnoye Razvedyvatelnoye Upravleniye or GRU). Ms. Schofield asked the general some tough questions and received some startling answers. For example in one response, Gen. Mikhailov explained that the "GRU is responsible for purely military intelligence... the Committee [referring to the KGB] has nothing to do with it." Ms Schofield then asked, "If the security of the army as a whole is not a function of GRU, is the security of GRU also guaranteed by an outside agency?" The general replied that "There is no one from the KGB in the GRU. I guarantee it. And as far as who is concerned with questions of security in the country in general, you should take a look at other organizations." The general goes on to admit that "In Stalin's time and in Beria's time, it was totally different." One wonders what happened to the KGB's third directorate (CI), although since the coup, the General's answer may be viewed as prophetic.

When asked about GRU officers aboard, General Mikhailov responded a bit ambiguously, that "there are perhaps no GRU officers working abroad. There is the military attaché system" which comes under "the foreign relations directorate of the Ministry of Defense." General Mikhailov shares the Western view that "the role of our intelligence and of NATO intelligence will be increasing because we should be following carefully and precisely the condition of the Armed forces on both sides. So it is my personal opinion that at present intelligence should not be reduced." Ms. Schofield responds, "Has it been?" "No," says the general, "Up to now it has not."

More recently the June 1991 issue had an article on North Korean Intelligence Agencies and infiltration operations, and another on Military Intelligence in the new Germany.

JIR editor Henry Dodds is interested in contributions from experts on intelligence subjects not normally covered by his staff.[99]

JIR is a glossy journal with a 3 color cover and about 50 pages per issue (and black and white). The pages in each volume are numbered consecutively. It uses an 8 1/4 x 11 1/2" format and is well illustrated with high quality photographic reproductions and line drawings. *JIR* is available by

---

99. Conversation with the author July, 20 1989.

subscription only for $175.00 annually. For subscription and editorial information in the USA, write Jane's Information Group, 1340 Braddock Place, Suite 300, P.O. Box 1436, Alexandria, VA 22313-2036; telephone 1-800-321-5358; FAX: 703 836-0029. For the UK call 44 81 763 0413, FAX 44 81 763 0276. *JIR* may also be obtained on-line using your PC. For information on this service in the USA call David Flint 703 836-3700, FAX 703 836-0029; in the UK call Mike Hobbs, 44 81 763 1030, FAX 44 81 763 1005.

LOBSTER - a journal of parapolitics

The provenance of *LOBSTER* is as unusual as its name. In 1982, Robin Ramsay and Stephen Dorril, two of Great Britain's self-proclaimed eminent conspiracy theorists, decided to emulate the radical anti-CIA Professor Peter Dale Scott (University of California, Berkeley), whom they admired.[100] They did so by publishing a small anti-establishment, "newsletter for about 50 like minded friends;" something "we wanted to read and no one else would do it." The problem of what to call their publication was solved by Dorril, a writer and sometime British probation officer, who "maintains a list of nonsense names for such occasions;"

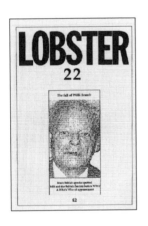

LOBSTER was the choice. Mr. Ramsay, who once worked for the Independent Television Network (INT), insists the name has no special significance and serves only to identify their publication, which it very nicely does.[101]

According to Ramsay, *LOBSTER* is a labor of political love that provides no salary and there is no outside subsidy, or "Moscow gold" as some British papers have hinted; subscriptions pay publications costs. Ads are not solicited though they are printed "if someone sends money." Despite this unconventional approach from "a couple of weirdos in the North of England... that's all we are," as Ramsay and Dorril have characterized themselves, each issue sells out, many have

---

100. This information, and that which follows, on the provenance of *LOBSTER* was provided by Mr. Ramsay during a telephone conversation with the author on 12 July 1989.
101. Stephen Dorril is the co-author with Anthony Summers of *Honeytrap: The Secret Worlds of Stephen Ward* (London: Weidenfeld & Nicolson, 1987). Dorril and Ramsay have recently published, *SMEAR!: Wilson & the Secret State* (London: Fourth Estate Limited, 1991).

been reprinted; some are out of print and "won't be reprinted, whatever the demand."

The editors see *LOBSTER* as a "member of the international brotherhood of parapolitics mags." The other members are *TOP SECRET - GEHEIM, Intelligence Newsletter,* and *Covert Action Information Bulletin,* which *LOBSTER* describes as "about as good as it gets."[102] Despite the fraternity, *LOBSTER* is distinctive in its depth of coverage, its detailed documentation, and in the absence of the rhetoric of the radical left so prevalent in its brother publications.

Beyond its unabashedly anti-establishment tenor in general, *LOBSTER* is anti-intelligence services in particular; those of the West, not the East. The Soviet Union, the KGB and the Eastern Bloc countries (when they existed) are largely ignored. The main focus is on the "bad" MI6 and MI5, with the CIA close behind, and other services with ties to these principals. The articles are written from the British political left and it is assumed the reader is familiar with the events and the cast of characters. Those wishing to grasp all the subtleties and innuendo, will have homework to do. A British journalist recently wrote that, "much of its content is impenetrable."[103] He is almost right, but *LOBSTER* is also intriguing. A good example is issue # 11 (April 1986, 55 pp.), which is devoted to "Wilson, MI5 and the Rise of Thatcher," or, "covert operations in British politics 1974-78." Despite the up-front political slant, it is a comprehensive account which should be included in serious study of these matters.[104]

LOBSTER has also been a frequent source of stories related to Philby and the Cambridge spies. Issue #16 has an interesting discussion of the possible role of Lord Rothschild in this regard, as seen by the press, and authors Nigel West and Chapman Pincher, among others. Also included is a translation, done by the FBI, of Philby's 1971 interview in Estonia.[105] Many articles are heavily footnoted, an element of scholarship Ramsay and Dorril have made an art form that the

---

102.*LOBSTER,* #9. p. 4, and conversation with Ramsay.
103.Jim White, *The Observer,* 1990, p.
104.*LOBSTER,* #17, footnote #7, p. 3. See fn #96 regarding the authors recent book on this subject which they describe as "essential for a full understanding of the Wilson plots."
105.ibid., #16., pp. 9-15, n.d.

documentation does not always support the conclusions which they candidly admit. An article in issue #19 contains the comment, "The material above is incomplete, under researched and does not sustain the following conclusions. Nevertheless, this is how we believe, this is how it feels."

As Julius Mader did in 1968 with his *Who's Who in CIA*, *LOBSTER* published its own "A Who's Who of the British Secret State,"[106] giving names and biographical data about British government officers "with indications of intelligence background." Perhaps in order to be fair, lists of alleged CIA officers stationed in London were reprinted from its German brother, *GEHEIM*.

LOBSTER issues frequently contain book reviews and news items. A recent review of the Hugh Thomas book, *Hess: A Tale of Two Murders* (London: Hodder & Stoughton, 1988),[107] lays out an account recently challenged on British television by Cambridge historian, Dr. Christopher Andrew. Dorril and Ramsay attack Andrew and academics like him for "refusing to distinguish between conspiracy theories and conspiracy research."[108] In another review, Richard Deacon's book, *The Truth Twisters* is taken to task, rather unfairly, to put it mildly, "as a classic of Western disinformation purporting to describe Soviet disinformation."[109] In short, *LOBSTER*'s reviews are not just descriptive of content. They are to the point, analytical, and reflect the political position of the authors.

In the news category, issue #19 has an obituary of Greville Wynne which is a balanced account of his life by any measure. They have also commented on American newsletters, like *FILS* (see page 46), which they characterize as "mainstream, (by contemporary American standards centre-right), academic, orthodox anti-communist, anti-Soviet, [and] anti-left."[110]

---

106. This document is the 111 page May 1989 issue. It is not the first time *LOBSTER* has done something like this. Issues #9 & 10 contained earlier attempts and #16 has a few. The consolidated May 1989 (unnumbered) issue covers some of the same ground (mostly the A & Bs), though some names have been added and others deleted. A supplement to the May 1989 issue included in issue #19, 19 May 1990.
107. *LOBSTER*, #17 pp. 20-1 & #20, pp. 29-31.
108. *LOBSTER*, #19, p. 26.
109. ibid., pp. 20-21.
110. *LOBSTER*, #17, p. 22.

Finally, there are articles on the problems of the world's intelligence services, and the personalities who served them. In the former category (in addition to the continual thumping on Britain's own) is the story of the French Secret Service and the Rainbow Warrior episode. In the latter group, there is an interesting account of the career of George Kennedy Young (MI6), "written by a close friend of his."[111] The author remains anonymous, but hints of Anthony Cavendish abound. In issue # 21, guest author Jeffrey M. Bale takes on the Unification Church and the KCIA.

LOBSTER has not been the victim of over planning. No charter has been publicly articulated. It began in 1983 and has averaged just under 3 issues per year. Only a few of the early issues are dated, most are numbered though beginning with #17 (November 1988) they have both. Topics, says Mr. Ramsay, are selected from "current news, subscriber comment, and leaks," which appear plentiful. Contributions, like Jeffrey M. Bale's "The Ultranationalist Right In Turkey and the Attempted Assassination of Pope John Paul II," are welcome,[112] but no compensation is paid.

LOBSTER issues contain from 20 to 50 black and white pages (20 x 30 cm). The printing is small, with a two column format and some photographs; starting with issue #17, desktop publishing has been abandoned for typesetting. Annual subscriptions (2 to 3 issues) are £7.00 in the US; Europe £6.00, Britain £4.0. Dollars and credit cards not accepted; international money orders in pounds will do nicely. Some back copies are available, prices vary with issue number. Subscriptions and further information can be obtained from *LOBSTER*, 214 Westbourne Avenue, Hull, HU5 3JB, U.K. Telephone: Robin Ramsay 0482 447558; Stephen Dorril 0484 681388.

---

111. *LOBSTER*, #16, pp. 30-32; and Issue #19, pp. 15-19.
112. Ibid., #19, pp. 28-41. Bale has an extensive bibliography and 257 footnotes, many annotated. He looks at the question of whether Agca's connections with the Turkish right could have provided motive for his acts. He allows, however, that this does not mean others were not involved. The evidence on that question is still not sufficient to say.

MILITARY INTELLIGENCE (MI)

MI is published by the U. S. Army Intelligence Command and School at Fort Huachuca, Arizona. It is something more than a magazine and less than a journal. While it does not ignore history as Lt. Steven J. Martin's article, "Custer Didn't Listen," (April-June 1989, pp. 17-20) shows, its principal emphasis is on the military intelligence problems of today and tomorrow as seen through the eyes of experienced participants and military scholars. In short, *MI* is an illustrated magazine with footnotes in many of its first hand accounts, think pieces, and articles.

The spectrum of topics is wide and ranges from deception, cross cultural communications and international security issues, to tactical intelligence effectiveness and the impact of glasnost, the latter gained during first hand contact in the Soviet Union.[113] *MI* also serves as a forum for exposing new ideas and doctrine while encouraging comments from those involved. As an example, Lieutenant Colonel Bob Hunt in his article, "Counterintelligence Analysis — The Rest of the Story," responds to an earlier article on the same topic by Major E.H. Coet. CI analysis is a relatively new career field in the military, though not a new function, and the growing pains are well laid out in these offerings.[114] Another relatively new topic is discussed in "Military Intelligence in Low Intensity Conflict," by Captain David B. Collins, USAF.[115]

---

113. See the April-June 1989 and July-September 1989 issues for typical coverage. General John A. Wickham, Jr., "Viewing Gorbachev from Inside and Outside," *Military Intelligence*, Vol. 15, No. 2, April-June 1989.

114. Major E.H. Coet, "Counterintelligence Analysis — The Untrained Discipline," *Military Intelligence*, October, 1988.

115. Ibid., July-September 1991, p. 10.

MI has regular columns on language training, book reviews, intelligence training, and an occasional Army favorite, the "Lessons Learned" article. Examples of the latter is "The Union's Blind Eyes: HUMINT in the Civil War," by John P. Finnegan, and "Operation Just Cause: The Divisional MI Battalion, The Nonlinear Battlefield, and AirLand Operations-Future," by Victor M. Rosello.[116]

Military Intelligence was called *MI Magazine* in 1974 when it was first published, and it remained so for the first three volumes. It is a quarterly with two color cover, about 50 pages per issue, in 8 1/2 x 11" format. It is available to all for $6.50 per year, MasterCard and Visa accepted. For subscriptions, information about availability, author requirements and back issues, write to, USAIC&S, ATTN: ATSI-TD-MIM, Fort Huachuca, Arizona 85613-7000.

---

116. Ibid., October, 1988, p. 29 and July-September 1991, p. 28.

MILITARY INTELLIGENCE CRITICAL ATTRIBUTES (MICA)

Nearing its 40th year, *MICA* is described in several databases (e.g., *DIALOG*, see page 239) as "irregularly" published. The British publisher, Aviation Studies Atlantic, says cryptically, that there are "periodic updatings every year." *MICA* promotional material says its contents include: "AF Leadership/Intelligence Advisories, Chiefs, organization, roles, missions, costs, manpower, NIE planning, kinds of intell."

The topical index is only somewhat more specific with its list of subjects like: "Agency intelligence, Army intelligence, C cubed I, Crypto, DIA, DIS, DMA, Murder International, National Intelligence, Space Intelligence, Security Intelligence, Subversion, U.K. Intelligence, and USSR Intelligence." Entries are short descriptive comments on these and other topics. In short, it is a printed reference database or order of battle estimate.

MICA is about 70 pages (8" x 10") and comes in a loose-leaf 2 ring binder with an index. The "periodic updatings" amount to 4 to 5 updates per year totaling about 30 pages. Initial and annual costs are $450.00 per year, postage included; sample sheets are available on request. The Library of Congress does not have a copy. For further information write: Aviation Studies, Sussex House, Parkside, London SW19 5NB, England.

MILITARY & SUBVERSIVE THREAT ANALYSIS (MISTA)

A Northern Newsletter

Writings on the Soviet intelligence threat routinely acknowledge the world wide pervasiveness of the KGB and GRU. Nevertheless, the actual extent of their operations in

the countries of Scandinavia does not get much attention in the English speaking press. In the early 1980s, Swedish lawyer and author Bertil Haggman, concluded that even for those interested

[t]here was at the time a lack of reliable information and analysis of Soviet subversion in Scandinavia in light of the ongoing Moscow pressures mainly on the two non-aligned countries Sweden and Finland. But also the three Scandinavian NATO countries Denmark, Iceland and Norway [which] were subject to Soviet threats.[117]

These circumstances led Mr. Haggman to begin publishing *MISTA* in 1983 as a window for the English speaking world; there are no Swedish subscribers.

Now in its ninth volume, *MISTA* has tracked the espionage and disinformation activities of the KGB, the GRU, and their former surrogates in the Warsaw Pact countries. This policy will continue no matter what organization undertakes the former KGB foreign intelligence mission.

Typical topics include the expulsion of Soviet agents like Igor Nikiforov, a KGB general who was ordered to leave in September 1991. Other examples are the appointment of a new counterespionage chief in Sweden, and the decision of the Swedish Communist Party to change its name in light of the

---

117. Letter from Mr. Haggman to the author, dated 8 August 1990

events in Eastern Europe and recent defectors. The May-June 1991 issues looks at Swedes who worked for the Stasi, and among other topics, comments on a conference that considered "The Moral Responsibility of the Left" under the new socialist/communist reality.

Most issues of *MISTA* have reviews of Swedish books on intelligence (unfortunately few are translated into English, including a recent one by Mr. Haggman.)[118] There are also short items, or historical footnotes, like the admission by the Soviet Union that it was a mistake to attack Finland in 1939.

For many, the amount of terrorist activity in Sweden will come as a shock. *MISTA* reports and documents numerous "connections between Moscow and international terrorism [that] have been unearthed in Sweden." One example involved Professor Joyce Blau, second-in-command to Soviet agent Henri Curiel (George Blake's cousin).

Computer security and domestic political intelligence operations are also problems as the May-June 1988 issue demonstrates. *MISTA* notes that the Swedish security service discovered the Soviet Union and its allies have copies of the computerized register of the entire Swedish population, including those who have committed crimes. On the domestic scene, a Swedish security officer was searched at the Danish border and found to be carrying "bugging" equipment which is illegal in Sweden. The officer involved had links to the Swedish minister of justice. *MISTA* outlines the political and intelligence service consequences of the apprehension.

In the "whatever happened to" category, *MISTA* reported in its May-June 1989 issue that the "Soviet submarine commander, Pjotr Gushchin, who commanded the submarine stranded outside the Swedish naval base Kalskrona on October 27, 1981, has reportedly died in a Soviet prison camp" while serving a three year sentence of hard labor.

Considerable attention is given to Soviet Disinformation and political influence. The May-June 1990 issue tells of Nikolai Neilands, currently the Latvian Vice Foreign Minister. The Swedish security police describe him as a "Latvian

---

118.Bertil Haggman, ***Desinformation*** (Stockholm, Contra Forlag & Co., KB, 1990), 125 pp.

disinformation agent," who once served in Sweden and was then suspected of being an "agent of the KGB." A number of his contacts are mentioned. Later interviewed by a Swedish newspaper, Neilands said elliptically, "I have heard that there are more democrats and enlightened people within the KGB than in the party apparatus."

An example with more far reaching implications appears in the *MISTA* September - October 1991 issue that leads off with the subject: "Don't Trust Foreign Minister Boris Pankin - A Swedish Warning." Pankin was Ambassador to Sweden before moving to Czechoslovakia. The article notes Pankin's role in a disinformation scandal in Greece when he was "head of the Soviet Copyright Organization, Vaap, with close ties to KGB...." Then its states that "informed Swedish observers say that Pankin was and is a KGB General." The article ends with a list of political statements made by Pankin he probably wouldn't make today.

In sum, whether the interest is in history, international relations or comparative intelligence services (a must for those concerned with counterintelligence), *MISTA* provides a singular source of information and a new perspective on Scandinavia. The articles are not signed; sources or references are almost always given in the narrative.

MISTA is published bimonthly 5 times per year (not in the summer) at a cost of $40.00. Issues are single spaced, black and white xeroxed, on legal size paper, from 4-6 pages in length. Sample copies are available. For further information and subscriptions write to: Mr. Bertil Haggman, Editor, P.O. Box 1412, S-251 14, HELSINGBORG, Sweden.

NAVAL INTELLIGENCE BULLETIN (NIB)

The *Naval Intelligence Bulletin* is the professional bulletin of the Naval Intelligence with the mission of keeping all Naval Intelligence personnel informed on current intelligence issues." The terms current intelligence issues should not be misinterpreted. The NIB is not a source of current intelligence in the traditional foreign and domestic meanings of the terms. It is the in-house newsletter, so to speak, for the Director of Naval Intelligence (DNI) and the naval personnel serving in the field. Evidence of this can be seen in the parochial use of terms like CINCLANT, LANTJIC, FICEURLANT, FOSIC, FICPAC, AND NAVMILPERSCOMINST, NAVRESECGRU, not always with translations. Its focus is on Naval intelligence personnel and their careers and may well be of interest to students of military or defense intelligence generally.

Issues contain messages from the Director of Naval Intelligence (DNI), articles on ONI policy, the outlook for the future, a section on career and assignment related issues, and comments on ONI organization including charts. There is also a professional development section with contributions from Naval intelligence personnel serving in the field. This often reflects current changes in activity locations due to budget cutbacks. It can also include comments from squadron intelligence officers, informal evaluations of training programs, and problems getting SCI clearances in time for personnel to be productive. One issue included comments from the "Navy Liaison Officer at NSA." Other sections contain short book reviews, letters to the editor, and data on where intelligence personnel are serving.

The Naval Intelligence Bulletin is published quarterly by the Commander, Naval Intelligence Command. Send questions concerning subscriptions and submissions to the Editor, NIB, NIC-12, 4600 Silver Hill Road, Washington, D.C. 20389-5000.

NAVAL INTELLIGENCE PROFESSIONALS QUARTERLY (NIPQ)

The Naval Intelligence Professionals (NIP), Inc., is an organization of active duty and former naval intelligence persons and interested col-leagues who want to stay cur-rent. The *Quarterly*, as they call it, is how they do it. It is more than a newsletter that tracks member activities, although there is some of that. But it is not a journal with long articles and footnotes, though there are seri-ous contributions to Naval intel-ligence history and reviews of important books. Nor is it a magazine, in the sense of short unattributed pieces full of pictures, though it does use photos and has a "Where Are They Now?" column. In fact, the *Quarterly* was not even published quarterly until volume six. Whatever its precise category, its job is "well done." And, says editor G. H. Hancock, neither the NIP nor the *Quarterly* have any PAC (political action committee) functions or agenda.

The articles are principally first person historical accounts and opinion pieces by noted naval experts. Some have been or will be printed elsewhere in greater detail, and their appear-ance in the *Quarterly* is for reader convenience. For a recent example see, "A Code Break And The Death Of Admiral Yamamoto," by Capt Roger Pineau, USNR (Ret).[119]

In other cases, original material is published, sometimes in parts over several issues. Interesting examples in this category include a two part piece by Capt E.D. Smith Jr., USN, "A Naval Intelligence Strategy," and Alan N. Schneider's, "Ian and I Part VI."[120] Schneider was a wartime colleague of the James Bond

---

119. Captain Pineau was a co-author, with John Costello and RADM Edwin T. Layton, of, *"And I Was There"* (NY: Morrow, 1985).
120. Capt. E. D. Smith, Jr., USN, "A Naval Intelligence Strategy, "Part I,

author and tells of their adventures in a six part series. A recent issue contains articles on "Operation Desert Storm: Naval Intelligence in Riyadh," and "Naval Intelligence Organizations in Washington, DC."

If there is an overall emphasis to the *Quarterly*, aside from a slight list toward matters Naval in general, it is intelligence history. In addition to articles on the subject, like "U.S. Grant Goes to Shiloh,"[121] and an oral history program, members are encouraged to commit their recollections to paper. If they are too sketchy for the *Quarterly*, they will be forwarded to the Naval Historical Center for integration into its database. Even a summary of intelligence billets (assignments) is a contribution to the big picture. Such a database will be of real value to the intelligence scholar and ultimately his readers and students.

Most issues contain book reviews that cover intelligence subjects as well as related naval topics and history. A recent exemplar is the Dick Bates (Captain, USN, Ret.) review of *The Pueblo Surrender: A Covert Action by the National Security Agency*, by Robert A. Liston.[122] A typical Liston conclusion, from data provided by his "informants," is that "NSA runs the United States." Bates finds this, and the book generally, hard to take seriously. He suggests, tolerantly, that some of Liston's informants were "pulling his leg." In the related subject category, Dean W. Given has taken a lessons learned look at *Soviet Submarines — Design, Development and Tactics* (London: Jane's, 1989), by Jan Breener.

One of the several regular columns in the *Quarterly*, "Writing About Naval Intelligence," by Dick Bates, is of general interest and worth the reader's attention. The title is misleading since Capt. Bates discusses subjects outside Naval Intelligence like the Institute for Policy Studies, ARDIS (the Association for Responsible Dissent), and The Christic Institute as well as "professional organizations either solely or partially dedicated to intelligence." His treatment is dispassionate and apolitical; references and sources are given in the narrative.

NIPQ, January 1989, volume 5, #1, pp. 1-3.

121. Bob Curts, "U.S. Grant Goes to Shiloh," *NIPQ*, Winter 1989, p. 5-8.

122. Robert A. Liston, *The Pueblo Surrender: A Covert Action by the National Security Agency*, (NY: M. Evans & Company, 1988).

The *NIPQ* issues run about 28 pages (8 1/2 x 11"). The black on gray cover with the name and NIP logo has a very professional look. It is available with NIP membership, $18.00/year, which is open to active duty and retired military and civilians, and "others" with similar interests who are not former naval persons.

For general information write, *NIP*, P. O. Box 9324, McLean, VA 22102-9998, or call Mr. A.D. Sesow (see-so) (703) 938-1765. For details regarding manuscript submission policies, use the same address, Attention: G.H. Hancock, Editor, or call 703 437-7487. All numbers are for office hours.

NMIA NEWSLETTER

This is a traditional newsletter aimed at keeping members apprised of organizational events and activities. But it also contains items of interest to the scholar and general reader such as the regular columns, "Allied Information Tidbits" and "Soviet Information Tidbits." The views of senior intelligence officials and members of the diplomatic corps on contemporary issues are included.

One issue in 1988 (Vol 3, #2) contained a "1990 NMIA Intelligence Assessment Quiz," where members were asked to answer questions about intelligence and national security issues like "Will Gorbachev stay in power?" Items from other periodicals are reprinted to keep members apprised of related activity. A recent example in this category asks is the "Rumanian Secret Service Using Radiation Device?"[123] In addition, the newsletter publishes notices of NMIA symposia, like the recent one on Intelligence and Low Intensity Conflict.

The *NMIA NEWSLETTER*, is a 16 page quarterly in 8 1/2 x 11 format with photos, and some advertising. Published by the National Military Intelligence Association, it encourages reader comments and contributions. Editorial, subscription and other information may be obtained by writing to: NMIA, Pentagon Station, P.O. Box 46583, Washington, D.C. 20050-6583.

123.*NMIA Newsletter*, Vol 3, #2., page 8.

The NUMBERS FACTSHEET (TNFS)

The *Numbers Factsheet (TNFS)* is "compiled and edited by Havana Moon," and "published by Moonbeam Press." These names were chosen to catch the reader's eye and have nothing to do with the former governor of California.

From the name alone one might not, understandably, associate *TNFS* with intelligence. In fact, the first issue (June 1990) stated only that the newsletter would be "devoted to Numbers Stations [hence the name] and related topics." By the fourth issue (April 1991), however, the "devoted to" topics included "SIGINT, covert radio, intelligence, cryptography, computers as they relate to all of the above and other topics not generally covered elsewhere." This expanded scope begins to make sense when it is realized that

"*numbers stations*" is a term used by the "Shortwave Listening Community" for what they also call "*spy numbers transmissions.*"[124] From the shortwave listener viewpoint, *TNFS* explains that *spy numbers transmissions*

are a shortwave oddity which have been around for the last 25 years. They are commonly heard in English, German, Spanish and the Slavic languages and take the form of four and five digit groups of numbers which are preceded by a three digit 'identified' and 'group count.' They are generally broadcast by a mechanical-sounding female voice, although more code (CW) 'cut number transmissions are also frequently reported.[125]

---

124. Quote from the Masthead of the *The Numbers Factsheet*, Vol. 2, #1, July 1991, p. 2. Vol. 1 #1 contains a tutorial on numbers stations.

125. *The Numbers Factsheet*, VOl. 1, #1, p. 2. To hear a "numbers" transmission (in Spanish), "tune your radio to 11468 kHz any Saturday" at 1600 EST to hear a "classic transmission" for 15-30 minutes.

From this description, students of intelligence will recognize that the so-called *spy numbers transmissions* are one form of agent communications which have been around much longer than 25 years.

Persons who record and try to make sense out of *"spy numbers transmissions"* are called, among other things, *"numbers chasers."* They operate what are in effect amateur intercept stations, not because they want to penetrate espionage operations (although that clearly would be fun), but because of the challenge posed by these mysterious transmissions. *Numbers chasers* are intrigued, inter alia, by the meaning of different formats, frequencies used, operator expertise, human errors, and clues to the originator; in other words, they are traffic analysts. The guru of this merry band, Havana Moon, is also the creator of *TNFS*, which in turn is the outgrowth of Moon's earlier column on unusual radio transmissions written for a Newark radio club bulletin. *Havana Moon* is indeed a pseudonym chosen as an attention getter while protecting the author's true identity for reasons not explained.[126]

The Numbers Factsheet reports on the results of the *Numbers chasers* efforts while giving advice on how to improve technique and skills. Issues include short articles on numbers stations and related topics from Europe and the Middle East to the Caribbean and the Far East. Some, like "Spy Transmitter of the GDR Silent" (Vol 1, #2) are historical. Others like "Babes, Beautiful Babes," are contemporary and tell of curious intercepts in Jerusalem.

TNFS also has a number of interesting columns and in the recent issues several new ones have been added. One, called *The Crypt*, presented an excellent tutorial on the one-time-pad (Vol 1, #2). There is another a regular column called *Spies on Stamps* which shows pictures and gives short accounts of recent stamps related to espionage (acquisition data are provided). The recent additions include *"RF Mysteries: Things That Go Bump Wheedle 'n Tweet,"* by Gary Bourgois, and *"Silhouettes,"* which provides historical perspective on

---

126. The Masthead of each issue explains that **"Havana Moon** is the pseudonym of a former US intelligence officer who is well known for his expertise in the area of Numbers stations and other shortwave mysteries."

cryptology and cryptanalysis. The latter is contributed by Dr. Felix Lof, a retired Brit who worked on "the fringes of professional crypto community" (Vol 2, #4).

Book reviews are also a regular feature. They are generally of two types, the "briefly noted" variety with minimum discussion, and the longer descriptive version, usually signed, like the review of David Kahn's *Seizing The Enigma*, by Zel Eaton (Vol 2, #1).

Each issue of *TNFS* begins with two feature articles on the front page. The range of topics is wide: from "mysterious Numbers Station from the Far East," to an interesting analysis of the unexpected transmissions from the former Soviet Bloc countries which continue to this day. Both feature articles in the April 1991 issue looked at the Bay of Pigs Anniversary. The emphasis of one is on COMINT and the other is a "Requiem for Brigade 2506" (Vol 2, #1).

As a rule the articles are signed but no sources are given. An example is Donald E. Kimberlin's *"The Day The Spooks Stepped on Ma Bell"* in which the author implies conflict with CIA communications without ever saying so directly (Vol 2, #1). On occasion pseudonyms are used as in the case of "Poco Coyote" who writes on "SIGINT tales" and "King Kasten" author of "A Warrenton Primer" (Vol 2, #1). The latter purports to be an expose of CIA communications facilities. Havana Moon attempts to add credence to "Kasten's" contribution by noting that the his knowledge of the "Virgina sites... is astonishing." The reader must make is own judgment as to veracity.

TNFS incorporates a practice which is likely to catch on with other periodicals: the signed articles usually give an electronic mail (E-Mail) address where the author can be contacted directly. Questions about unsigned articles can be sent to *TNFS* via one of its E-Mail addresses (see below). I have tried this method and the response is quick and encouraging.

In a relatively short time *TNFS* has grown from an 8 to a 20 page publication. In the process it has absorbed two other periodicals which covered similar territory - *Umbra et Lux* [roughly 'light in the shadows'] and *Bits, Bytes & BBSs*. The latter was concerned with "computers as they relate to radio, defense and intelligence." The *BBSs* stands for bulletin board systems and will prove of interest to those with personal computers. The former editor of *Bits, Bytes & BBSs*, Kristin Kaye, now writes the *RF Bits* column for *TNFS* which focuses on SIGINT and computer related items like the US Army's search for computer hackers to "develop a potential to break into enemy computer systems." *Umbra et Lux* was a quarterly newsletter which reported on SIGINT and covert shortwave communications. Its editor, Harry L. Helms, is now a regular contributor to and the Associate Editor of *TNFS*.

According to Havana Moon *TNFS* will continue to evolve with more new columns and perhaps a name change to just *The Factsheet*, though this would seem to confuse rather than clarify. Its format — two column, lettersize — has remained constant, however, as has it use of newsprint (single color, black print). Current subscription rates are $20.00 per year in the USA, $30.00 in Canada and overseas. Contributions are encouraged though no guarantee of publication is given. Questions concerning advertising, compensation, and other matters should be sent to the Editor, *The Numbers Factsheet*, PO Box 149, Briarcliff Manor, NY 10510. Contact may also by made by calling 914-923-1862 or E-Mail: havanamoon@cup.portal.com; ckp@cup.portal.com; Havana.Moon (*GENie*); or harry_helms@cup.portal.com.

PERISCOPE

*P*ERISCOPE, the once quarterly Journal of the Association of Former Intelligence Officers (AFIO), became a ten issue per year *monthly* newsletter in January 1992. Although the

number of pages per issue was reduced to 4 (from about 30), the currency of its content and publication has improved. *PERISCOPE* contains much of benefit to future careerists, those with a desire to better understand the intelligence profession, and scholars or writers looking for first hand views and even an outlet for their own viewpoints.

In addition to feature articles, the monthly version will add regular columns to cover current events, member profiles, chapter news and letters to the editor. The result of all the changes, according to AFIO executive director David Whipple, will better serve the membership in these times of rapid change.

As part of a now 17 year tradition, *PERISCOPE* will continue to include, on an occasional basis, historical essays (some with photographs) and remarks, sometimes verbatim, made by intelligence community notables. Examples in the latter category include comments by former DCI William H. Webster on the status of the Intelligence Community and the issue of congressional oversight, Dr. Fritz Ermarth, Chairman, National Intelligence Council, on "The Role of Analysis," VADM William O. Studeman, Director NSA, on intelligence performance in the Gulf war, and Douglas Gow, Asst. FBI Director on the foreign intelligence threat.[127] As a rule sources

---

127. William H. Webster, *PERISCOPE*, VOL., XIV, No. 2, Spring 1989 and VOL XV, No. 1, Winter 1990. The date is misprinted on the Spring issue as 1988 (it should be 1989). Fritz Ermarth, "The Role of Analysis," *PERISCOPE*, Fall 1988, pp. 7-11. For Studeman and Gow,

are not cited though, where appropriate, they may be obtained by contacting AFIO.

PERISCOPE also informs the readers about opposition activities. A recent piece comments on the new publication *Campus Watch* (see page 19) which, among other things, quotes Philip Agee, on "why it is so important to turn off this [the universities] faucet of new recruits" for the CIA. Former CIA officer John Stockwell is also quoted blaming the CIA for the AIDS epidemic and charging that the films *Rambo* and *Red Dawn* were created as CIA propaganda so that children "would learn to glorify war."[128]

The August 1991 issue describes the amazing experiences of Professor Philip V. Fellman and his successful battle against the phenomenon of *Political Correctness* when he taught a course on intelligence at Dartmouth College. The irony is inescapable — as communism died in its homeland, its tradition of 'questions not open to argument' is alive and prospering in a major American university.

For the two months each year that *PERISCOPE* is not published, editor Mary Scully states that AFIO members will receive *PERISCOPE's* sister publication, *The Intelligencer* (see page 76) which, though aimed primarily at academia, will have items, especially the book reviews, of interest to all.

PERISCOPE uses a 8 1/2 x 11" format in two colors (blue and black). Subscriptions come with AFIO membership ($35.00 per year) which is open to all. Submissions are encouraged though compensation comes solely from the satisfaction of publication. And, as with all periodicals, the decision rests with the editor. For further details about *PERISCOPE* contact AFIO executive director David Whipple, 6723 Whittier Ave., Suite 303A, McLean, VA 22101. (703) 790-0320.

---

see Vol. XVI, No. 1, 1991.
128. Ibid., p. 10.

POLITICAL WARFARE (PW)
Intelligence, Active Measures & Terrorism Report

Political Warfare was originally called *DISINFORMATION: Soviet Active Measures and Disinformation Forecast*. With issue # 14 (Spring 1990) it became *Soviet Intelligence & Active Measures (SIAM)*. The change was primarily because of the new circumstances in the Soviet Union and eastern Europe. Then, in early 1991, "given the multi-polarity of world affairs and the wide ranging nature of US interests," the editor, Georgetown University professor Roy Godson, decided to "enlarge the publication's focus to include related types of hostile or covert efforts," such as terrorism, "'to wage war' on public opinion in the West and other democratic states."

Thus, with the Spring issue of 1991, *Political Warfare* was born with the objective of tracking and documenting "the unconventional tactics that states and terrorist groups use to adversely affect the security of the US and other democracies." Moscow's efforts in these areas will still be reported, but the scope will be expanded to include the "threat from other non-democratic states and groups." Now that the Soviet Union has taken steps toward democracy, it may be expected that Political Warfare will monitor closely its policies concerning disinformation, terrorism, and active measures.[129]

PW is distinguished in part from the monthly *New COUNTERPOINT* by its emphasis on the future, articles written by a variety of experts in the field, its publication frequency (3 issues per year), and by its impressive two-color

---

129. The quotes above are from the Spring 1991 issue of *Political Warfare*.

presentation. *PW* recognizes *COUNTERPOINT*'s contribution to the field and the Spring 1991 issue of *PW* included
excerpts from the January 1991 issue of *COUNTERPOINT* (see
page 28).

An international advisory board works with the *PW* editor
to achieve its goals. Its membership includes French Soviet
historian and political philosopher, professor Alain Besancon;
former KGB officer Ilya Dzhirkvelov;[130] Boston University
professor Ladislav Bittman, a disinformation specialist
formerly with the Czech Intelligence Service; professor
Richard Shultz;[131] Boston University professor Uri Ra'anan;
former KGB officer and active measures specialist, Stanislav
Levchenko; Sidney Hook, and Adam Ulam, Director of
Harvard's Russian Institute.

In the past, in one issue each year, *PW* has anticipated the
likely Soviet activities in active measures for the coming year.
In the future this objective will be expanded to include other
countries and groups. A companion column called, "Our Track
Record," presents a candid evaluation of the previous years'
predictions; successful and unsuccessful. Included in the
success is the 1987 story on "the Soviet AIDS-made-in-the-USA
campaign." In the missed calls category for 1987, they "did not
anticipate the extent to which the Soviets would confess to past
deception practices." Looking back over 1989, a good job was
done predicting the disinformation themes like the need for a
"common European home," and the "Gorbachev should be
helped with investments" pitch. The number of new front
groups also increased as predicted and the old ones remained.
On the other side of the coin, the level of Soviet emphasis on
environmental issues to garner support was not foreseen, nor
was the Soviet reaction to East Europe's upheaval.

For the 1990s, *PW* predicted, among other things, that the
Soviets will work hard to convince the world that they should
not be viewed as the enemy; that NATO should be a political
"transmission belt;" the Soviets will use "business diplomacy"
to weaken the American geopolitical position; and they will

---

130. Dzhirkvelov served in both the first and second Chief Directorates of
the KGB, and was Deputy Secretary General of the Union of Soviet
Journalist where he worked extensively with disinformation projects.
131. Director of the International Security Program at the Fletcher School
of Law and Diplomacy.

continue their campaign to reduce restrictions on technology exports from America. The recent revolution will, of course, require a rethinking of these arguments. But some of their assessments were on the mark as when the Spring 1991 issue predicted that Gennadiy Yanayev (the coup leader), who said he was a "communist to the depths of my soul," was "the man to watch."

Typical *PW* feature articles include Adam Ulam's, "Countering Soviet Propaganda," or "Anticipating Moscow's Use of Emigres," by former International Department officer, Evgueni Novikov, and "When Are Active Measures Effective? or "KGB 'Back Channel' Documented."[132] The Winter 1989 issue has a valuable fold-out chart of the Soviet active measures organizational superstructure which now provides a basis for comparison with future changes. Other articles, reprinted from Soviet publications and *FBIS*, frequently give surprising Soviet views. Perhaps the winner in this category is the item on the proposal by KGB Colonel Igor Prelin to form an international organization of former intelligence officers (*SIAM*, Spring, 1990, #14, p. 10). Patrick Watson's, the "Changing Foreign Intelligence Threat: FBI Assessment," is an excellent example of the solid intelligence articles that may be found in PW.[133]

PW also provides solid book reviews like those on the new series edited by Dennis Bark on "Moscow's orchestration of its own and its allies active measures resources." The first volume, The Red Orchestra: Instruments of Soviet Policy in Latin America and the Caribbean, has been published.[134] The review of Edward Jay Epstein's new book, *Deception: The War Between the KGB and the CIA*,[135] gives some perceptive comments on his view of the historical meaning of glasnost and the epistemology of deception. A more recent contribution is the review of *KGB: The Inside Story*, by Christopher Andrew

---

132. *DISINFORMATION*: Summer 1989, No. 12, pp. 1, 12; Winter 1989, No. 11, pp. 1, 14-16.
133. *PW*, Spring, 1991, p. 1, 10-11.
134. See review in *DISINFORMATION*, No. 5, Winter 1987, p. 5.; Dennis L. Bark, *The Red Orchestra: Instruments of Soviet Policy in Latin America and the Caribbean* (Stanford, CA: Hoover Institution, 1987). The next volume will be on Soviet involvement in Africa and is due for publication in 1990.
135. Edward Jay Epstein, *Deception: The War Between the KGB and the CIA* (NY: Simon and Schuster, 1989).

and Oleg Gordievsky, which notes their prophetic conclusion that the only solution for the KGB is to abolish its current structure.

Some issues also contain articles devoted to particular topics; e.g., "Soviet Priorities in '89," and "Soviet Use of Fronts: The Old and the New," and the Stasi penetration of Der Spiegel.[136] Documentation of specific active measures is a regular feature and provides an excellent source of recent thinking on the subject.

PW is printed on coated 8 1/2 x 11" stock and well illustrated with photographs and charts in its 24 pages. It is available in some magazine and bookstores and can be obtained by subscription, $35.00/year (or by single issue for $10.00) from the Institute for International Studies, *PW* Editorial Office, 1815 H Street NW, Suite 600, Washington D.C., 20006; (202) 466-2849.

---

136. *DISINFORMATION*, Winter 1989, No. 11, pp. 1, 17-20; Summer 1989, No. 12, pp. 6-8; Spring 1991, PW.

PROPAGANDA - DISINFORMATION - PERSUASION (PDP)

The Boston University Program for the Study of Disinformation was established in 1986 with Ladislav Bittman as Director. Its objective is to:

> study current disinformation campaigns — their methodology, world wide orchestration, and misuse of democratic communications systems — and to serve scholars and journalists from democratic countries with literature and expertise on the subjects of international propaganda and disinformation.[137]

The *PDP* is a journal for publishing the results of research on these topics by experts in the field.

The Summer 1990 issue is typical although there is no standard subject mix. An article by Stanislav Levchenko surveys Soviet active measures in 1989, including the KGB's role, throughout the world. Branka Lapajne examines the official Canadian view of the Soviet Union as a "benign world power seeking peace and detente," and the effectiveness of Communist organizations in Canada to propagandize this view. Pierre Rigoulot looks at "Soviet Propaganda and Disinformation in France," contrasting the ineffective overt propaganda with the more successful indirect propaganda and disinformation. USIA Soviet disinformation expert, Todd Leventhal, reports his own views of "U.S. - Soviet Talks on Disinformation." He discusses the major "crude Soviet disinformation" themes, the steps the U.S. has taken to counter them, and looks at Soviet charges of U.S. disinformation. His comments about two 1988 Soviet books, in English, with a "veritable smorgasbord of disinformation," are instructive. The first, *Once Again About*

---

137. This statement appears on the title page of each *PDP* Journal.

The CIA (Moscow: Progress Publishers, 1988), repeated the claims that, inter alia, the United States has a "genetic weapon that kills only non-whites," and that it was the U.S. that tried to kill the Pope. The second, *The CIA In Asia* (Moscow: Progress Publishers, 1988), claimed, among other charges, that the U.S. had killed its own Ambassador in Afghanistan. Leventhal notes that they later charged that the U.S. had killed Pakistani president Zia.

PDP editor Ladislav Bittman, a man with firsthand experience in the disinformation business before his defection from the Czechoslovak intelligence service, has considered the potential impact of the political changes in Eastern Europe and the Soviet Union on his program. Although the term disinformation is closely associated with the Soviet Union in many minds, he notes that it actually characterizes a worldwide phenomenon, as do the more familiar terms persuasion and propaganda. Consequently the "1991 revolution" in the Soviet Union is not expected to result in diminished study of these fields. Perhaps a more likely event is the increased participation by scholars from the former Eastern bloc countries and the Soviet Union. Of course, these views are subject to change.

The first volume of *PDP* appeared in 1988. At least one issues has been published each year since. The most recent, Spring 1991, was distributed in the Fall 1991 due to publishing delays. The number of issues per year has varied from 6 in 1988 to one in 1990 and one in 1991. The format is 5 x 9," with three-color covers. Copies are available at no charge to those interested in the field. For further information write Boston University, College of Communication, Program for the Study of Disinformation, 640 Commonwealth Avenue, Boston, MA 02215, or call 617 353-3945.

THE RIGHT TO KNOW & THE FREEDOM TO ACT

NCARL's First Amendment Monitoring Service

This is another newsletter published by the National Committee Against Repressive Legislation (NCARL). *Right To Know* focuses on infringements of First Amendment Rights by federal law enforcement/intelligence agencies. Coverage includes analyses of activities of the three branches of the federal government and the private/voluntary sector, but it includes much more in intelligence than its cousin, *FBI News* (see page 146).

Right To Know takes unambiguous positions. It is for increased oversight of law enforcement and intelligence agencies, opposed to covert action and CIA contacts with university students on campus, supports the "October Surprise" theory, alleges "truth decay" at the CIA, and asserts that the FBI has a "right to kidnap." The September/October 1991 issues states, without any documentation, that Robert Gates "lied to Congress regarding Iron-Contra. Its pieces are unsigned, without any indication of sources.

The Right To Know masthead states it is published bimonthly, but CIA Off Campus First Annual Update (see page 23) says it is published in alternate quarters with *FBI News*. *Right To Know* is in its fourth volume, is presented on two legal size pages (front and back, black on white), the items are unsigned and no editor is indicated. It is available with a $15.00 contribution and this apparently entitles the subscriber to two issues of *FBI News* which is printed on alternate quarters. For further information write NCARL, 236 Massachusetts Ave., NE No. 406, Washington, D.C. 20002, or call 202-543-7659.

SECRECY & GOVERNMENT BULLETIN (S&GB)

The *S&GB* is published by the Federation of American Scientists "to challenge excessive government secrecy and to promote public oversight and free exchange in science, technology, defense and intelligence." Its immediate origins lie in the frustrations experienced by Federation members trying to assess Pentagon accountability when the program budgets are classified. More generally, the topic is an old one and with the "end of the cold war," so their argument goes, the time may be right for major reform. Since no other periodical is devoted to the subject, *the Bulletin* was created to provide a forum and serve as a catalyst for discussion and presumably action.

S&GB's statement of purpose in issue #1 (July 1991) makes clear that the "primary objective is to promote reform of government practices involving secrecy." *S&GB* seeks comment on ways to explore the extent of secrecy in government and science, "its uses and abuses," proposals on how to roll it back, and "reports on newly declassified documentation." Key among the intended audience are those "in a position to help reform the practice of secrecy." It is not clear whether some effort will be given to considering the bounds of legitimacy for secrecy or whether the ultimate goal is an unclassified government.

Typical issue topics include problems and legislation concerning Special Access programs, the classified budget and the law, Congressional oversight and notification of covert actions, disclosing the intelligence budget, classifying unclass-ified information and the "Black Budget and the Constitution." The battle over the Senate proposal to establish a "black pro-gram czar, " promptly called "czar wars" by *S&GB*, gets a thumbs down because it would institutionalize black programs. The "Congress Gives CIA a Free Ride" item in Issue No. 4 (November 1991) is revealing of *S&GB*'s position while raising serious questions about its grasp of the role of intelligence in government.

Items are short (about one-half column on a two column legal page at most) and discuss important issues which all, in and out of government, must face. The implied assumption that classified government programs would be monitored better if not classified, or at least much less so, is probably justified, but neglects the purpose of classification in the first place. Similarly, while the argument that the end of the cold war means the end of the need for government secrecy has an intuitive attraction, it does not necessarily follow logically and *S&GB* has not made its case on this issue. But the debate should be interesting.

In its current 2 page (legal size) format, *S&GB* has no space for sources, but is willing to provide them on request, assuming, presumably, they are not secret. Readers are asked to "notify us of stories, documents, or events or related interest for use in future issues." They do not say whether the identity of the suppliers will be kept secret if requested.

For information about *S&GB* write Steven Aftergood at the Federation of American Scientists, 307 Massachusetts Avenue, NE, Washington, D.C. 20002, or call 202 546-3300.

SECURITY INTELLIGENCE REPORT (SIR)

SIR was formerly known as *Counter-Terrorism & Security Intelligence*. The content and approach did not change with the name — it remains a biweekly newsletter that reports on the fast growing fields of counter-terrorism and security. It provides the information (i.e., intelligence) needed to monitor events in both fields throughout the world, before they become newsworthy. And then, when they do, *SIR* supplements the media coverage with details in follow-on stories of concern to specialists.

Although coverage is broad geographically and in terms of terrorist groups, activities and related security matters, those concerned with specific topics or events will have to augment the coverage with research of their own or by requesting further data from *SIR*.

Each issue begins with a page headed SCOPE which contains one or two line comments on current issues; some are followed up inside. Typical SCOPE coverage includes current worldwide terrorist incidents, Congressional activities, comments on leading terrorists, US-USSR cooperation against terrorism, a new Soviet "true spy" magazine, follow-up on previously mentioned terrorist acts, aviation security and Israel's request to pardon Jonathan Pollard.

The balance of the ten page issue usually has a terrorist incident log by location and date, a World View section with short paragraphs on items like death squads in Brazil or the KGB fomenting unrest in central Asia, a summary of Active Groups and Cases, and periodic statistical reports on terrorists attacks. On occasion, terrorist profiles and training camp locations are also provided.

From time to time *SIR* includes special reports — succinct pertinent comments on a single topic. The 25 February 1991 issue had a 5 page "report card" on "US Intelligence In the Gulf and Into the 1990s," attributed to a "senior US official." The 22 April 1991 issues discussed "X-Ray Technology, Marketing and Security."

Most articles and comments are written, though not signed, by *SIR*'s founder and editor Frank McGuire, a specialist in aviation and space matters. There are contributions from guest authors and they are usually signed. As a rule references and sources are not indicated, but McGuire notes that subscribers may contact him for this kind of information as well as back-up material and he will provide it where possible.

SIR was begun in 1986 and is published 24 times annually in 8 1/2 x 11" format. The first page is two-color black and red (logo and border) on white, the balance is black on white. The basic subscription rate is $290.00 annually, plus $30.00 for airmail. An electronic edition is available via *NewsNet* (see page 246). For further information or subscriptions, write the publisher, Interests, Ltd., 8512 Cedar St., Silver Spring, MD 20910, call 301-588-7916; FAX: 301-588-2085, or make contact via Compuserve 71067,1407, MCI electronic mail 170-1412, or telex via WUI 6501701421.

THE SHIELD

The Shield is the quarterly newsletter of the National Intelligence and Counterintelligence Association (NICA)." The NICA (a spin-off of the NCICA, see page 49), was formed in 1986 by a group of former intelligence officers in Las Vegas to permit the inclusion of members with other than counterintelligence corps experience. Thus *The Shield* contains items on intelligence, CI, law enforcement and security matters.

While there are occasional original articles (usually based on firsthand experience) and book reviews, the majority of each issue consists of reprinted material from national newspapers and other intelligence periodicals. There are also some "gossipy" items like the comments on Peter Wright's cousin, author James Rusbridger, and the difficulties he had with the British government over his book, *The Intelligence Game: The Illusions and Delusions of International Espionage* (London: The Bodley Head, 1989). Most of the time the original sources are cited, but not always, though this information can be obtained from the Editor.

Printed in standard 8 1/2 x 11" format, *The Shield* runs from 5 to 20 black and white pages per issue. Like some of its cousins, publication is a bit irregular but they strive for 4 issues per year. Questions concerning membership and subscriptions should be sent to NICA, P. O. Box 60448, Las Vegas, Nevada 89160 (tel: 702-734-9698).

SPECIAL OFFICE BRIEFS
An Early Warning Intelligence System

This newsletter is different in at least three ways. First its name has a most singular acronym. Second, its deals in part with religious matters effecting world politics. Third it has a sliding annual subscription rate: from $6000.00 for corporations to "$15.00 or so" for "Clergy of limited means."

SPECIAL OFFICE BRIEFS deal with topics ranging from SWAPO terror, ecclesiastical revolutionaries, Boris Yeltsin and the KGB, propaganda in the Middle East, Soviet front groups like the World Youth Festival, to polar scientists in the Antarctic.

Subscriptions include receipt of "Special Reports when possible, average twice weekly." These cover topics like "Gorbachev's Triumph," which deals with the question, can Gorbachev survive at home?

The history of *SPECIAL OFFICE BRIEFS*, as given, is unusual, even spectacular. It has been published since 1935, when according to the publisher (name not divulged), the Special Office was set up with the concurrence of the "War Office (Intelligence)." Subsequently, "Colonel Stewart Menzies, then Deputy Chief of the Secret Intelligence Service... suggested informal collaboration between himself and the Special Office which continued for many years." In 1936 "the U.S. Ambassador in London asked the Special Office to establish a close relationship with the U.S. That was done and we had the support of Mr. Thomas J. Watson (then head of IBM), Ambassador James W. Gerard and many others. Elsewhere keen support was given by R. A. Butler, Sir Thomas Inship (Cabinet) and John Buchan first Lord Tweedsmuir." After conducting a number of studies, Stalin "was obsessed by the accuracy of the Special Office. After the war, the "Special Office reported Russia's first Atom Bomb detonation three weeks before President Harry Truman."[138]

Although "technically" published by Intelligence International Ltd., the same group that publishes the *Intelligence Digest (UK)*, it is sponsored by "The Second Marquis de Verneuil Trust. Requests for subscriptions and further information should be sent only to *SPECIAL OFFICE BRIEFS*, Longborough, Moreton-in-Marsh, England, GL56 OQG. "The Trust must see all applications."

---

138. From *Special Office Briefs*, Memorandum, dated "Fall of 1989," Subject: "Re: What Stalin Feared," p. 2 of 4.

SURVEILLANT

Acquisitions For The Intelligence Professional

SURVEILLANT is a bimonthly publication that provides a single source of information about books, video tapes, and selected periodicals (English and foreign languages; fiction and non-fiction), on or related to intelligence. It also contains news and anecdotes about publishers, authors and their books. The first issue noted, among other things, that former KGB officer Viktor Sheymov has a book in search of a publisher.

This is a periodical that will clearly be of value not only to collectors, booksellers, libraries, and intelligence professionals (in and out of government), but also to authors, students, academics, and the general reader. Aside from the obvious benefit of having a single source of current and upcoming books, there is a second equally, if not more important, advantage. *SURVEILLANT* lists books many of us would not otherwise know about. Examples from other countries include: *Circle of Fear: From the Mossad to Iraq's Secret Service*, by Hussein Ali Sumaida, with Carole Jerome, (Stoddart Publishing, Canada, 1991; David Porter's *The Man Who Was Q: The Life Of Charles Fraser Smith* (Paternoster, UK, 1989); *National Security: Surveillance and Accountability in a Democratic Society*, (Canada: Les Éditions Yvon Blais, 1989), edited by Peter Hanks; Harvey Barnett's *Tale Of The Scorpion [the story of Australia's Secret Intelligence Service]* (Australia: Allen & Unwin, 1988); *The Rhodes Scholar Spy*, by Richard Hall (Random Century: Australia, 1991) and *OYSTER: The Story Of The Australian Secret Intelligence Service*, (Australia: Heinemann, 1989).

American titles in this category include, Tom Moon's *This Grim and Savage Game: OSS and the Beginning of U.S. Covert Operations In WWII* (Mission Hills, CA: Burning Gate Press,

1991); Curtis Peebles's *The Moby Dick Project: Reconnaissance Balloons Over Russia* (Washington, D.C.: Smithsonian Press, 1991); Tom Gilligan's *CIA Life: 10,000 Days with the Agency* (Guilford, CT: Foreign Intelligence Press, 1991) and David W. Doyle's translation of Boris Bazhanov's, *BAZHANOV and the Damnation of Stalin*, published by Ohio University Press earlier this year.

The range of topics contained in *SURVEILLANT* goes beyond the traditional fields of espionage, security, counterintelligence and covert action. The entire spectrum of intelligence related literature is included; memoirs, biographies, intelligence history, SIGINT, military and strategic intelligence, hi-tech collection, photointerpretation, tech transfer, computer security, terrorism, and congressional oversight. Thus, Clifford Stoll's, *The Cuckoo's Egg*, was mentioned, as was Joseph Douglass's *Red Cocaine: The Drugging of America* and Viktor Suvorov's, *ICEBREAKER: Who Started the Second World War?*. Although *Red Cocaine* is mainly concerned with Soviet and Chinese involvement in Latin American drug trafficking in the United States, there are intelligence aspects of the story involving many countries. Similarly with *ICEBREAKER* which deals with the GRU/NKVD role in Stalin's plans regarding Hitler.

The "Book News" portion of *SURVEILLANT* reports on upcoming books and comments on some of those that recently hit the shelves. In the latter category, the May/June 1991 issue discussed the ramifications of breaking the government's secrecy agreement by serving and retired members of intelligence agencies. The same issue notes that David Wise's new book, *MOLEHUNT: The Secret Search for Traitors That Shattered the CIA* (NY: Random House, 1992) will "disclose startling new facts about the CIA's most valuable asset in the Kremlin during the Carter and Reagan years."

Although the original purpose of *SURVEILLANT* was announced as providing advance notice of books to be published, the policy has changed and nearly all entries refer to books recently or about to be published. In most cases items are accompanied by a short descriptive, sometimes critical, summary or review of the book or event. The intent is to help the potential reader decide if the item is one worth having. For relatively detailed critical reviews, however, one should consult *FILS* (see page 46), *IQ* (see page 72), or one of the major newspaper book review sections.

SURVEILLANT is published by the National Intelligence Book Center. Each issue has 32 pages, black on white, in 8 1/2 x 11" format, punched for a three ring binder and contains a book order form with postage-paid return envelope.[139] Page 32 has a title and author index and a cumulative index is published separately at the end of each volume. A complimentary copy will be provided potential subscribers on request. For advertising rates and policy contact the managing editor, Elizabeth Bancroft. Annual subscriptions are $48.00 for US delivery, all other addresses $55.00. For further information write *SURVEILLANT*, 1700 K Street, NW, Suite 607, Washington, D.C. 20006, or call 202-785-4334, or FAX 202-331-7456.

---

139. The NIBC no longer sells books. Consequently, although the return envelope is addressed to the NIBC, the book order is not filled there but is sent on to Olsson's Books, a Washington D.C. firm that will supply most of the titles listed in *SURVEILLANT*. For fastest book ordering contact Olsson's directly: 1200 F Street NW, Washington, D.C. (tel: 202-337-8084; FAX: 202-342-2342).

TOP SECRET
International News and Analyses

TOP SECRET (TS) is the international English language edition of the German language *GEHEIM-magazine*.[140] In its first editorial, *TS* is described as a magazine "for people who need to know." While few will argue with "need to know" in principle, some will question the spirit and veracity of its application in a periodical that accuses the USA of originating AIDS in a US military laboratory and editorializes about the United States "secretly intervening in country after country to topple governments, to corrupt politicians and to promote political repression." And that is just a small sample. TS boldly states that it intends to follow in the footsteps of its German language cousin "which reports on and denounces... destabilization and intervention" by the United States of America that is "dominating a 'New World Order'... and threatening all of us."

In a regular column *TS* proudly "features 'Naming names' of CIA agents [sic] working under diplomatic cover." Thus it will come as no surprise that former *CounterSpy* staffers Philip Agee, John Kelly and Konrad Ege are among its contributors. Despite the focus on the CIA, names allegedly part of the Drug Enforcement Agency (DEA) or "INR," which *TS* calls the "Intelligence Service of the State Department," are sometimes mentioned. The rationale for including any of the names is as follows:

The world-wide infrastructure maintained by the CIA intervenes in the affairs of other nations on a daily basis, not from time to time as the National Security Council may direct. Our naming names

---

140. *GEHEIM* began publication in 1985 with a German language edition.

column will in future regularly expose CIA agenty [sic] working under cover world-wide.[141]

Entry format and content vary somewhat from issue to issue, but generally follow the Agee-Marks *CAIB* tradition — Name, current position, cover, assignments (location and dates), and name of wife, though not necessarily in that order. In some cases at least, denials of those previously named have been printed.

The summer 1991 issue broke new ground in two areas of "Naming Names" policy. In the first *TS* added a "living together with" category to accommodate unmarried roommates.

The second policy change is somewhat more significant, if not astounding. *TS* is not happy with the recent changes in the Soviet Union. Or, in its own words, the "political, economic and military degradation of the Soviet Union to the status of a beggar whose clothes are starting to turn to rags," has made the Soviet Union a "direct or indirect accomplice of Washington's plans to gain hegemony." Therefore, *Top Secret* will *"when necessary, extend our Naming Names feature from case to case so as to include the KGB agents who are responsible for destabilization activities and/or work together with the CIA, MOSSAD, NIS, and DMI (emphasis added)."*[142] The editorial announcing this new policy concludes with, "We are prepared to break a few taboos as we pursue these goals." If will be interesting to see if only taboos are broken and who does the damage.

A review of the *TS* issues reveals a consistent editorial approach. All 8 articles in the first issue (labeled 0/89) are concerned in varying degrees with the CIA. The second issue (labeled 1/89), with its expanded title, *TOP SECRET: International News and Analyses*, continues the policy, with 11 of 13 articles focusing on the CIA, although two of the 11 also involve Canada and South Africa. Subsequent issues confirm the trend while broadening the geographic scope to

---

141. TOP SECRET, Summer 1991, Number 1/91, p. 31. The word agenty appears elsewhere in TS and the context suggests it is the result of translating from Spanish to English, not a misspelling.

142. *TOP SECRET*, Editorial, Summer 1991, Number 1/91, p. 2.

include the southern hemisphere and Ireland, with occasional mention of other Northern hemisphere nations.

To get a sense of *TS* and its radical political rhetoric or — depending your viewpoint — calculated disinformation, one could pick an article at random and not be misled. A particularly good candidate is the two part article, "AIDS: US-Made Monster." It is characteristic of the direct *TS* attack. The first part, actually two articles, is a survey of the allegations spread by selected anti-American "scientists" and political groups, with emphasis on the "racist origins" of the AIDS story. Six citations are provided. Few, if any, of the key allegations are supported by fact.

The second article is a mix of technical jargon with social and political analysis. Among its claims one reads that AIDS is the result of "gene manipulation at Fort Detrick, Maryland," and that the AIDS virus was "tested on prisoners at Fort Detrick, Maryland, and spread from there to New York City." *TS* also asserts that "Western experts are actually helping to spread the disease in Africa." Efforts to rebut these assertions as disinformation are included in the articles, but are quickly dismissed as "false propaganda."

The authors of the second part, Prof. Dr. J. Segal and Dr. L. Segal, have claimed links to East Germany and France, and are now rumored to be in Sweden. They provide a bibliography but no citations for their charges. Furthermore, neither the authors nor *TS* acknowledge the Soviet admission in the late 1980s that the story was false from the beginning.[143]

The theme of US imperialism is argued in "The US Intelligence Community in Pakistan" which alleges that Pakistan was "built up by the CIA and the Pentagon into one of the most important espionage headquarters in the world." Other articles typical of *TS* coverage include one by editor Michael Opperskalski in which he attacks one of his favorite targets, "The Structure of South African Military Intelligence." A recent contribution by Dr. Julius Mader (remember him from *Who's Who in CIA?* Berlin, 1968) discusses the US Special Operations Command at "MacDill Airbase in Florida." The latter article was written before East Germany collapsed and Mader

---

143. *TOP SECRET*, Winter 89, Spring/90; and Summer/Autumn 90.

exposed as a paid scribe of the Stasi. The anti-CIA theme finds its way into each of these contributions.

TOP SECRET also writes negatively about other Western services like, for instance, the Mossad. It is, however, effusive over the Cuban DGI, and about the "old" KGB it writes nothing critical at all.[144]

As to sources, some are not cited in order to protect them. Those that are mentioned are mostly secondary works (magazines, books, newspapers), although US Congressional publications, Army Field Manuals, and *FBIS* reports have been cited. Supporters are encouraged to make contributions. Articles are often based in part on interviews but those on "The CIA's Endless War against Cuba" were taken from a Cuban television series. Most issues have a section called Documentation, but this includes items like a speech by Fidel Castro, or a piece on covert action by the Christic Institute, none of which are documented.

TS also published a special issue (October 1989) on the "Namibia Election." It too contains attacks on South Africa and the CIA. Under the heading DIRTY TRICKS, it had an account of a 5 day penetration of the "Democratisie Turnhalle Aliansie (DTA) by editor Opperskalski and Nick Wright (a contributor). The "DTA propaganda chief," Nico Basson, and his staff, were cooperative apparently because Opperskalski and Wright were white and therefore assumed to be sympathetic to DTA. During this time, Basson is said to have "admitted his connections to South African intelligence."

A curious item in the Summer/Autumn 90 issue alleges that editor Opperskalski was the victim of a CIA plot to assassinate him during a visit to the Philippines. It goes further alleging that

A special CIA team has already compiled a detailed list of up to 5000 names that includes addresses, personal data or photos etc. of activists of democratic and revolutionary organizations.... The CIA station at the US Embassy in Manila is fully involved in the plan.

No source is identified.

144.*TOP SECRET*, Winter 89, Spring/90.

Like its predecessor *GEHEIM*, *TOP SECRET* is published in the "tradition of *Covert Action Information Bulletin (CAIB)* [see page 32], and *CounterSpy*," (see page 183) and it "cooperates with Soberania" published in Nicaragua [still, one wonders?]. TS is also sympathetic to *LOBSTER*, though it uses far less footnotes, and it expands on themes which have appeared in *Intelligence Newsletter* (and some that do not), but apparently has not specifically mentioned that periodical.

Looking to the future, *TOP SECRET* intends to set up teams of "interested people, including journalists... to research all forms of destabilization [and] prepare articles, analysis and discussion... as well as organizing a distribution network around the globe" especially to acquire names of CIA personnel. With disarming seriousness we are told that

> The founders of this journal are not interested in superficial attacks, but rather in serious research, analysis and observation in the best traditions of progressive investigative journalism."[145]

Only the Top Secret editor-in-chief, Michael Opperskalski (V.i.S.d.Pr.)[146] is named on the masthead. No publisher is identified there or on the subscription form (last page). This, plus *TS*'s political bent, and Oppperkalski's co-author Kunhanandan Nair [in their book, *CIA: Club der Mörder: Der U.S. Geheimdienst in der Dritten Welt* (*CIA: The Murderers Club: The U. S. Secret Service in the Third World*)], who worked for an Indian communist newspaper well known for printing Soviet disinformation stories, has led to speculation that "Moscow Gold" may be involved. If so, the new Russian regime may mean changes are coming at *TS*.[147]

TS is published twice a year. Articles like the one by Opperskalski in the Summer 1991 issue defending Sadaam Hussein, are generally signed. When signed articles do not use

145. *TOP SECRET*, Editorial, Number 1/89, p. 2.
146. Editor M. Opperskalski kindly furnished (FAX 23 Sep 91) the meaning and explanation of the abbreviations (v.i.S.d.Pr.) which appear after his name in *TS*. In German they stand for "verantwortlich im Sinne des Presserechts." In English this means the person legally responsible for editing the magazine. The German legal system requires this designation for each periodical.
147. See *IN*, February 15, 1989 and Aleksandr Kaznacheev, *Inside A Soviet Embassy: Experiences of a Russian Diplomat in Burma* (Philadephia, PA: J. B. Lippincott, 1962). For the reference to Nair, see Leventhal op. cit. *TS* denies the "Moscow Gold" charge.

the true name explanations are given. Issues are 32-40 pages (21 x 30cm) long and are simply but nicely laid out. The cover page has the title in red, but the rest is black on white, with photos, drawings, and some advertising. Single copies are available for $3.50; subscriptions are $32.00 (2 years/4 issues), payable in US dollars. Both are obtainable from: *TOP SECRET/GEHEIM-magazine*, Mr. Michael Opperskalski, P. O. Box 27 03 24, 5000 Köln (Cologne) 1, West Germany; telephone 011-49-221-513-751, FAX, 011-49-221-529-552.

UNCLASSIFIED

Newspaper of the Association of National Security Alumni

The Association of National Security Alumni (ANSA) was "organized in January 1989 as successor to the Association for Responsible Dissent (ARDIS)."[148] It is "composed of

people who have worked in foreign and domestic intelligence or national security related agencies, and who have come to oppose the secret policies and activities in which they once were participants."[149] In general, what "the Association opposes absolutely is the misuse of the 'intelligence system' for the conduct of covert operations employing force... and misinformation, subversion, terror and corruption for illegal intervention in the affairs of other nations." A recent "Restatement of Principles" added "secret conduct of or support for... assassination, kidnapping, torture, sabotage, black or gray propaganda, and the use of 'plausible denial'" to the list.[150]

UNCLASSIFIED is ANSA's periodical voice of opposition to a U.S. intelligence community which it views as a perpetual violator of these principles. Toward this end it is a newsletter of "information on and analysis of the continuing struggle to eliminate covert operations as a tool of United States foreign policy."[151] And, as editor David MacMichael notes, with a

---

148. *UNCLASSIFIED*, Vol 1, No. 1, May 1989, p. 1. In a sense, ANSA is ARDIS without John Stockwell.

149. Covert Action Information Bulletin, Number 34 (Summer 1990), p. 54.

150. *UNCLASSIFIED*, Vol. 2, No. 3. June-July 1990, p. 11. The remainder of the quotation gives further insight into ANSA's thinking: "The Association recognizes, as it has always done, the need to gather information for the purpose of national decision making. It is skeptical... about the need for much of the secrecy and hocus pocus involved in the collection of information and its concealment from public knowledge via the classification system."

touch of humor, "since we oppose covert activities and covertness, this publication is for unofficial eyes only."[152]

An examination of *UNCLASSIFIED's* issues reveals that it interprets "covert operations" in the broadest sense. At one extreme is the story attributed to the *Toronto Star* which stated that *"a CIA team knowingly allowed the bomb to be placed on Pan Am Flight 103 as part of a plot to get rid of another CIA team that was on board the flight"* (emphasis added). Furthermore, says *UNCLASSIFIED*, "[A] major source for this story is former CIA officer Victor Marchetti... [who] confirmed the accuracy of the *Toronto Star* report to *UNCLASSIFIED*."[153] At the other extreme *UNCLASSIFIED* does genuflect in the direction of reality as when it allowed that "secret information gathering... is an acceptable practice."[154] But that kind of rhetoric appears infrequently. More typical of the editorial view, beyond specifically anti covert action remarks, is the statement that ANSA "strongly recommends that the United States... abolish... the insertion of CIA stations in US embassies."[155]

For a recent example of *UNCLASSIFIED's* outlook, approach and tone, one should read its commentary on the Senate confirmation hearings of Robert Gates to be Director of Central Intelligence (DCI). These hearings, says *UNCLASS-IFIED*, revealed a

squalid, mendacious, confused, badly-divided system, wracked by internal division, compromised by politics, corrupted by outside money, misled and mismanaged throughout the 1980s by an evil genius (William Casey)... The Gates hearings made the disclosures of the Church and Pike Committees 15 years ago pale by comparison.[156]

---

151. *UNCLASSIFIED*, Vol 1, No. 1, May 1989, p. 1.

152. Quoted in *Covert Action Information Bulletin*, Number 34 (Summer 1990), p. 54.

153. Ibid., Vol. I, No. 4. December 1989, p. 2. *UNCLASSIFIED* links the story to the *Toronto Star* (November 12, 1989). Marchetti is best known for the book which he co-authored with John Marks, *The CIA and the Cult of Intelligence* (New York: Dell, 1989) pb.. According to *UNCLASSIFIED*, he is "continuing his investigation with the support of Congressman James Traficant (D-OH).

154. ibid.

155. *UNCLASSIFIED*, Vol. 3, No. 3. June-July 1991, p. 2.

156. *UNCLASSIFIED*, "Gates — What Price Confirmation?," October-November 1991, Vol. 3 #5, pp., 1, 3-6.

Many will disagree with the "Church and Pike" comparison, but the anonymous author leaves little doubt as to his position.

But beyond that, the article goes on to quote much of the negative press while adding its own pejorative commentary about Gates, such as, "To Know Him Is To Loath Him," a statement for which the author offers not a bit of evidence. The subject of intelligence "politicization" is discussed as if it were a fact rather than a perception, the term used during the hearings. Finally, many of those who testified against the nomination are quoted or discussed at length while opposing views are almost entirely ignored. It must be noted, however, that another view was presented in a separate article by former CIA analyst Allen Orton, who takes a less strident more balanced view of the hearings.[157]

Turning to other issues addressed regularly in **UNCLASS-IFIED**, one finds that the impact on the US of the fall of the Eastern European governments and the Soviet Union has not been neglected. In response to arguments that the need for intelligence would likely be greater under the "new world order" than the old, **UNCLASSIFIED** promptly invoked the memory of the Palmer raids, the McCarthy era, and "the paranoid style" after World War Two, while omitting the historical background. According to **UNCLASSIFIED** "the enemy is abandoning the field" and the United States "has panicked in the face of victory." America, we are assured, should not repeat these errors by creating or identifying new spurious threats to justify unneeded intelligence capability.[158]

Some of the other topics that receive at continuing attention in **UNCLASSIFIED** include Congressional oversight, the Oliver North case, CIA recruiting on campus, the Defense Intelligence Agency, and the "October Surprise." The latter topic is the subject of a long article in the October-November 1991 issue. It attempts to show, inter alia, that "key witness" Ari Ben-Menashe, the alleged former Israeli intelligence officer, has more credibility than some of the press allows. But **UNCLASSIFIED** fails to mention the very strong evidence against Ben-Menashe recently published by Frank Snepp.

---

157. Allen Orton, "Allen Orton On The Gates Nomination," **UNCLASSIFIED**, Vol. 3, No. 5, October-November 1991, pp. 12-13. Orton is described as a retired CIA analyst, now the ANSA Secretary.
158. **UNCLASSIFIED**, Vol. 2, No. 3, June-July 1990, p. 10.

At various times *UNCLASSIFIED* has columns called "Trashing the CIA," "Shadow Justice," "Drugs and Thugs," and "Campus Follies," which report on various elements and personalities in the intelligence community currently in the news. A more general column called "Quotable Quotes" is at times serious and humorous in conveying its message. One edition quoted "Former CIA liaison officer to Congress, Charles Briggs," from his talk at the popular Smithsonian lecture series on intelligence, as saying that "My most challenging and frustrating job was dealing with Bill Casey. He was no shrinking violet, and he filled all vacuums." Another quote cites General Paul Gorman saying, "The fact is, if you want to get into the subversion business, collect intelligence and move arms, you deal with drug movers."

UNCLASSIFIED does recognize that some former intelligence officers have views contrary to those of ANSA. In one case, in its "We Must Be Doing Something Right Department," it quotes the "director" [sic] of the Association of Former Intelligence Officers (AFIO), John Greany. When asked for his opinion of the members of the Association [ANSA], Greany replied, "Shark bait is about the best use I have for them. They are useless traitors who gather people about them to think evil thoughts." A more substantive exchange of contrary views on a new book by Peter Dale Scott is printed in the August-September 1991 issue.

Book reviews are a regular feature in the *"Required Reading"* column. The October 1989 issue departs from the norm of anti-intelligence works to "focus on a short guide to the literature, a *'Suggested Reading List on the Intelligence Agencies,* by Linda Lotz & Chip Berlet.'" Among those suggested are William Blum's, *The CIA, A Forgotten History: U.S. Global Intervention Since World War 2* (Zed Press, 1987), Wilber Crane Eveland's book, *Ropes Of Sand: America's Failure in the Middle East* (W.W. Norton, 1980), and "classics" like the *Dirty Work I* and *Dirty Work II* by [sic] Philip Agee and Louis Wolf.[159] A more recent selection, with a testimonial

---

159. Lotz & Berlet are in error as regards the Agee and Wolf statements. The first of the *Dirty Work* books was edited by Agee and Wolf, the second was edited by Ellen Ray, William Schaap, Karl Van Meter and Louis Wolf. Agee was a contributor to the second volume. Copies of the reading list may be obtained by sending $0.45 to The National Lawyers Guild Civil Liberties Committee, 14 Beacon Street, Suite 407,

by former DEA agent (now author) Mike Levine, is *Cocaine Politics: Drugs, Armies, and the CIA in Central America*, by Peter Dale Scott and Jonathan Marshall.

The review of John Stockwell's new book, *The Praetorian Guard* (Boston: South End Press, 1991), provides a glimpse into ANSA internal politics. After characterizing the book as "excellent and thought provoking," the anonymous reviewer challenges Stockwell's theory that the dissolution of ARDIS, which led to the formation of ANSA, "was a possible result of government penetration of the organization and manipulation of some of its members." Moreover, says the reviewer, "Stockwell did not 'close the association down lest it lead to a major scandal,' he resigned...."

In sum, like former DCI General Walter Bedell Smith who was said to have been the most even tempered of men — always mad, *UNCLASSIFIED* has a parallel element of consistency in its treatment of intelligence and clandestine operations — always negative — well, almost always. This approach, of course, follows naturally from its statement of principles. And while it echoes many of the political views of the *CAIB* and *TOP SECRET* (see pages 32 and 125), there is much less of the radical-left Marxist rhetoric. One should read *UNCLASSIFIED* closely, it presents one side very well.

UNCLASSIFIED is published bimonthly. Some articles are signed, some not; most are think pieces although sources are cited where appropriate. Occasionally, items are reprinted from other sources. Format size has varied but is now fixed at 8 1/2 x 11" (black and white, newsprint). Issue length has varied from 8-24 pages and is expected to average about 16 pages.

The subscription notice in recent issues reads, without further explanation: "Free six month subscription to prisoners (renewable)." For all others, "contribution[s] of $20.00 or more entitles" one to an annual subscription (six issues). Send checks or write for further information to Verne Lyon, 921 Pleasant St., Des Moines, IA, 50309. For all other questions contact editor David MacMichael, 2001 S Street NW, Suite 704, Washington, DC 20009; tel: 202 483-9325, FAX: 202-483-9314.

Boston, MA 02108.

INTELLIGENCE-RELATED PERIODICALS

The 24 periodicals in this section frequently contain articles on various aspects of intelligence, though in some instances their names give little indication of potential intelligence content; *Diplomatic History*, *International Security*, and the *Radio Liberty* publications are examples. On the other hand, some of the publications have intelligence terms in their titles but even so, contain only an occasional article directly on intelligence — *Intelligence Report*, *Clandestine Tactics and Technology*, *Information Digest*, and *Soviet Analyst* are in this category. In both instances the main focus of the periodical is not intelligence, it is elsewhere.

Nevertheless, most of the intelligence articles that do appear are valuable. They are the product of private information services, government agencies, scholars, think tanks and the like. Such articles tend to deal with geopolitical, economic, military, legislative, current events, public controversy on intelligence, history, or some mix of these categories. Thus they provide insights on viewpoints and topics related to intelligence that won't be found elsewhere.

As with the periodicals in the first part of this guide, the quality of the substantive content (as related to intelligence) is mixed. Moreover, the frequency of articles on intelligence varies with events. The recent changes in Eastern Europe have resulted in a steady flow of *FBIS* items (page 150) on the intelligence services involved, and a similar surge is now underway concerning the former Soviet Union as it redefines its intelligence policy.

Two of the periodicals included are worth special mention here; the *FBIS Reports*, and the products of Radio Free Europe/Radio Liberty (see pages 163-6). Both contain translations of current stories in the foreign press and timely analysis by experts that don't appear elsewhere in the public press, at least in part because there is so much. But for the student, scholar, author, etc., they are a veritable gold mine.

Examples of periodicals in this category from the domestic front include *First Principles*, which has many intelligence related articles, *SIGNAL* which has a special intelligence issue each year, and *Military History*, which has a regular column on intelligence in each issue.

AIM REPORT (AR)

The *AR* is a biweekly newsletter published by Accuracy In Media (AIM), whose editor Reed Irvine, was one of the founders in 1969. Irvine, a somewhat controversial figure who once circulated petitions to "impeach Dan Rather," is seen by his supporters as a man unfettered by self-interest, intent on exposing "serious media abuses." To Irvine's critics, mainly on the left, he is an irritating itch they can't scratch; a man possessed by "paranoid anti-communist fantasies" according to AIM's own press releases.

A typical *AR* controversy in an intelligence related matter concerns the major network reaction to the dismissal of the $24 million Christic Institute suit against MG John K. Singlaub and 28 others, on the basis of "unsubstantiated rumor and speculation from unidentified sources." The *AR* of March-A 1989 wrote that "the networks (ABC, NBC, and CBS) had not reported one word about the Christic suit being thrown out of court," and thus not a word critical of the Christics. Representatives of ABC and NBC could not or did not explain the omission; ABC said, "We don't do a lot of stories out there. Let's face it we are limited."[160] Without this "otherside" viewpoint provided by *AR*, the public would be left with a much narrower, some would say distorted, perspective.

The *AR*'s have also been critical of PBS for its anti-intelligence programs like "On Company Business," a three part series in 1980 "from the point of view of Philip Agee, a former CIA agent [sic] who had developed procommunist sympathies." Notwithstanding *AR*'s anodyne description of Agee, it underscores the producers distorted characterization of the film as "the story of 30 years of CIA subversion, murder, bribery and torture...." Not to be outdone, the PBS public affairs director, insisted it was "a highly responsible overview of the CIA's history."

160.*AIM Report*, February-B 1989, XVIII-4, p. 1.

The same issue of *AR* also examines a four part 1988 PBS program, "Secret Intelligence," where Agee is described "only as a former CIA officer." This program, suggests the *AR* optimistically, so distorts the facts that most viewers can sort out reality since the events are relatively well known and documented, by others.[161] A recent issue of *AR* exposes a relatively unknown radical left group called Fairness and Accuracy In Reporting (FAIR). The disinformation and "politically correct" line it peddles throughout the journalism industry includes, inter alia, charges that the CIA ran drugs in Vietnam and Central America.

AR is distributed to all members of Congress, and all editors and reporters; the two American institutions that reject outside supervision and interference. While it is viewed by some as constructive, provocative and controversial, *AR* is ignored, whenever possible, by the news media, perhaps because it is seldom shown to be in error. *AR* is an extremely valuable source for those concerned with the public image of intelligence and how that image is affected by the major media. For an alternative view of AIM, see Louis Wolf's article, "Inaccuracy In Media: Accuracy In Media Rewrites The News and History," *CAIB*, Spring 1984.[162]

AR, with its title and logo (a target) in red, has 6 pages (8 1/2 x 11") per issue. Irvine's co-editor is author Joseph C. Goulden. Subscriptions are free to AIM members, $35.00 per year for non-members; single issues, $1.25. For more information write AIM, 1275 K Street, N.W., Washington D.C. 20005.

---

161. Ibid. This article also discusses Bill Moyers's contribution to CIA bashing with "inaccurate and misleading accounts" of the overthrow of Mossadegh in Iran and Arbenz in Guatemala; unfortunately, the article didn't identify the inaccuracies.
162. This article is reproduced in Richard O. Curry, ed., *Freedom At Risk* (Philadelphia, PA: Temple University Press, 1988), pp. 355-383.

COMPETITIVE INTELLIGENCE REVIEW (CIR)

This is a new publication of the Society of Competitor Intelligence Professionals. It is included here as a borderline case, not because it lacks quality or substance, it has plenty of both. Rather it is because of the way "intelligence" is used — what it means to the Society members. To the readers of *CIR*, intelligence refers to the analyzed information or data a business needs to be competitive. *CIR*, is therefore concerned with communicating information about collection practices, analytic techniques and their results. This is business intelligence not national security intelligence, but there are obvious parallels. The question then comes up, is *CIR* of value to those concerned with national security intelligence?

If similarity of terminology were the criteria, the answer would be an unqualified, yes. One will find in volume 1, #1 of *CIR*, references to CI (competitive, not counterintelligence), ethics, foreign intelligence, strategic intelligence, collection and analysis (can sources and methods be far behind?); but the constant here is business, the search for commercial advantage, something that has gained more importance internationally with the recent upheavals in East Europe and the Soviet Union.

But there are other more substantive reasons why the national intelligence advocate will find utility in *CIR*. The first is the link to economics and the need to know how corporations function to achieve their goals. This is of concern to analysts and operations officers (the latter when serving overseas), and to students of both fields. The article by Jerold Owen, "Competitive intelligence gathering in Japan: lessons from the Japanese," is a good example. The discussion of building networks, contacts, and having a sensitivity for the culture, is common to both professions.

Those considering a career in national security intelligence would do well to follow the *CIR* articles concerned with the use of open sources; the literature, TV, books, the sales force (people in the field), databases, etc. Several examples are given on how to employ sources for studies, to acquire a database and to monitor the competition. This, plus the emphasis on collecting, analyzing, and presenting the results is good solid groundwork. A command of these techniques will certainly help enhance one's professional skills and career.

The process apparently also works the other way around; several contributors to the first issue of *CIR* have national security intelligence backgrounds. One, Professor Steven Dedijer, of Lund University, Sweden, is on the editorial board of the *International Journal of Intelligence and Counterintelligence (IJIC)*.[163] In *CIR*, however, he writes on "The Intelligent Corporation: a global survey of a 1990s business innovation."

On the basis of the first issue, one can say *CIR* has a number of regular features including book reviews, software applications, an editorial, letters, and a "foreign intelligence" briefing. The journal itself is 40 pages (two color, 8 1/2 x 11"), uses photos, some cartoons, and contains advertising. No foot or end notes, but each article lists the phone number of the author who may be contacted with questions.

The first and subsequent issues of *CIR* may be obtained by joining the Society. Membership is $100.00 annually, except for students where $25.00 will do. For further details write the Society of Competitor Intelligence Professionals, 818 18th Street, NW, Suite 225, Washington, D.C. 20006.

CEO/International Strategies

CEO/IS "Monthly Magazine of the CEO Institutes of International Media Partners, Inc. Currently in its fourth volume, *CEO* focuses on global international economic and political issues and those activities which effect them — national security, geographical, military, and social.

Of particular interest to those in the field are the occasional articles on various intelligence issues. An example of the latter

---

163. Professor Dedijer's "The Rainbow Scheme: British Secret Service and Pax Britainnica," appeared in *Clio goes Spying: Eight essays on the History of Intelligence*, edited by Wilhelm Agrell and Bo Huldt, and published by the University of Lund in 1983. It is one of the many articles he has contributed on the history intelligence.

with the not too original title of "The Spies Who Won't Come In From The Cold," by Jen Sacks,[164] is a well done piece on what can be expected from the KGB foreign intelligence directorate under the new circumstances in the Soviet Union. The same issue has another article by Richard Pipes, "Turning the Clock Back in Russia," which looks at the CPSU and the KGB in terms of maintaining power. His assessment is that over the long run it can't be done and recent events have shown him to be correct.

In his regular column called Intelligence, former Director of Central Intelligence, William Colby, plays the role of analyst as he looks at economic issues and geopolitical roles of regions like the Middle East.

CEO is a polished high gloss product, perhaps the Architectural Digest of its field. Its format of 8 1/2 x 12" is impressive as are its four color photographs. In addition to Mr. Colby, its regular contributors include Paul Goble, perhaps the nation's foremost expert on Soviet (C.I.S.) Nationalities, Marshall Goldman, former CIA analyst Herbert Meyer, economist Henry Nau, journalist Kevin Phillips, and Soviet analyst Judy Shelton.

DIPLOMATIC HISTORY

Diplomatic History is a first rate professional journal that is worth monitoring for at least two reasons. First, from time to time it publishes original papers on various aspects of intelligence and diplomacy. Warren F. Kimball's, "Roosevelt and Prewar Commitments to Churchill: The Tyler Kent Affair," is an excellent example, and John Gaddis's, "Intelligence, Espionage, and Cold War Origins," is another.[165]

A second reason is that the organic functional link between diplomacy, military attachés, and intelligence is reflected in its pages. So are the frustrations of getting at primary sources, a

---

164. *CEO*, May/June 1991, pp. 40-43.
165. Warren F. Kimball, "Roosevelt and Prewar Commitments to Churchill: The Tyler Kent Affair," *Diplomatic History*, 5, (Fall 1981), pp. 291-311; John Gaddis, "Intelligence, Espionage, and Cold War Origins," *Diplomatic History*, 13 (Spring 1989), pp. 191-212.

problem which is less of an issue in America, relative to the
U.K. and other European countries, but which, even here, too
often becomes more an exercise in bureaucratic blimpery than
the logical application of the 30 year rule.

There is no apparent pro or anti intelligence bias in the
editorial policy of *Diplomatic History*, and the need to factor
in the intelligence contribution is recognized. This in turn
presents historians with some problems peculiar to the subject,
as Professor D. Cameron Watt suggests in a recent essay. "The
sheer unhistoricism of most of the literature" about intelligence, what Professor Christopher Andrew has termed "the
airport bookstall school of historiography," tends to inhibit
historians from "working the field by implanting in them the
fear of losing their professional reputations."[166]

While the emphasis in *Diplomatic History* is definitely on
diplomacy, the contribution of intelligence is mentioned
frequently and the quality of the work is high. It has earned the
attention of scholars, intelligence officers, and the general
reader of history.[167] Several of the anonymous referees have
themselves taught courses and published on aspects of intelligence. Dr. Sandra Taylor, Professor of History at the University
of Utah, who has done research on intelligence and the Viet
Nam war and Professor Richard H. Immerman, University of
Hawaii, the author of *The CIA in Guatemala*, are but two
examples.[168]

Diplomatic History welcomes papers. Submission
requirements are contained in each issue. Subscriptions, which
include membership in the Society for Historians of American
Foreign Relations (SHAFR), "are $20.00 for employed persons,
$9.00 for retired and unemployed, and $7.00 for students."

---

166. D. Cameron Watt, "Intelligence and the Historian: A Comment On
John Gaddis's 'Intelligence, Espionage, and Cold War Origins,' cited
above, pp. 199, 204.
167. For example see, Joseph M. Siracusa and Glen St. John Barclay,
"Australia, the United States, and the Cold War, 1945-51: From V-J
Day to ANZUS," *Diplomatic History*, volume 5, #1, Winter 1981, pp.
39-52.
168. Richard H. Immerman, *The CIA in Guatemala* (Austin: University of
Texas Press, 1982).

For further information write, SHAFR Business Office, Department of History, Wright State University, Dayton, OH 45345, or call (513) 873-3110.

EARLY WARNING (EW)
& THE INTERNATIONAL REPORTS (TIR)

The monthly *EW* and the weekly *TIR* are the foreign news counterparts of *Information Digest (ID)* [see page 155] with a twist; they concentrate more on the present and the future, assessing what is likely to happen in time to plan and take effective action. These are not publications for neophytes or the uninformed, the reader is assumed to know the territory and the players. They deal with economic, social, political, technological and national security issues throughout the world, evaluating risks and opportunities.

TIR in particular does not seek "to emulate *Time* or *Newsweek*, but to bring you important information omitted, overlooked, ignored or misinterpreted by the media."[169] Each 8 page issue contains short items about 30-40 countries, with information not usually seen elsewhere in the open literature. For example, *TIR* issue # 98-29 announced that the head of the Cuban intelligence service, the DGI, has lost his organizational head, being replaced by Jesús Bermúdez Cutino, former head of Cuba's military intelligence.[170] Other typical topics include, annual aid to Fiji, sabotage in Nigeria, financial problems in Chad, politics in Burma, terrorist policy in France and Italy, planning for a Mars space mission in the Soviet Union, and the lifting of Japanese export bans to China. An "As we go to press" column covers late breaking items like the recent events in Soviet Union/C.I.S..

The 16 page *Early Warning (EW)* provides more detailed analysis of current foreign problems and the likely effect of various options. One issue included a look at "Bush's Latin American Inheritance," and a piece on Gorbachev "Looking Good Compared to Stalin." The latter article contained some interesting insights on the expanding roles of the KGB and the

---

169. Author conversation with John Rees, 20 July 1989.
170. *TIR* issue # 98-29, July 21, 1989, p. 6.

military in the economy. It also predicted, contrary to most other analysts, greater not less KGB invasiveness into the lives of the citizens, a topic eventually commented on in the Soviet press when reporting the story of former KGB Major General Oleg Kalugin.

A column called "Flashpoints," highlights items which are developing and of general interest like a proposed "Spy Swap" involving the Pollards, or the note that Argentina's intelligence service, Secretaria de Información del Estado, (SIDE), "turned up indications that president elect Carlos Menem's recent campaign was heavily bankrolled by Syrian president Hifiz al-Assad." A very nice feature of *EW* for the reader is the printing of names in bold type.

In order to service these publications, *Early Warning*, which staffs both, has established what amounts to a private intelligence service using stringers around the world. Editor John Rees explained that their stories are printed only after verification with the governments involved, checking with the Foreign Broadcast Information Service (FBIS) and U.S. media organizations. The intent is to provide accurate risk analysis and predictions. The publications are privately produced "finished intelligence products," specific enough so that long term accuracy can be tracked.

EW & *TIR* are published by Mid-Atlantic Research Associates, Inc., a political risk analysis group whose founders and directors are Robert Moss, Arnaud de Borchgrave and John Rees. Rees is an editor for both publications. He is joined by Robert Moss and Arnaud de Borchgrave (on leave) on *Early Warning*, and by M.C. Gabriel and Managing Editor M.C. Powers on The International Report.

Both newsletters are black and white, 8 1/2 x 11" format. *EW* has an "antenna logo" in the upper left-hand corner with the word Confidential just to the right. It is not likely to cause concern going through a security check. An annual subscription for non-clients is $250.00 for *TIR* (50 issues), and $1000.00 for *EW* (12 issues). For further information write the publisher, Mid-Atlantic Research Associates, Inc., P.O. Box 1523, Washington, D.C. 20013, or call (301) 366-2531.

FBI NEWS

For readers looking for news about the FBI generally, this periodical will come as a disappointment. Those who find the FBI a tool of oppression and a threat to the exercise of first amendment rights, and do not want contrary views, should subscribe. The focus of *FBI News* is very narrow and fixed in its views. Published by the National Committee Against Repressive Legislation (NCARL), it contains "news of the latest constitutional violations by the FBI... includes organizing and lobbying ideas, as well as legislative updates."

The masthead has the statement: "To enact legislation that will prevent the FBI and other federal criminal law enforcement agencies from undertaking investigations that threaten the exercise of First Amendment Rights." Technically, this definition or objective excludes the CIA and other elements of the intelligence community who are not law enforcement agencies. But the FBI News contains many counterintelligence and counterterrorism related items and for those reasons, at least, it will be of interest to students of intelligence.

Examples include comments on the FBI battle with the Committee In Solidarity with the People of El Salvador (CISPES), the National Lawyers Guild and NCARL itself; the "reinterpretation" of the "executive restrictions" on assassination; the FBI library awareness program; and the so-call FBI Snatch program. This is a mono-viewpoint periodical with a mix of alleged facts and opinion. Items are not signed or sourced. It is edited by Kit Cage.

The publication frequency is not mentioned in the *FBI News*, but an item in *CIA Off Campus First Annual Update*, (see page 23) states it is a "quarterly newsletter, alternating [with] *'Right To Know'* (see page 114)." *Right To Know*, on the other hand, states on its masthead that it "is sent bimonthly... " with no mention of *FBI News*. Whatever the frequency, a contribution of $15.00 to the NCARL, 236 Massachusetts Ave. NE Suite 406, Washington, D C 20077-0678, will apparently cover an annual subscription to both newsletters. For questions write the address above or call tel: 202 543-7659.

FIRST PRINCIPLES

The Center for National Security Studies (CNSS), was founded by the Institute for Policy Studies (IPS) in 1974. It is now "jointly sponsored by the American Civil Liberties Union Foundation and The Fund for Peace;" the latter is also linked to the IPS.[171] The CNSS "is a non-profit public interest organization that utilizes litigation, research and public education to ensure that our civil liberties are not eroded in the name of national security."[172] The role of *First Principles* is to convey the CNSS message and help focus public attention on its activities.

With regard to intelligence matters, CNSS is concerned that secrecy in government is misused and that tighter controls on covert action, counterintelligence and the clandestine collection of intelligence would benefit American civil liberties and foreign policy. At the top of each issue of *First Principles* there is a quote by Thomas Paine from which its name is taken. This is the same Paine who was dismissed as secretary of the Congressional Committee of Secret Correspondence for leaking information from its files to the press during the Revolutionary War.

In some respects the viewpoints expressed in *First Principles* are similar to those found in the *CAIB* (see page 32). But whereas the *CAIB* tends to be sensationalist, and melodramatic with a radical tone, *First Principles* is more reasoned and sophisticated, with emphasis on corrective legal actions and legislative solutions. The viewpoints taken are clearly articulated and timely.

A typical 12 page issue contains two or three articles, most signed. They are usually written by a member of the staff (directed by Morton Halperin), but occasionally by a guest contributor. In most cases, at least one of the articles will

---

171.Steven Powell, *Covert Cadre: Inside the Institute for Policy Studies* (Ottawa, Ill: Green Hill Publishers, Inc., 1987), pp. 19-21, 57.
172.This quote appears on the *First Principles* masthead.

involve intelligence; not the details of espionage, of course, but the legal, political, and ethical aspects of the profession. Oliver North and the Iran-Contra case have been the subjects of these articles; the April 1990 issue devoted several pages to excerpts from the independent counsel's report.

Intelligence related items may also be found among the four "In The..." sections in *First Principles*; in the "Courts," "Congress," "Literature," and "News." Topics range from legal cases involving the right of the government to deny security clearances to homosexuals; to intelligence oversight, computer security, book reviews, plus news items about the CIA, suspected spy Felix Bloch, and proposed changes in the spy laws. The final section is called, "Guest Point of View," and has included Jay Peterzell on terrorism and Congressman John Conyers, Jr., on the FBI Library Awareness Program, Executive (not congressional) secrecy agreements, and the CIA Fernandez case.

But the theme that receives the most persistent attention is covert action. It has been the lead topic in articles by, among others, Professor Loch Johnson, Gary M. Stern, CNSS research associate, and in excerpts from Lawrence Walsh's second interim Iran-Contra report in April 1990. The thrust of these arguments varies from better control to abandonment. Stern contends first that covert military operations should not be conducted without Congressional approval. Then after Iran/Contra, he sees "Graymail" in the Oliver North trial and suggests the need to ban all covert operations.[173] Other intelligence related topics which receive attention include government secrecy (too much), privacy (too little), and security regulations (too intrusive). Most of the articles are signed and some are footnoted.

First Principles is published in a two color (colors change each year), 8 1/2 x 11" format, with issues of 12 to 16 pages. It is available by subscription for $15.00 ($10.00 students), four

173. See for example the cover story, "Congress and the Control of Covert Operations" with views by Rep. Wyche Fowler, Jr. and Professor Loch Johnson, *First Principles*, March/April 1984, vol 9, No. 4; Gary M. Stern, "Covert Paramilitary Operations," *First Principles*, Feb/Mar 1988, Vol. 13, No. 1 and "Secrecy on Trial in North Case," *First Principles*, March 1989, Vol 14, No. 1; and "'Fictionalized Secrets' Protect Iran-Contra Defendant," *First Principles*, April 1990, Vol 15, No. 2.

issues per year. Sample copies are available on request, back issues $1.00 each. Written commentary and contributions are welcomed. For further information write to CNSS, 122 Maryland Avenue, NE, Washington, D.C. 20002, or call 202-544-1681.

FOR YOUR EYES ONLY (FYEO)

FYEO is published biweekly to provide "[A]n Open Intelligence Summary of Current Military Affairs." It is a concise digest of current defense industry news with national and international security implications. Items are pulled out of magazines, journals, computer bulletin boards, the Defense Department's *Current News*, and the wire services. In most cases sources are indicated, but with the proviso they account "for only a portion of the information presented, the remainder is developed by the staff of *FYEO*."

While *FYEO* is not devoted to the intelligence profession, it does report items of intelligence interest; a recent issue had espionage items on Iran, Yugoslavia, and the USA. It is itself a source of unclassified commercial-industrial intelligence that gives the reader a way to stay up to date with the major defense related publications which are identified. Those of interest can then be read for detail. The emphasis is on reporting events and data with bumper sticker succinctness. Hardware, order of battle, contracts and personnel items are stressed, detailed analysis is left to others in their particular context.

Contents are arrayed in functional and geographic categories; e.g., Iran-Contra Crisis, Soviet Armed Forces, New Israeli Bomb, Espionage, Nicaragua, Eastern Europe, etc. Capsule book notes and book reviews are sometimes presented, including novels (they like Red Phoenix). A typical 6 page issue will have 45-50 items varying in length from a few lines to half a page (the Chinese Army order of battle summary consumed just over half a page). On occasion an 8 page special issue is published.

FYEO is a copyrighted publication owned and edited by Stephen V. Cole who is assisted by his wife Leanna. Mr. Cole began as a reporter for *FYEO* and eventually took over the publication. They subscribe to all the publications summarized and retain the sources in their database; *FYEO* subscribers can request a list of sources.[174]

FYEO is available for $60.00/year, 26 issues. For subscriptions and information on how *FYEO* can be obtained electronically via *NewsNet* (see page 246), write Tiger Publications, P.O. Box 8759, Amarillo, Texas, 79114-8759, or telephone: 806 655-2009.

FOREIGN BROADCAST INFORMATION SERVICE
DAILY REPORT *(FBIS-DR)*

The organization that eventually became FBIS was created in 1939 as a research project of the Princeton Listening Center to study Axis radio propaganda. The Center was taken over and expanded in 1941 at the suggestion of the State Department by the Federal Communications Commission (FCC). Renamed the Foreign Broadcast Monitoring Service, and subsequently the Foreign Broadcast Intelligence Service, its task was to record, transcribe, and translate foreign broadcasts, news items, and speeches which were then sent to various agencies of the government. After the war it was transferred briefly to the State Department, then to the Central Intelligence Group as a service of common concern, and finally to the Central Intelligence Agency where it became and remains the Foreign Broadcast Information Service.[175]

The FBIS *Daily Report* contains current news (usually within a week of occurrence) on political, military, economic and sociological affairs of the major world nations. "All

---

174. The quotations concerning *FYEO* production were obtained from Mrs. Leanna Cole during a 19 July 1989 phone conversation with the author. The Chinese order of battle item appears in Issue # 216, dated 26 June 1989, p. 216-2.

175. For the historical background of FBIS see: House of Representatives, *Hearings before the Select Committee to Investigate the Federal Communications Commission, Study and Investigation of the Federal Communications Commission*, 78th Congress, 1st session, part I, pp. 1-27, 1943; Thomas F. Troy, *Donovan and the CIA: A History of the Establishment of the Central Intelligence Agency* (Frederick, MD: Aletheia Books, University Publications of America, 1981), pp. 209, 268.

information has been obtained from foreign radio and television broadcasts, news agency transmissions, newspapers, books, and periodicals." All sources are identified and they often include Reuters, *Moscow News*, *Die Welt*, AFP France, and the *Financial Times* reporting on the same story. *FBIS-DR* is published Monday through Friday in eight volumes (hardcopy and microfiche versions) covering specific countries and regions of the world.

The frequency of intelligence related items varies with the country concerned. Since the upheaval in Eastern Europe and the Soviet Union, and the demonstrations in China considerable *FBIS-DR* space has been devoted to domestic news accounts of the activities of the intelligence services and the public reaction to the reforms instituted. While, as FBIS correctly points out, all the reports must be considered secondary sources, the accounts are invaluable in gaining an appreciation of just what is happening. Much of what appears in the *FBIS-DR* is never printed in the American press, or at least not in the same detail, there is just too much. The coverage of former KGB Major General Oleg Kalugin is a good example. The *FBIS-DR* items makes it possible to see the reaction to General Kalugin's remarks from the perspective of many countries.

The coverage of the gradual disintergration of the KGB since the Soviet coup has been excellent. Ten interviews with the new chairman, Vadim Bakatin, provided extraordinary insights which would not have been available to non Russian readers any other way. *FBIS-DR* provided similar coverage of Bakatin's successors and of the changes in the intelligence services of the former Eastern Bloc countries.

In short, this is a fine source of material, and for breadth and depth of coverage, even better than CNN, just not quite as current.

Weekly, monthly and supplemental regional reports are also published. FBIS publications can be found in all land grant and most other university libraries. They are also available to private subscribers and institutions.

For further details and subscription rates write FBIS, P.O. Box 2604, Washington, D.C., or by phone: 202-338-6735. FBIS does not publish an index, but one may be obtained (in hardcopy or microfiche) from NewsBank, Inc., 58 Pine Street, New Canaan, CT 06840 (tel: 802-875-2910).

FULL DISCLOSURE (FD)
For Truth, Justice, and The American Way

"The Federal, State and Local governments... The Corporations... Are all taking advantage of you! In every way imaginable. Why? They are simply bureaucracies out of control. Your only safety is in information. Knowing your rights... etc." Relying on the press is not the answer because "most of the major press coverage is superficial in nature. The nuts and bolts type of information is missing." So says *Full Disclosure* (issue #22, 1991), a tabloid-like periodical which, of course, is the solution to the problem. It wants to be "your source for inside, in depth, information that you need. Information that you can't get easily elsewhere."

Editor/Publisher Glen L. Roberts began *FD* in 1985 after various experiences getting information via the Freedom Of Information Act (FOIA). He decided to pass on, in newsletter form, what he learned following FOIA procedures. Today the content of *FD* is provided by private sources and the publication has become a fulltime endeavor.

The principal emphasis of *Full Disclosure* is "inside information on electronic surveillance" devices, their specifications and applications. Typical article topics include the "telephone splicing boot," subminiature bugs, burst communications, and other "suppressed information" such as "Narga miniature tape recorders" that Corporations and the government, according to *FD*, want kept secret. It also covers related issues like "privacy, constitutional rights... corporate scams," wasteful government programs and "how the privacy invaders do their jobs," and computer security.

A recent special issue (special price $5.00) entitled, "Citizen's Guide On How To Use The Freedom Of Information And Privacy Acts," gives the historical and legislative background on the topics, plus procedures for requesting documents. It also provides examples of material that may be requested, reasons for Agency denial, and a discussion of the appeal procedures. Addresses of many government agencies are also included.

A feature article in issue #22, 1991, is concerned with "government's fear program," in connection with the treatment of computer hackers. It reflects a definite political or anti-government secrecy slant that is pervasive in *FD*. Another example titled, "CIA, FBI Nuclear and Chemical Sunburn," attempts to link America to Nazi era eugenics and racial hygenics, while confusing the OSS and CIA in a post WWII period dominated by mind control experiments and FBI COINTELPRO, among other things. A final example is an article on "Mail Surveillance" which discusses the dos and don'ts about Drug Enforcement Agency (DEA) mail cover (and in some case opening) programs.

A section on surveillance describes "high tech" devices exhibited at the 1990 meeting of the National Technical Investigators Association (NATIA) [sic], none of which are exclusive to *FD* coverage. There is also a section called surveillance equipment buys which lists government "bid specifications" for "electronic surveillance equipment."

FD has a full page devoted to letters to the editor, with replies. Advertising is encouraged and varies from items like the "world's smallest lapel microphone" ($139.00) and book ads (*How To Get Anything On Anybody*), to *"How To Become A Millionaire-By Mail!"* and magazine ads like the one for *The Cyberpunk Technical Journal*. Advertising rates are published in each issue.

Full Disclosure is currently published irregularly about 5 times per year, though plans are to make it a 12 issue per year periodical. Consequently, since subscriptions are for 12 issues, the effective subscription period is 2 years plus. *FD* is printed on newspaper stock in tabloid format, black on white, with photos usually of hardware. Efforts are underway to expand distribution to magazine stores. Subscriptions rates are regularly $24.00 for 12 issues, $36.95 for 24 issues. As of issue #22, 1991, a special 25% discount is in effect. For reasons not fully (or partially) disclosed the order form states that "Sorry, no Canadian subscriptions accepted." On the other hand, complimentary copies are provided to prison inmates. Authors are encouraged to submit articles for publication. Questions regarding author compensation, and subscriptions should be sent to *Full Disclosure*, Box 903, Libertyville, Illinois 60048; tel: 708-395-6200.

THE HARRIMAN INSTITUTE FORUM

Alexander J. Motyl's, "Policing Perestroika: The Indispensable KGB," in the August 1989 issue of *The Forum*, considers why "few observers of the USSR attempt to incorporate the security police into an overall analysis of the Soviet system." His conclusion that "the farther perestroika proceeds, the brighter the KGB's future," though not likely popular with many of his academic peers, was correct until the coup.[176]

The Forum began publishing in January 1988 under the editorship of Paul Lerner, to provide the students, faculty, and guests of the Institute a vehicle for discourse on the Soviet Union and real meaning of glasnost and perestroika.[177]

The Motyl article is the only one to date primarily on a Soviet intelligence service. Papers in other issues have mentioned the KGB, but many have not, despite topics one would think involved a KGB role.[178] Whatever the balance finally achieved, *The Forum*'s initial contribution justifies continued reader attention.

In its 8 1/2 x 11" two color (blue & black) format, each issue of *The Forum* contains a single paper, 8 pages, well footnoted. Personal subscriptions (US and Canada) are $20.00 per year, $30.00 elsewhere (checks payable to Columbia University). Institutional subscriptions are $30.00 US and Canada, $40.00

---

176. Alexander J. Motyl, "Policing Perestroika: The Indispensable KGB," *The Harriman Institute Forum*, August 1989, Vol 2, Number 8, pp. 1-8.

177. Copy of an announcement of *The Forum*, undated, with a subscription form at the bottom, supplied by the editor, 8 August 1989.

178. For an example of a paper mentioning the KGB role see, Robert B. Cullem, "Human Rights: A Millennial Year," *The Harriman Institute Forum*, December 1988, Volume 1, #12, pp. 1-8. For an example of a paper omitting mention of the KGB see, "The Dynamics of Emigration and Nationality in the Soviet Union," Volume 2, #2, February 1989, pp. 1-8.

elsewhere. Subscription orders and requests for further information should be sent to, The Harriman Institute, Columbia University, 420 West 118th Street, New York, NY 10027.

INFORMATION DIGEST (ID)

ID has been published continuously since 1968. Publisher John Rees with his Editor and wife Louise, earned their credentials the old fashioned way; they penetrated the radical left — SDS New York and the National Lawyers Guild — for four years beginning in 1969. At the same time they continued publishing *ID*, using their firsthand knowledge to reveal what was happening, chapter and verse. Although their former activist colleagues were rather displeased when they discovered the Rees's true allegiance, the "director of the ACLU's Project on Political Surveillance termed Rees 'a sort of Renaissance man of countersubversive intelligence.'"[179]

Rees describes *ID* as "concerned with political and social movements in the United States (including those which may aid foreign governments or movements to the detriment of U.S. interests) and with extremism, public disorder and ter-rorism." Its intent is to provide a "historical analysis" of events involving the "background, grievances, operations and real capabilities of social movements and political groups" such as the Institute for Policy Studies, neo-Nazis, and the National Lawyers Guild.

With regard to intelligence in particular, *ID* has reported extensively on "campaigns to destroy the foreign intelligence and counter-intelligence capabilities" of the U.S. In this connection, *ID* frequently does verbal battle with *CAIB* (see page 32). The article "Covert Action v. Anti-Communism," which discusses a *CAIB* conference[180] at Harvard attended by

---

179. Rael Jean Isaac and Erich Isaac, *The Coercive Utopians: Social Deception by America's Power Players* (Chicago: Regnery Gateway, 1983), pp. 133-38. All the quotes are from an *ID* undated publicity release and a 20 July 1989 phone conversation with the publisher, John Rees.

180. Sponsored with the participation of Philip Agee, John Stockwell, Angela Davis, Gus Hall, Daniel Ellsberg and Joel Kovel, the Alger

students, academics, and "more than 100 journalists," being a good example. Although it is not fair to say that two views were represented equally in the article, it was not *ID*'s fault. Those who supported "the theories of Marx" and "the practice of Leninism," dominated the affair.

ID's coverage was reportorial not editorial. There was one, perhaps the only one, incident where a U.S. institution, the press, was defended. In that case, *ID* reported that Professor Edward Herman of the Wharton School attacked the U.S. government for publishing disinformation on Central America. Carl Bernstein, though "booed and jeered by the audience," told the professor he was wrong. Those concerned with the current tactics of the anti-establishment left will gain insight from *ID*'s reporting.

A timely example of *ID* intelligence coverage is the story on "Perestroika and Industrial Espionage." It summarizes KGB efforts to bring the USSR the hi-tech of the West, efforts which are not likely to decrease in the new Soviet Union.[181]

While the editorial policy of *ID* can be fairly described as anti-communist, that is not the entire story. A more complete descriptor would be anti-radical or anti-smash-and-destroy extremists. The rhetorical tone, however, is calm and balanced compared to *CAIB* and *EIR*, whether the subject be the denial of Libyan links to terrorism, or "Skinhead Violence."[182]

The *ID* articles are neither signed nor are sourced. Rees says veracity comes with their solid track record; but when subscribers ask for a source, it is provided, unless it is confidential. He adds that though they have been the object of considerable litigation, especially since 1976, "the accuracy of *ID* has never been successfully challenged." Nevertheless, *ID* should not necessarily be considered a primary source. The student and general reader would do well to confirm any information of interest.

ID is published biweekly in 8 1/2 x 11" format, 10-15 pages and 3-4 articles per issue. The first page is a cyan color and

---

Hiss Professor of Social Studies at Bard College, among others. See: *ID*, Vol. #25, December 2, 1988, pp. 273-279.

181.*ID*, Vol. XXI #26, December 16, 1988, pp. 289-290.

182.See *ID*, Vol XXI #25, and #26, December 2 and 16, 1988, pp. 273-279, 287-288, respectively.

contains the table of contents with short synopses. It is available by subscription, $300.00 for individuals, $500.00 for institutions. Subscribers may reprint and distribute articles, have access to most source material, and take advantage of the monitoring service to obtain articles and press analysis. For subscriptions and further information write, *ID*, 2805 St. Paul Street, Baltimore, MD 21218, or call (301) 366-2531.

INTERNATIONAL SUBCOMMITTEE REPORT (ISR)

A Quarterly Newsletter From
The International Subcommittee, JIGSAG

The *ISR* is published by the *Joint Industry-Government Awareness Group (JIGSAG)* "a volunteer non-profit organization... with interagency intelligence and security sponsorship which was organized to assemble and disseminate security and threat awareness information." The "International Subcommittee passes to its audience information on the overseas travel threat and issues related to technology transfer, loss [sic], exploitation and licensing." The primary target groups are "small and midsize companies who might not have full time security managers," but who have "contractual U.S. Government relationships."

Each issue contains reprints from government and private publications, newspapers, and information presented at security-related seminars. An example of the latter is found in the Spring 1991 issue which leads off with a summary of a presentation by "Mr. Raymond Mislock, FBI Hqs" during the "Government/Industry ASIS Seminar," on the subject of "Threat: Groups, International Travel Publications, and Videos." Subjects covered include the changing Soviet threat and the activities of surrogate intelligence services, the intelligence service of the Peoples Republic of China, the new role of "friendly" intelligence services, counterterrorism, and the resultant counterintelligence problems. The FBI's worldwide role in combatting these problems receives considerable attention.

Other typical items include articles like George Lardner's "CIA Seeks To Define New Role," originally published in *The*

Washington Post, and a section which looks at databases from which risk assessment information may be obtained and which gives information on costs and responsible individuals. A considerable portion of the Spring 1991 issue is devoted to economic and related technology transfer problems. There are also lengthy discussions on the role of COCOM (Coordinating Committee for Multilateral Export Control) and the European Community. Curiously, there is a section titled "State Secrets" which does not contain any, it merely summarizes or reprints articles from *Defense Trade News*. Finally, from time to time items appear here and there on miscellaneous subjects like sources of books, frequent flier issues, and "notable and quotable" comments.

Since *ISR* is a quarterly it lacks the timeliness and detail many security managers require, and which is normally associated with risk assessment and analysis reports. When this is coupled with the fast changing circumstances in world intelligence and security today, the reader should, at a minimum, get an update from the Chairperson of the JIGSAG. Alternative courses of action include contacting the State and Commerce Departments for advice.

Although references are made to "interagency intelligence and security sponsorship" and the "individual members," no identification of these organizations or persons is provided. Furthermore, the term "membership" is not defined, and subscription requirements are not mentioned. Issues of *ISR*, now in its 4th volume, are about 22 pages, letter-size, black on white. For more information on the JIGSAG International Subcommittee, "contact Robert Gass or Ray Glover, Atlantic Research Corporation, 5390 Cherokee Ave, Alexandria, VA 22312 — 703-642-4238."

JOURNAL OF ELECTRONIC DEFENSE (JED)

The *JED* is the "Official Publication of the Association of Old Crows (AOC)." The "Old Crows" are descendants of the WWII operators of RAVEN radio countermeasures equipment, known originally as "RAVEN operators." The term RAVEN came from the definition, to seek out the prey with intensity. It was a cover name for those involved with radio counter measures, but was not invented by the British as some believe, but by the Americans. The term CROW, used to refer to electronic countermeasures operators, "did not come into common use until the early 1950s."[183]

The "Old Crows" journal is predominantly oriented toward electronic warfare (EW) hardware and its use, but often contains articles of intelligence interest. For example, the July 1989 issue has one article on the National Security Agency's TEMPEST information security program and how it impacts industry, and another on the Air Force's implementation of the program, called SMART TEMPEST. From time to time there are articles on what the Soviets are doing about EW problems. Those concerned with SIGINT and security matters will want to monitor *JED*.

The *JED* is not sold on newsstands nor is it a common item in local or university libraries, though it is found in most military and defense contractor libraries. Subscriptions come with membership in the AOC for $15.00/year and for others are $60.00/year. For further information write the Association of Old Crows, The AOC Building, 1000 North Payne Street, Alexandria, VA 22314-1696, or call (703) 549-1600, 1-800-262-6958.

MILITARY HISTORY

For many, the term military history invokes an image of great battles and famous campaigns as related by Thucydides and Creasy, or renowned treatises like Quincy Wright's *A Study of War* or Clausewitz's *On War*. And although intelligence was a factor in every engagement, most accounts tend to give it less than proportionate attention. Clausewitz devoted a single chapter to the subject; one and one half pages. *Military History* takes a different approach. It has a column in each issue devoted to espionage in the broadest sense of the term, and often includes feature articles on various aspects of intelligence as well.

---

183. Alfred Price, *The History of U S Electronic Warfare: The Years of Innovation-Beginnings* [sic] *to 1946* (Alexandria, VA: The Association of Old Crows, 1984), p. 84.

A few examples of the Espionage column in 1990 and 1991 will show the range of subject matter covered. The June 1990 issue has an article by Alice S. Wentzell, about the controversy over whether John Jay influenced James Fenimore Cooper's decision to write, *The Spy*, by telling Cooper about one of his [Jay's] agents, Enoch Crosby. The August 1990 column, by Ronald McGlothlen, examines Gen. Nikolai Skoblin's role in the Tukhachevsky affair. In the April 1990 issue, by Kenneth P. Czech, relates the little known story of Augustus Agar, a British naval lieutenant working for the British Secret Intelligence Service (SIS). Agar was tasked to rescue another SIS officer, Paul Dukes (ST-25), from the Bolsheviks in 1919. The rescue failed, but Agar managed to disable the Soviet Navy in the process and Dukes escaped on his own. The attack on Pearl Harbor is the subject of an article by Raymond Callahan (October 1991) in which he argues that it should not have been unanticipated and was not without precedent.

The regular contributions by intelligence historian John H. Waller should not be missed. One example is in the October 1990 issue and tells the story of "horse doctor" spy, William Moorcroft. As players of Kipling's "Great Game... of espionage and political maneuver" between two great imperial powers, England and Russia, Moorcroft and his party were sent to Bokhara to collect intelligence, not buy rugs. Their cover was transparent, their route circuitous, their adventures hazardous and their mission, unsuccessful. A second piece (December 1991) deals with the bizarre story of Le Chevalier d'Eon, a male whose cover as a spy was to pose, successfully, as a woman at the imperial Russian court. One can only imagine how this must have strained the abilities of the French central cover staff. Waller's telling is great reading.

These articles are well done, but with the exception of the Wentzell piece, where her sources are clearly identified, the others have no citations or references to enable the interested reader to explore the topic further. This is especially curious with the story about Agar and the Waller pieces. Agar has written two books about the adventure and Dukes mentioned it in one his own. Waller has recently published *Beyond The Khyber Pass*, and the Moorcroft article is an expansion of his treatment of it in the book, which is fully documented.[184] A

---

184. John H. Waller, Beyond The Khyber Pass: The Road to British Disaster

short description of the authors credentials or background would be helpful in this regard.

Another regular feature of *Military History* is the article-interview providing first hand accounts and discussion of historical events. The April 1990 issue interviews a former OSS Sergeant, the late Jack Risler, who tells of his recruitment, training (under the legendary British Colonel William Fairburn) and parachute operations with OSS in France in support of the Maquis. Articles in general are well illustrated and this one has photos and maps. Suggestions for further reading are provided.

For just plain entertaining reading with a bonus of history included, the bimonthly *Military History* is a genuine bargain. Subscriptions are $16.95 annually; it is sold at some books stores for $2.95 a copy. Articles are encouraged. Submissions and requests for further information should be sent to Military History, 602 King St., Leesburg, VA 22075; (703) 771-9400. Subscriptions should be sent to *Military History*, Circulation, P.O. Box 373, Mt. Morris, IL 61054-7967, or call (815) 734-6309.

NATIONAL SECURITY LAW REPORT (NSLR)

The newly named *NSLR*, formerly the *Law and National Security Intelligence Report* is a monthly newsletter of the Standing Committee on Law and National Security of the American Bar Association (ABA). The name change, effective with the October 1991 issue, "does not reflect any decreased emphasis on intelligence matters — which remain a major focus of the committee's attention — but it does the committee's broader mandate.[185]

The idea for *IR (NSLR)* originated during the turmoil of the late 1970s among three lawyers; Morris I. Leibman, Antonin Scalia and Raymond J. Waldman. Mr. Waldman, its first editor,

---

in the First Afghan War (New York: Random House, 1990). Much has also been written about d'Eon. See for example, Edna Nixon, *Royal Spy: The Strange Case of the Chevalier D'Eon* (New York: Reynal & Company, 1965).

185. The new name was announced in the Summer 1991 issue of the Intelligence Report, p. 8.

got publication underway in March 1979; the first volume had only nine issues. The general purpose was and is "consciousness raising" with regard to the law and intelligence, a once neglected field. In practice it reviewed "court cases and books concerned with (1) national security, and (2) intelligence" in the U.S. and abroad.[186]

The early issues in particular followed the activities of the Congressional select intelligence committees. For those concerned with the historical or contemporaneous legal aspects of intelligence law or law making, the changing role of the select intelligence committees, or the role of Congress and the courts in intelligence practice, these issues of *NSLR* provide a rich source of introductory material. The recent volumes give somewhat less attention to Congressional intelligence issues while looking more closely at "Congressional Activism" and separation of powers.

The *NSLR* is six to eight pages long, two color (blue logo) in an 8 1/2 x 11" format. Editor, John J. Shenefield, is redesigning the newsletter, thus the description above is likely to change. Subscriptions to *NSLR* are free and may be arranged by writing the Editor, at 1501 Trombone Court, Vienna, VA 22182, FAX 703-938-1727; or calling tel 703-242-0629.

OPEN EYE
"— A *NEW* MAGAZINE CHALLENGING MEDIA CENSORSHIP"

The recent inaugural issue of *Open Eye* has contributions from Phillip [sic] Agee (**"Gulf War Launches 'New World Order'..."** a "comprehensive analysis of American military operations") and [John] Stockwell plus articles on "N.A.T.O.'s Terrorist Network," "CoIntelPro," the "CIA & the drug trade," "Economic League: Political Surveillance," and the "Falklands War Plot." This rich fare puts in context *Open Eye's* claim to be "a magazine of non-ideological analysis, unsensored investigative journalism, Green issues... global politics, psychology.... "

---

186. The historical information on the Standing Committee was provided to the author by Mr. Waldman.

As of January 1992 only one issue has been published. Like *TOP SECRET* and the *Covert Action Information Bulletin* (see pages 125 and 32) which, along with other politically left periodicals are shown on the back page, *Open Eye* has a glossy cover with red letters and contains 38 pages size A-4, slightly larger than standard American 8 1/2 by 11". With its nicely done layout and use of photos, editors John Murray and Mathew Kalman have put together an impressive first effort.

Open Eye also includes book reviews and items not directly related to intelligence ("Green" issues and the "scandal of surpressed cancer cures"), but if the first issue is a guide all elements of intelligence will be regularly atttacked.

At present *Open Eye* appears to be operating out a of bookstore in London and does not have a telephone listing. It is available from "your local alternative bookshop, cafe etc." in Britain for £1.20. Copies may also be obtained from **Bookmarks**, 265 Seven Sister Road, Finsbury Park, London N4 2DE for £1.34; "discount on 5 or more copies," how much is not specified. Annual subscription rates are not given in the advertisement appearing in *LOBSTER* (#21, p. 3), nor is the price for overseas purchase which will probably be about £2.00 or $3.75. The ad does invite authors and readers to "send in any of your own articles, ideas, art-work, comments etc.," with no mention of a compensation policy. All quotations included here are from the *Open Eye* ad mentioned. For further information write the address given above.

RADIO FREE EUROPE/RADIO LIBERTY (RFE/RL) PERIODICALS
RFE - REPORT on EASTERN EUROPE (REE)
RADIO LIBERTY - REPORT ON THE USSR
RFE/RL - DAILY BACKGROUND REPORT

These periodicals are among the most informative in their area of concern. Both Radio Free Europe (RFE) and Radio Liberty (RL) were initially independent public corporations created with secret agendas; the product of a covert action sponsored by the Defense Department, the State Department, and the CIA/Office of Policy Coordination (OPC), whose organizers had links to the wartime Office of Strategic Services (OSS).

RFE (originally the National Committee for a Free Europe) was formed in 1949. RL (originally the American Committee for Freedom for the Peoples of the USSR, Inc. [Amcomlib]), was formed in 1951. Their purpose was to provide employment for talented East European émigrés and to serve as a source of intelligence for the West. The secret financing of RFE by CIA was exposed by *Ramparts* magazine in 1967. Unsuccessful efforts in Congress to shut them down did succeed in eliminating a publishing operation and a research institute. Left with their broadcast mission and a small research element, they were merged in 1976 as RFE/RL, Inc., both nonprofit corporations funded by Congress.[187]

From the public perspective, RFE/RL operates as two distinct parts of the same corporation. The RFE part is concerned with Eastern Bloc countries, the RL part with the Soviet Union. Research required to support their broadcasts is published by both parts, in the form of reports with different names. The reports published by both organizations are summarized below.

RADIO FREE EUROPE

For thirty years RFE published a weekly *Situation Report (SR)* on each of the Eastern bloc countries, and monthly *Background Reports*, on several of the bloc countries. Beginning in 1990 both were replaced with the weekly *Report On Eastern Europe*. The range of topics is dependent on the events of the day, but special theme issues are published from time to time. Reports are based on materials from wire services in Europe and the West, plus 800 newspapers and periodicals from 11 East European countries, and the daily monitoring of radio and TV by RFE.

---

187. For a history of RFE and RL, see: Sig Michelson, *America's Other Voice: The Story of Radio Free Europe and Radio Liberty* (NY: Praeger Publishers, 1983). The balance of the data on these organizations and publications came from the documents and the Washington editor, Jane Lester.

Examples of articles in *Report on Eastern Europe* of interest to intelligence readers include: "How Dead Is Ceausescu's Secret Police Force," by Mihai Sturdza (April 13, 1990); "New Minister Dissolves State Security" (in Czechoslovakia), by Jan Obrman (16 February 1990); "Changing Views on Security in Eastern Europe," a regional overview by Jan B. de Weydenthal (July 20, 1990); and "The Polish Internal Affairs Ministry Adapts to Changing Political System," by Louis Vinton.

The average issue of *Report On Eastern Europe* is about 50 pages, two column, with fully documented analyses. Most issues end with a "Weekly Record of Events," a chronology of activities in each country which often include items on intelligence. Annual indexes are available. Coverage includes the Eastern Europe countries minus the Baltic nations which are the domain of Radio Liberty publications.

REPORT ON THE USSR

Until December 1988, Radio Liberty (RL) published the weekly *Radio Liberty Research Bulletin*, with occasional special subject supplements. Then in 1989 the name was changed to the *Report on the USSR*. In either case, the content is generally the same. The reports are prepared by staff analysts, and guest Soviet specialists like Amy Knight of the Congressional Research Service, Jack Dziak from DIA and journalist Hendrick Smith. They cover Soviet personalities, and all facets of Soviet social, economic, military and political life, including intelligence, though mainly the KGB. Past reports have discussed changes in KGB leadership, organizational problems, anniversary celebrations, abuse of powers, and nationality issues. The September 6, 1991 issues deals with the KGB and MVD roles in the "attempted coup" in a series of articles. While the coverage is not as broad or timely as the *FBIS* publications (see page 150), the Report provides expert analysis not available from other sources.

The sources for the *Report on the USSR* are mainly the more than three million entries in what is known as the RL's "Red Archive." This archive is comprised of material collected over more than 30 years from over 600 Soviet, Western and emigre newspapers, journals, official bulletins, broadcasts and wire services. The documents in this archive are available on microfiche from Chadwyck-Healy of Cambridge, England. This massive database is the source of over 500 reports each year, the best of these are available in *Report on the USSR*.

Each issue of the *Report on the USSR* ends with a 10-15 page summary of the major events of the week. The summary for the week of April 13, 1990 had four items of direct intelligence interest; one on the KGB Chairman meeting with Progressive Deputies at KGB headquarters; another on the announcement that "more than 30 subdivisions of the KGB third Directorate [responsible for military counterintelligence] had been abolished," and the overall military counterintelligence reduced by 10%; the third referred to the NKVD and its the Katyn victims, and the fourth to rumors about the East German Stasi.

The Report on the USSR articles are well documented and an index is published annually. Fifteen reports were published on the KGB in 1989, none on the GRU (no surprise here). Typical examples include: Alexander Rahr's "KGB Attack on Gorbachev," (April 13, 1990); Amy Knight's, "Personnel Changes in KGB as Public Relations Campaign Continues," (February 20, 1989); Mikhail Tsypkin's, "From State Security to National Security?," (October 9, 1989); Elizabeth Fuller's, "New KGB Chief Appointed in Azerbaijan," (August 22, 1989); Jan B. de Weydenthal's, "A Split in the KGB?," (June 13, 1990); and Victor Yasmann's "Reshuffle at the Top of the KGB" (March 1, 1991).

The *Report on the USSR* is printed on glossy white paper in two columns and varies in length from 40-50 pages. They are provided in the slightly larger than 8 1/2 x 11" European format.

OTHER RFE/RL PUBLICATIONS

For those wishing to monitor daily highlights of Soviet events, RFE/RL publishes *The Daily Report* which, because of the time difference, can be on one's desk with morning coffee. Items are short, 1/4 to 3 or 4 pages. Frequently topics of intelligence interest are included. Typical headlines are: "KGB Attack On Reform and Gorbachev," (March 9, 1990); and

"Kalugin Turned Down Sobchak and Popov Offers," (July 31, 1990).

There is another RFE/RL periodic publication worth knowing about called, *A Biographic Directory of 100 Leading Soviet Officials*. It will be of great value to some readers and researchers. The first four editions (1981, 1984, 1986, 1989) were published (softbound; legal size) and distributed by RFE/RL. They provide life history data, including their assignments and writings, on selected personalities. Beginning with the fifth edition, February 1991, several changes were imlemented. First, the Directory is now published by Westview Press (Boulder, CO) in hardbound book form, 211 pages; $42.85. Second it now has photos with most entries. Third, each entry was submitted to the individual involved for comment prior to publication. Some, like Presidents Gorbachev and Yeltsin, did not reply. Others, like the then KGB Chairman V. A. Kryuchkov, and the current Chairman of the Foreign Intelligence Committee, E. Primakov (former Director of the Institute of World Economy), provided photos and content approval. For further information call Westview Press, 800-456-1995.

DOCUMENT ACQUISITION

The *Report on Eastern Europe* and the *Report on the USSR* are available by subscription for $150.00 per year each; the special student rate is $75.00, again for each. For information about the *Daily Reports* write RFE/RL, 1201 Connecticut Ave, NW, Washington, D.C. 20036 or call (202) 457-6900).

In the United States, for subscriptions and information about all the other publications mentioned (and some not mentioned, like monitoring transcripts) write RFL/RL, 1775 Broadway, New York, New York, 10019 or telephone (212) 397-5318. In Europe the address is: RFE/RL, Oettingenstr. 67, D-8000 Munich 22, Germany.

A final note: the reader should be alerted that although the Library of Congress card index lists a full set of the RFE/RL documents, not all copies are available.

SECURITY MANAGEMENT (SM)

SM is the periodical voice of the American Society for Industrial Security (ASIS). It looks at all aspects of security: personnel and physical, software and hardware, in both industry and government. The articles deal with matters of policy and management as well as the more practical hardware oriented problems, often in a "how-to" format. Both are worth your attention. In the former category, one finds an article by FBI Director William S. Sessions on the issues and problems of enforcing drug laws.

Like those of policy and law, the more practical case oriented problems are also of direct intelligence interest at all levels of expertise. The topics range from security surveys, computer viruses and PC security, to personnel screening during hiring, and "bugging or being bugged." On the latter subject an article by CIA veteran, Glenn Whidden, "A Raid On Bugs," takes a top down approach in an example dealing with executive suite security. He stresses using basic concepts and terms within the grasp of the CEOs, flag officers, super grades, those on the way up the ladder, and yes, the Congress. For example, he asks who has had the courage to tell the boss that it is impossible to give him a tap free phone?[188]

When it comes to industrial undercover operations, the circumstances and techniques are typical of those encountered in intelligence as are many of the solutions, particularly where acquiring proof is concerned. In his well documented article, "Undercover Operatives and the Crux of Credibility," Brook I. Landis discusses these points and the pitfalls associated with actual cases. The questions of due process, corroborative evidence, impact on employees and management, and the demands on the undercover operative are considered. One can see, by inference, why it is so difficult to initiate legal action against suspects like Felix Bloch.[189] In a final example, Leonard M. Fuld takes a case study approach in his article, "Can You

---

188.Glenn Whidden, "A Raid On Bugs," *Security Management*, vol 33, #6, June 1989, pp. 85-88.

189.Brook I. Landis, "Undercover Operatives and the Crux of Credibility," *Security Management*, vol 33, #6, June 1989, pp. 59-62.

Plug The Leaks," about loose lip leaks and how Hewlett-Packard got an accidental break on the competition.[190]

SM has several regular columns which will also be of interest. One, "The Pentagon Corner," recently explained the new interim security clearance procedures. Another worth checking is called the "Legal Reporter." It includes "intelligence activities," and often reports on bills in Congress, like those on surveillance issues, which may effect security officers. The "On The Market" column has short descriptions of new technical equipment for security operations like fingerprint verification, access systems, shredders, removable PC hard disks, and laser communications devices. This is hardware aimed at dealing with problems common to all security organizations.

A typical issue of *SM* varies from approximately 110 to 150 pages (8 1/2 x 11"). It is a four color, professional, well written glossy publication, with advertising, photos, etc. Some articles are think pieces, others are well documented. Technical detail is kept to a minimum, this is more an "understand the problem" magazine.

Article contributions are encouraged, see instructions with each copy. Subscriptions to *SM* come with membership in ASIS, which is open to all, for $20.00 per year; forms in each copy. For non-members the rate is $36.00 per year. For further information write ASIS, Suite 1201, 1655 North Fort Myer Drive, Arlington, VA 22209-9958; or call 703 522-5800, FAX 243-4954

SIGNAL

The Armed Forces Communications and Electronics Association (AFCEA) was founded in 1946 as a non-profit professional organization to improve cooperation between government and industry in what has become the area of command control, communications, computers and intelligence (C4I). *SIGNAL* is its monthly journal which contains at least one intelligence related article per issue, and one issue

---

190. Leonard M. Fuld, "Competitor Intelligence: Can You Plug the Leaks?," *Security Management*, vol 33, #8, August 1989, pp. 84-87.

each year is devoted to intelligence (usually September). As might be expected the topics are management and technologically oriented. A recent example is a story about NSA's in-house microelectronics fabrication capability which allows it to manufacture chips with its own classified circuits. Although the article is unsigned, there is little doubt as to its accuracy since it is an extract from the agency's NSA Newsletter.[191]

On the management side, the January 1990 issue had a short article describing the organization of the Intelligence Community Staff (ICS). The ICS is seldom written about and this brief presentation with "wiring diagram" will be helpful to many.

SIGNAL uses an 8 1/2 x 11" format, with more than 100 pages per issue, has high quality color photos, charts, and informative advertising. Copies are sent to all AFCEA members as part of the $20.00 dues. Membership is open to all. Subscriptions for non-members are $32.00/yr (12 issues); foreign $44.00. For further details write, AFCEA, 4400 Fair Lakes Court, Fairfax VA 22033-3899.

---

191. *SIGNAL*, "Intelligence Agency Makes Special Classified Chips," May 1990, pp. 117-18.

SOVIET ANALYST (SA)

The *Soviet Analyst*, is "A Fortnightly Commentary," published (biweekly) since 1972. Coverage includes all aspects of Soviet life from politics and economics, religion and nationalities issues, to the military and the KGB. Until recently, its importation in the Soviet Union was forbidden.[192] Perhaps this was because it has referred to the Soviet Union as "the fantasy world of Marxist/Leninist historical processes,"[193] and has frequently mentioned "the mess the country finds itself in."[194] For the Westerner though, *SA* aides in understanding the politics and political culture of a state in the midst of important changes which will affect us all.

SA reports the circumstances, sometimes critically, sometimes not. The story of the progress and problems of glasnost and perestroika provides ample room for both. It also includes people type items like the story on one of Stalin's eight grandchildren, an illegitimate grandson, who "has only respect and admiration" for the former dictator.[195] To maintain perspective, coverage goes beyond the USSR to what were the Soviet Bloc nations and the People's Republic of China.

Of particular importance to those concerned with intelligence are the frequent articles on the KGB and GRU. A recent example discussed a letter to the editor of Izvestiya, which stated: "To be quite open, we often hear of secret employees of the KGB in almost every major collective. Please would you explain how the concept of glasnost squares with the activity of the system of state security?" The candid answer was, in part, that it was a constitutional duty to help the state and "our operatives work openly."[196]

Before the August coup *SA* warned that the new KGB law would benefit the KGB most by reinforcing its current role in all aspects of Soviet life.[197]

---

192. Moskovskiye Novosti, No. 10, 1989.
193. *Soviet Analyst*, Vol. 18, No. 8, 19 April 1989, p. 1.
194. *Soviet Analyst*, Vol. 18, No. 10, 17 May 1989, p. 1.
195. Ibid., p. 7-8.
196. *Soviet Analyst*, Vol 18, No. 11, 31 May 1989, p. 4.

On the subject of "tech-transfer," *SA* noted in its 13 September 1989 issue that the KGB and GRU activity in this area has increased, not decreased, as many would have the West believe. Moreover, even the Soviet scientists were concerned about the problems thus created.

Each issue of *SA* concludes with a column called "Survey," or "In Brief" which contains short items of interest. One mentioned that KGB Chairman Kryuchkov said that the "KGB is lifting the traditional veil of secrecy over its work." It is ensuring, Kryuchkov continued, "that its personnel act within the framework of the law."[198]

Soviet Analyst is printed on onion skin weight paper, light red or pink in color. It is about 8 1/2 x 12", 8-10 pages, and available in major libraries. Subscriptions may be obtained by writing to *Soviet Analyst*, P.O. Box 39, Richmond, Surrey, England. Overseas rates are $200.0 per annum, $100.00 for students of the Soviet Union.

STATEWATCH

STATEWATCH is a relatively new (March/April 1991) interesting and informative bimonthly "bulletin and on-line database" with a section on "security and intelligence" matters. Each issue also contains sections on civil liberties and related topics such as the law, policing, military, terrorism, the state and politics. Intelligence matters can also be found under one or more of these sections, as in the case of "Spycatcher and the press" in the law section of issue #3. Although concerned primarily with the United Kingdom, there is a section on Europe which treats the basic topics as they apply there, including intelligence.

STATEWATCH is "produced by an independent research group of journalists, writers, lawyers, lecturers and community activists." Issue #1 contains two items on the Dutch security service, one involving a whistle-blower, and the other on the "clean up" of the Dutch service archives. Issue #2 has articles on "MI5's secret search warrants," the Dutch

---

197. Ibid., June 1991, pp. 7-8.
198. Ibid., p. 8.

parliamentary debate on the internal security service (the Binnenlandse Veiligheiddienst (BVD), and the intelligence gathering powers of the German customs investigators. Issue #3 looks at telephone tapping in the UK with comments on MI5 and GCHQ. The Dutch security service is again mentioned in connection with its battle with the Dutch police in the fight against terrorism.

Sources are cited in the text or after each section. Book reviews and comments on relevant articles from professional journals appear in each issue. American books and journals (like the *IJIC*, see page 78) are cited, sometimes with comments, sometimes just the basic citation. Some of the books on intelligence mentioned to date are by well known authors such as Chapman Pincher, Nigel West, Richard Deacon, Jeffrey Richelson, John Stockwell and George Blake.

But *STATEWATCH* also includes titles less likely to be widely publicized in the USA such as *Reforming The Secret State*, by Patrick Birkinshaw (Open University Press, UK), *State Security, Privacy and Information*, by John D. Baxter (Harvester Wheatsheaf, 1990), and *Surveillance in the Stacks: the FBI's Library Awareness Program*, by Herbert Foerstel (Greenwood Press, 1990), although readers of *SURVEILLANT* would have been alerted to most. Issue #1 mentioned four new British official histories on the Special Operations Executive (SOE), a British WWII organization involved in supporting resistance movements.[199]

STATEWATCH also provides a number of research services like bibliography preparation and article reproduction from its archives, on and off line. The "on-line database includes references to books, pamphlets, articles, Hansard written answers, and Acts of Parliament." Key word (provided by customer) searches will also be made. Each Bulletin also lists "background document files which subscribers can buy. When ordering subscribers have to complete a copyright declaration form" supplied by *STATEWATCH*.

A *STATEWATCH* subscription outside Europe costs $35.00/year for an individual, $35.00 for voluntary groups

---

199.*SOE in Greece*, by R.R.M. Clogg (1991); *SOE in the Low Countries*, by M.R.D. Foot (1991); *SOE in Yugoslavia*, by M.C. Wheeler (1992); and *SOE in Italy*, by C.M. Woods (estimated 1992-93).

(non-profit), and $50.00 for institutions; payable in US dollars. Rates for the UK and Europe are £12 and £14 respectively for individuals, voluntary groups (non-profit) £16. For institutions it is £20 in the UK, and £22 for Europe. The cost of on-line access to the *STATEWATCH* database for individuals is 20p/min in the UK, $0.50/min in the USA. For voluntary groups it is 30p for the UK, $0.50 elsewhere. For institutions the rate is 50p/min in the UK and $1.00/min elsewhere. For further details write *STATEWATCH*, PO Box No. 1516, London N16 OEW; call 081-802-1882 or FAX: 081-880-1727.

LIMITED DISTRIBUTION INTELLIGENCE PERIODICALS

The 4 periodicals in this category are not generally available in public libraries and newsstands. Some will be found in, or can be obtained by, university libraries that are depositories for government periodicals and reports. Details on possible accessibility are given in each entry.

They are included here for two reasons. First, they are cited in papers and books from time to time, often without comment on where they are published or how (and whether) the cited articles can be obtained. To the extent possible that will be corrected below. Second, some are available for the asking, but this fact is not widely publicized. The information below informs those interested how to request copies.

CURRENT NEWS - ESPIONAGE

Espionage is a "publication... prepared by the Air Force [SAF/AA] as executive agent for the Department of Defense (DOD) to bring to the attention of key personnel new items of interest in their official capacities. It is not intended as a substitute for newspapers, periodicals or broadcasts..."

The items of interest are copies of news clippings and articles on the subject of espionage and related topics. They are not current but they provide broad coverage nearly impossible for the individual to obtain on his own. Despite the title, topics include covert action, congressional issues, court cases, education, recruitment, technology and analyses of other articles on intelligence.

The 1 March 1989 issue carried 64 items published during November and December 1988, in periodicals from the USA, Canada, Australia, and Israel. It does not claim to be comprehensive, but for an overview of what has recently appeared in the printed press, it does a splendid job.

Espionage is black and white, published in 8 1/2 x 11" format, approximately 70 pages, about 6 times a year. It is edited by Ricky Fritz as a special edition of the DOD daily, *Current News*, which contains copies of national security related stories. Distribution of *Espionage* includes most government libraries. Copies are also supplied to some universities with government depositories, think tanks and contractors. For more information write Herbert J. Coleman, Chief, *Current News* Analysis & Research Service, SAF/AAR, Pentagon, Washington, D.C. 20330-1024; or call (202) 695-2884.

FACT BOOK ON INTELLIGENCE
(Central Intelligence Agency)

The CIA *Factbook On Intelligence* is published to provide the public with a source of basic information about this agency with the well known name and little known activities. The Factbook is reissued when warranted by some major change or event in the intelligence community, including Congress. The most recent one was published in September 1991.

By any measure, it is an attractive, polished, well done 36 page publication with color pictures and very useful information about the Agency. In addition to some background facts on the genesis of the CIA and its responsibilities as assigned by the President, the Factbook contains an organizational chart and a short history with an aerial color photo of the Headquarters compound. These are supplemented with pictorial vignettes of CIA facilities and memorials, an explanation of the Agency seal, and a chronology of selected events involving the Agency and its predecessors. There is also a list of all Directors and Deputy Directors of Central Intelligence (showing dates of service) with portraits and biographical data on those currently serving. Two pages are devoted to a description of the duties of the Director, his principal deputies, and the National Intelligence Council.

On the topic of the intelligence profession, the *Factbook* contains comments on the intelligence process, plus remarks and charts on the various elements of the Intelligence Community organizations, the intelligence cycle, and a list of the members serving on the Congressional oversight intelligence committees. The groups formed by the President to help supervise the CIA and provide Executive oversight — President's Foreign Intelligence Advisory Board and the President's Intelligence Oversight Board — are also described. Page 28 contains the nine point CIA Credo.

Pages 30-31 are devoted to answering questions "We Are Often Asked." These include, "How is the Central Intelligence Agency different from the KGB?," "How many people work for the Central Intelligence Agency?" (no numbers given, they explain why), "Does the Central Intelligence Agency give tours of its headquarters building?" (no, for logistical and security reasons), "Does the CIA spy on Americans? Does it keep a file on me? No.," "Who decides when the CIA should participate in covert actions, and why?," "Does the Central Intelligence Agency engage in assassinations?" (No, prohibited by Executive order) and "What is the Central Intelligence Agency's role in combatting [drug trafficking] and international terrorism?"

The *Factbook* is printed in four colors in an 8 1/2 x 11" format, with a CIA seal on the cover in color. The final page (32) contains instructions for obtaining Agency publications and maps available to the public. Copies of the *Factbook On Intelligence* may be obtained, without cost, from the Office of Public Affairs, Central Intelligence Agency, Washington D.C. 20505, (703-482-7676 or 703-351-2053). Those with questions on employment should write the Director of Personnel (same address) or call 703-351-2028.

RECENT ESPIONAGE CASES (REC)
Summaries and Sources

The *REC* is published aperiodically, as needed, by the Department of Defense Security Institute. Each edition summarizes a number of espionage cases in selected periods involving the various government services concerned.

The March 1989 issues contains 64 short summaries of all the cases reported "in the public media or in unclassified sources" since 1975. Also included is "information from the CIA, FBI and DIA as appended to the published Hearings before the

Permanent Subcommittee on Investigations of the Committee on Governmental Affairs, United States Senate (April 16-25 1985). A few references to open sources are cited after each summary.

Inquiries should be sent to the Department of Defense Security Institute c/o DGSC, Richmond, VA 23297-5091.

STUDIES IN INTELLIGENCE

Studies, as it is known by its intelligence community readers, is a quarterly professional journal published by the Central Intelligence Agency. It was started by Sherman Kent in 1955, as a forum for those who wished to add to the cumulative knowledge of a relatively new profession, even when writing on classified matters. It contains a mix of firsthand accounts, opinion pieces, scholarly articles and book reviews.

As a rule the issues are classified, though most contain some unclassified articles.[200] An exception to the rule was an un-classified September 1987 Bicentennial issue on intelligence and the constitution. It contained contributions from Congressman Lee Hamilton, "A View From The Hill;" Marquette University history professor Ralph Weber on "As Others Saw Us;" former CIA Director of Congressional Affairs, David Gries on "The CIA and Congress: Uneasy Partners," and DCI William Webster on "With Fidelity to the Constitution." Perhaps the article of most general interest was contributed by Linda S. McCarthy, a member of the CIA's Historical Intelligence Collection staff. She called it, "You're From Where and You're Doing What?", and it is about her contacts with people outside the CIA when she asked for their help for an exhibit on the Constitution at CIA Headquarters. Now out of print, copies of individual articles should be available on request.

Manuscripts may be submitted by anyone involved with, or interested in, intelligence, whether working for the US or

---

200. The early volumes of *Studies* were in the five-by-eight inch format and some had the unclassified material published separately as an annex. The current 8 1/2 x 11" format began in the late 1960s.

foreign governments, academia, industry or just doing private research. Retired KGB General Oleg Kalugin was published in *Studies* while still on active service, the first KGB officer in that position to do so. Articles by Cambridge historian Dr. Christopher Andrew and author Nigel West have also appeared. Submissions are reviewed by an editorial board. When the article is unclassified, the author is furnished with copies — of the article, not the entire issue.

Studies is mentioned here mainly because it is cited in the literature from time to time, often without comment on the origins or accessibility of the article mentioned.[201] A number of academics and journalists have obtained copies of the unclassified articles by filing FOIA requests in a particular subject area, and this probably accounts for most citations.

When the reader encounters such a reference and desires to obtain a copy, one may write to the CIA, Attn: Office of Public Affairs, Central Intelligence Agency, Washington D.C. 20505, or call 703-482-76776 or 703-351-2053. In most cases if it has been declassified, copies will be provided promptly. If it has not yet been considered for declassification, it will probably be handled under the FOIA procedures, which may lengthen the process.

201.See for example: Thomas F. Troy, *Donovan and the CIA: A History of the Establishment of the Central Intelligence Agency* (Frederick, MD: Aletheia Books, University Publications of America, Inc., 1981), p. 564; Nigel West, *Games of Intelligence: The Classified Conflict of International Espionage* (London: Weidenfeld and Nicolson, 1989), p. 1.

INTELLIGENCE PERIODICALS
NO LONGER IN PRINT

The 12 entries in this category are included because the reader may wish to know what happened to them and because their content may be of value to historical research. More information about most of the recent ones can be found in *NAMEBASE* (see page 230). There are a number of defunct magazines that were not directly related to intelligence but which frequently carried major articles on the subject. Most existed before TV became the primary source of public news. A few examples will be given here and not discussed anywhere else. The old *Blue Book* carried a 17 part series between January 1946 and October 1947 devoted to operations of the OSS. It is available on microfilm in the Library of Congress and a complete list may be found in the *Readers Guide To Periodical Literature (RGPL)* under the author's name, Richard M. Kelly. The *RGPL* is also a good source for other articles in this category. For example, Kim Philby wrote an 11 part series for *The New Republic* in 1956-1957, which commented on affairs in the Middle-East. At the time, Michael Straight, recruited at Cambridge as a prospective agent by Anthony Blunt, was still affiliated with the magazine, which his parents had founded, and his name still appeared on the masthead. Straight, however, denies having anything to do with Philby's assignment. Philby, of course, was supposed to be just a journalist but that was actually a cover for his re-employment by the British Secret Intelligence Service.

If one searches the *RGPL* for names like Walter Krivitsky, Whittaker Chambers, Elizabeth Bentley, Alger Hiss, Alexander Orlov, to name a few, entries will be found in magazines like *The Saturday Evening Post*, *Life* (weekly), *Colliers*, and *Look*. Much of the material in these articles appeared later in books, but many of the pictures used by the magazines did not.

While the Library of Congress has all of these magazines, copies may also be found in major libraries and even in out-of-print magazine stores like, *From Out Of The Past*, 6440 Rich-

mond Highway, Alexandria, Virginia (703-768-7827). A word
of caution, *Blue Book* is very hard to find anywhere.

BIG SISTER

One of the most unusual quarterly newsletters, *BIG SISTER*,
was distinguished as much by its name and country of origin,
New Zealand, as by its content. Its editorial purpose was made
clear in the name of its parent organization, the Organization
To Abolish The Security Intelligence Service (OASIS). OASIS
sought (1) to "provide information on the activities of the
Australian Security Intelligence Service (ASIS), particularly it's
'anti-subversion' investigations, and its links with overseas
intelligence agencies; and (2) to encourage greater scrutiny of
the ASIS by Parliament, the media and the public."[202] It went
on to assert that "incompetent and right-wing" ASIS agents
have failed to prevent terrorist attacks and that the ASIS
functions could be better carried out in a "politically neutral
manner by other Government Departments." After about three
issues, it is now out of business.

In its relatively short existence, *BIG SISTER* provided
articles with sources, editorial comment, selected statements
by MPs on various intelligence related matters. Issue number
3 discussed a proposed bill on international terrorism,
provided a hand drawn chart depicting New Zealand's intelligence community with its overseas links, and reprinted an
article from a local paper on effort by New Zealand's
government to prepare a report on overseas national security
threats. From time to time cartoons satirizing intelligence were
also included.

BIG SISTER also promoted visits by "foreign intelligence
specialists" like Ralph McGehee (see page 225),[203] a recent
guest of OASIS, who spoke on the CIA as an "anti-intelligence"
agency. Philip Agee "the best known former CIA agent [sic] in

---

202. See: *BIG SISTER*, No. 2, August 1986, p. 3.
203. McGehee, author of *Deadly Deceits*, a book whose title is reflected in
its content, is a former CIA officer who has become a favorite of the
radical left by making many anti-Agency claims, most of which he
cannot support.

the world," also accepted an invitation to make a speaking tour in New Zealand in 1987.

For those who detect a political orientation in the OASIS agenda, your suspicions are confirmed by its once close affiliation with the *Covert Action Information Bulletin* (see page 32) and what is now the *Intelligence Newsletter* (see page 65). In any case, *BIG SISTER* made its position clear, if not its staff and authors (which are not named), and provided useful insight into the workings of those opposed to intelligence organizations.

BIG SISTER was a bare bones operation ($5.00/ year subscription except for those who couldn't afford that; then it was free) and apparently just couldn't develop the support necessary to promulgate its views. A letter requesting its publication status was returned by the Wellington post office marked no such address. For those who wish to try for themselves, write OASIS, Box 1666, Wellington, NZ.[204]

CONFLICT: The Dorff Report

The Dorff Report, as *CONFLICT* was known, did not survive its first year, 1990. Its existence and content will be of interest primarily to scholars of conspiracy theory and unsolved mysteries related in some way to intelligence. *CONFLICT* placed emphasis on reporting rather than analyzing and predicting. The eight page (last page for address) issue #2 lead off with an unsigned piece about attempts to counter or discredit claims of conspiracy theorists regarding the Kennedy assassination. This was followed by a glowing and interesting review of Anthony Summers' most famous book, Conspiracy, on the occasion of the release of a revised paperback edition.

A second article, excerpted from the *Interfor Report*, prepared by Interfor Inc., concerns the Pan Am 103 tragedy. Interfor, according to *The Dorff Report*, "is headed by Juval Aviv, a former member of Israeli intelligence." In the article,

---

204. The masthead does not list an editor or any other names. OASIS uses the native name of NZ (AOTEAROA) in its letterhead, but not all US Post offices recognize the term and NZ is recommended.

Interfor mentions having sources and describes them generally, but does not identify them. Perhaps the most interesting aspect of this article is the seldom mentioned Interfor Inc. itself.

Another article concerns the S&L catastrophe in the USA. It has no byline an is largely a rehash of stories in the press alleging, inter alia, CIA links. It also includes comments by Richard Brenneke, lately of October surprise fame and exposed by Frank Snepp as having lied to authorities on that matter.

A fourth copyrighted contribution came from Bradley E. Ayers who describes himself as a former "CIA operative," and for two years an "undercover operative in the Reagan-Bush war on drugs, with, he implies, the Drug Enforcement Agency. Ayers, provides many assertions about problems in the DEA but no sources.

Just what Mr. Dorff was trying to accomplish is unclear. For those interested in learning more, he can still be reached at the address given in his Report: Robert Dorff Auctioneers, Inc., RDA-223 S. Beverly Drive, 202A, Beverly Hills, CA 90212.

COUNTERSPY /
NATIONAL REPORTER (CS/NR)

What began in March 1973 as *CounterSpy* and ended in the Fall of 1988 as *The National Reporter*, concluded nearly 15 years of CIA and FBI bashing at the "counter-publishing barricades." *CounterSpy* was initially known as Philip Agee's "naming CIA names magazine." After the 1975 assassination of CIA chief of station, Richard Welch, in Athens, there was a public outcry against *CounterSpy* which the editors still attribute to U. S. government disinformation. Earlier that year, *CounterSpy* had reported Welch assigned to the CIA station in Peru, and from that, so some would have it, an Athenian terrorist group learned he had moved to Greece. Others said there were better sources than *CounterSpy* in Athens. In the event, it ceased publication for awhile.

CS/NR will be of interest to those concerned with the history and thinking of the radical left and its arguments for, among other things, stopping U.S. covert action (including Afghanistan) and intervention, the need to end U.S. nuclear testing and "CIA drug dealing," U.S. "responsibility" for the famine in Chad, preventing the "unleashing" of the CIA and FBI, and stopping the U.S. economic "war" against Nicaragua. Reasons for *CS/NR*'s name naming policies are supplied in abundance. They range from Agee's intent to destroy the CIA, to the exposing "enemies of social progress;" that is from A to B.

If you look to *CounterSpy* or *The National Reporter* for criticism of the Soviet Union and its support for wars of national liberation, its disinformation and forgery campaigns, the KGB or the GRU, go elsewhere; there is none. Where there is some mention of these issues, it is passive or supportive. In short, *CS/NR* does not present a balanced view, in the sense the term is used elsewhere in the *RGIP*.

CS/NR's demise was due in part to new public attitudes toward intelligence in the 1980s, in part because of the Intelligence Identities Protection Act (IIPA) 1982, and because it ran out of money.

In the final issue of *The National Reporter*, the question of goals was addressed for the last time. "All *CounterSpy* ever wanted," wrote contributor Daniel Brandt, "was accountability under the law, but what it got was a law that tries to preclude accountability."[205] What *CS/NR* never realized, or accepted, is that the accountability of government agencies has been there all along; the IIPA applies only to those who would be unaccountable.

CounterSpy: The Magazine For People Who Need To Know, was published 4 times a year in 8 1/2 x 11" format on newsprint stock. The glossy cover sometimes used a second color and often photographs. Co-editors Konrad Ege and John Kelly contributed most of the writing, along with other lesser known figures of the left. Some articles had documentation but many did not. Back issues are no longer available for sale, but major libraries should have them.

---

205. Daniel Brandt, "Little Magazines May Come and Go...," *The National Reporter*, Fall 1988, p. 5.

DISINFORMATION
& SUBVERSION UPDATE (D&SU)

Apparently *D&SU* has not been published for about two years. All recent attempts to contact the publisher have been unsuccessful. D&SU began on 23 September 1987 as a one man, one page, (single space 8 1/2 x 11"), weekly publication. It was typed, xeroxed, and boldly labeled "Please Photocopy, and Distribute." Editor Thomas P. Cutler described it as a "newsletter" in the sense that it "tries to present information to allow the reader to understand current events." The stated purpose "of *D&SU* is to explain & expose the massive pro-communist campaign of disinformation & subversion within the US."[206] *D&SU* also attempted to provide a tutorial on disinformation for the general reader unacquainted with the topic; but he leaves no doubt that his political outlook is well to the right.

For the first year or so of publication the quality and organization was poor, the documentation even worse. In short, they are likely to lead more to befuddlement than understanding and are not recommended as references.

The substance improved in February 1990 when Mr. Cutler published a new edition of his "Updates" in three parts and a supplement. The first volume contains 33 single page (single spaced) issues plus a 12 page appendix and is labeled "Part I, 3rd Edition." It is intended to present an "overview of the goals, techniques and themes of the [communist] disinfo [sic] campaign." Issues 1-14 are devoted to a tutorial of sorts, definitions and examples. Issues 15-25 comprise a useful annotated bibliography of 75 items. The balance of the issues give Cutler's assessment of the problem and what the reader can do about it. The 12 page appendix, labeled "Interpreting the News," gives Cutler's often ad hominem responses to "disinfo" items in the news.

---

206. This quote appeared in a document entitled, "A Word About *D&SU*," distributed with copies of *D&SU* on December 22, 1987. Each of the subsequent issues contains a variation of it.

D&SU, Part II, 2nd Edition, contains 48 single page issues and a page and one-half bibliography. The principal subject is: "The Evidence for the Existence of A Massive Pro-Communist Campaign Of Disinformation & Subversion Within the United States." What this amounts to in practice is an "overview" of Cutler's appreciation of Marxism-Leninism which uses Lenin's and Marx's own writings to make its points. The quotations are short (but cited) and though some sense of the mood of the general doctrine can be acquired, its relevance to disinformation is not always obvious, although the general communist doctrine is clear.

Part III of the *D&SU* is concerned with more "Evidence," which consists of Cutler's statements and selected quotes; assertions would be a better title. For example, Cutler writes that the "Cheka-KGB has killed some 30-40M people in the USSR alone." No source is given. Suggested reading, mostly secondary sources, is cited at the bottom of each page, but it is not always linked directly to the points made.

The Supplement is a reproduction of a 1988 report to Congress by the United States Information Agency, Soviet Active Measures in the Era of Glasnost (about 100 pages), with an introduction by Mr. Cutler. It provides a summary of Soviet "Black," Gray" and "White" active measures, with examples.

During the analysis presented, Mr. Cutler mentions several times that "This evidence will necessarily be indirect" (emphasis in original). But he does not make it clear why this should be so when so much has been published on the subject.

Mr. Cutler, a graduate of Yale University, Johns Hopkins School of Advanced International Studies, and the George Washington University Law School is obviously devoted to, if not obsessed, by his subject. These three single spaced volumes contain a great deal of information, but in their current form represent a roughly ordered database. He has characterized his newsletter as a "book appearing one page at a time." An interesting concept but that does not remove the obligation for continuity from page to page, a continuing problem. In its current condition, D&SU could serve as a starting point for research, provided the reader-scholar does his/her own homework where unsubstantiated assertions are encountered.

The price of the first three parts as last published was $7.50 per part. The Supplement was $8.00. No subscription information is provided, questions and orders should be mailed to D&SU, P.O. Box 18423, Washington D.C., 20036.

THE DOSSIER

Subtitled, *The Official Journal of the International Spy Society*, *The Dossier*, came into being in 1982 and lasted only a few issues. Apparently the public response to in-depth articles on "The Man From Uncle," the columns on "gadgetry," the unlabeled intermixing of fiction and non-fiction, poor editing and dull writing, was not good.

The black and white covers were labeled TOP SECRET in familiar font. The format was 11 x 8 1/2", being bound on the short dimension. An issue was about 40 pages.

Whatever the obscure goals of *The Dossier*'s editor, Richard L. Knudson, English Department, State University of New York, Oneonta, NY, they were not achieved.

EXECUTIVE INTELLIGENCE REVIEW (EIR)

The *EIR* is described by author Dennis King, as an "attractively printed weekly newsmagazine" founded by former Trotskyite, Lyndon H. LaRouche,[207] and published since the early 1970s by the New Solidarity International Press Service (NSIPS). NSIPS operates a worldwide network of news bureaus, once called intelligence offices, that arrange normal official accreditation, including the White House, for its staff journalists.[208] Although *EIR* often reports on various world intelligence services, the primary focus of the magazine is the product of its own intelligence organization, described by one

---

207. LaRouche still contributes to EIR in the form of interviews over the phone from "the Alexandria Detention Center in Virginia where he has been a political prisoner since January 27, 1989." *EIR*, July 7, 1989, editor's note, p. 58.

208. Dennis King, *Lyndon LaRouche and The New American Fascism* (NY: Doubleday, 1989), p. 164.

former NSC staffer as, "one of the best private intelligence services in the world."[209] Topics covered include economics, national security, international politics, and book reviews.

The track record of *EIR* content is mixed and the problem for readers is knowing what is right in time to make use of it. This is a situation faced daily by intelligence producers and consumers. Their solution involves careful sourcing and reasoned arguments. This is not always the path followed by *EIR*.

For example, as King points out, *EIR* predicted the Iran-Contra scandal months before the article in the Lebanese newspaper, but no one paid attention. The reason *EIR* was ignored was, in part at least, because of a well earned reputation for articles like the one by Jeff Steinberg, in its July 7, 1989 issue. Under the headline, "CIA commissioned anti-LaRouche book," Steinberg (an *EIR* counterintelligence director), reviewed King's political biography, calling it a "book-length, slanderous diatribe" that "drew upon the resources of the CIA, USIA, the FBI and the NSC."[210] The funds, according to Steinberg, were funnelled through the Smith-Richardson Foundation. That is the extent of the support for the charge. Similarly, undocumented vicious ad hominem attacks on Henry Kissinger and the Queen of England have been relentless.

Like other news weeklies, *EIR* also has signed articles that often include quotes from unnamed sources, Congressional testimony, or named newspapers. What is provided then is analysis and in some cases it fails to meet the argument set out in the title, as with Herbert Quinde's, "U.S. Intelligence is blinded by joint CIA-China operations."[211] Nevertheless, articles can be thought provoking, sometimes audacious. In this category, Konstantin George's, "Moscow prepares the great terror as KGB sparks Uzbekistan riots," outlines the risks inherent in Gorbachev's policies and predicts another Stalinist terror and purge, "perhaps before the month of June [1989]

---

209. Ibid., p. 160.
210. Jeff Steinberg, "CIA commissioned anti-LaRouche book," EIR, July 7, 1989, p. 61-62.
211. Herbert Quinde, "U.S. Intelligence is blinded by joint CIA-China operations," *EIR*, vol 16, Number 28, July 7, 1989, pp. 63-64.

ends;" it didn't happen. Unfortunately, how he knows the KGB "played a major role in staging the unrest," is unclear.

Besides the articles on intelligence related matters, there is also a weekly column, "International Intelligence," but the content here is the product of *EIR*'s collection concerning world affairs, not intelligence matters.

EIR also publishes "special reports." Many are book length; some documented, some not. In the former category the upcoming "most fruitful, comprehensive examination of the [TRUST] story" in 70 years, promises to be at least a controversial contribution to the literature. It is over 600 pages, many endnotes and, inter alia, concludes Sidney Reilly was a Soviet agent in 1918. A preview appeared in the November 1988 *EIR*; "The First Chapter of the TRUST, The Lockhart Plot, by Allen and Rachel Douglas.[212]

An example in the no documentation category is "The Kalmanowitch Report: Moscow's Moles in the Reagan-Bush administration," prepared by the *EIR* Counterintelligence staff. It is an attack on the Mossad and the Washington based, Consortium for the Study of Intelligence (CSI), with Jonathan Pollard, "a joint Soviet-Israeli asset" tossed in.[213] In Appendix B, the Consortium is labeled a "key conduit for Soviet agents and Soviet disinformation into the Reagan administration."[214] Then the names of most of the conference attendees from 1979 to 1984 are given. This is pathetic scholarship and miserable journalism. Reader beware! Exercise extreme care when using *EIR* products. If the item is important to your work, the assertion or citation where one is given, should be checked.

EIR is often as extreme in its rhetoric as *CAIB*, but more eclectic in its attacks, taking on the CIA and the KGB and most governments and services in between. According to some political analysts, *EIR* reflects the political ideology of LaRouche which places it squarely in the fascist camp, although others see signs of his earlier leanings.

212.Allen and Rachel Douglas, "The First Chapter of the TRUST, The Lockhart Plot, *EIR*, November 1988, pp. 1-15.
213.No author attributed to "The Kalmanowitch Report: Moscow's Moles in the Reagan-Bush administration," *EIR*, Special Report, March 17, 1988. 120 pp., $150.00 per copy.
214.Ibid., p. 99.

Should you wish to see for yourself, *EIR* is available in some libraries (certainly the Library of Congress) and sometimes sample issues could be obtained in airports from LaRouche representatives, though that practice seems to have diminished. Annual subscriptions were obtainable for $396.00 (three months for $125.00). The reports often cost in the hundreds. For further information write, NSIPS, P.O. Box 65178, Washington, D.C. 20035, the last known address.

ESPIONAGE MAGAZINE

Espionage was founded by Bob Guccione (Penthouse Magazine) and his sister, Jeri Winston. It went out of business in 1987 while attempting to publish its third volume. The issues were about 50 pages (8 1/2 x 11") in length, four color, with advertising. Each contained approximately 20 articles plus features; about half were labeled fiction. Those not so labeled were sometimes pseudonymous or written by "a second year student at Yale University, majoring in random studies."[215] The overall quality of *Espionage* as a source of truth and accuracy is questionable and demonstrates that executive editor, Ernest Volkman, has genuine reasons for modesty.[216] Aside from some interesting book reviews, and Volkman's gossipy column, "Top Secret," there is little of interest and nothing to recommend it, unless one is concerned with espionage fiction.

FPI INTERNATIONAL REPORT (FPI-IR)

The Free Press International (FPI) International Report was begun in 1980 by Robert Morton, publisher of the *New York City Tribune*, to provide subscribers "A Background Briefing On Events Of Strategic Significance;" these events often in-

---

215. *Espionage*, September, 1987, p. 87.
216. Volkman has written one book and co-authored another; both merit intense skepticism. See: Ernest Volkman, *Warriors of the Night: Spies, Soldiers, and American Intelligence* (NY: William Morrow and Company, 1985); and Ernest Volkman and Blaine Baggett, *Secret Intelligence: The Inside Story of America's Espionage Empire* (NY: Doubleday, 1989), 265 pp., $19.95.

clude intelligence matters. While clearly conservative, it discusses issues on their merits, without automatically passing them through an ideological filter. *FPI-IR* stories generally have geopolitical implications rather than a focus on domestic politics.

Although the emphasis on foreign intelligence services is not as comprehensive as the *Intelligence Newsletter* (see page 65), it came close and offered a different slant. Typical stories in this category include the discovery of a Soviet spy in Japan, the terrorist activities of the Afghan secret police in Pakistan, reports on Soviet KGB defectors, and Spetsnaz operations. The international implications of national security issues such as arms control, verification, and strategic defense are routinely included.

Domestic intelligence turmoil with international side effects are also covered in some depth. For example, the 1987 shifts of intelligence personnel in the National Security Council staff which reduced its counterintelligence effectiveness received critical attention.

The *FPI-IR* "Backgrounder" column is frequently devoted to intelligence. In this regard the impact of the Peter Wright book, *SPYCATCHER*, on British intelligence and the CIA was given extended treatment.[217],

Although the articles are unsigned, source references are often given in the text. Like other newsletters, however, the readers will have to assess accuracy over its lifetime.

Sadly, *FPI-IR* apparently died with the *Tribune*. Issue format is 8 pages (8 1/2 x 11) long, black and white except for a green and blue logo, and uses photos and maps. It was published biweekly by Free Press International Inc., 401 Fifth Avenue, New York, NY 10016. (212) 696-4995; the phone number has been disconnected. Annual subscriptions were available for $80.00 (US & Canada), $90.00 overseas.

---

217. *FPI-IR*, July 29, 1987, p. 3. The article is wrong, however, when it states Peter Wright "as the first British counterspy to break the code of silence of the secret service [MI5]" by publishing a book. At least five preceded Wright, one, Sir Percy Sillitoe, was a former MI5 Director General. The others were Lord Rothschild, Sir John Masterman, Derek Tangye, and Steven Watts. Wright's was clearly the most detailed and controversial.

INVESTIGATIVE LEADS (IL)

IL was a newsletter "published by *Executive Intelligence Review (EIR)*," (see page 187), and the LaRouche organization. The only signed article in the December 1988 *IL* issue is by Lyndon H. LaRouche, Jr. In terms of content, *IL*, was in some respects the extreme right-wing political counterpart of the *Covert Action Information Bulletin (CAIB)*, though both, interestingly, attack many of the same people and organizations such as the CIA and the U.S. government. But there are several significant administrative differences. *CAIB* lists editors and authors, and often cites sources. It is available on the newsstands and by subscription. *IL* was available only by subscription ($75.00 for 12 monthly issues) and avoids naming editors, authors, and, with some exceptions, sources (Peter Wright was cited as a source in connection with comments on Lord Rothschild and his daughter Emma).[218] The failure to document, while not unprecedented, is particularly important in *IL* because of the often serious charges made about organizations and people.

A tactic used often by *IL* is the old "rational core" technique of deception discussed by disinformation expert Professor Ladislav Bittman (Boston University), among others. For example, one article mentions the 60 Minutes interview with convicted spy, Jonathan Pollard. It is, of course, easy enough to check what the anonymous *IL* author claims was said on the air; hence a presumed rational core of truth concerning these comments. But the assertions about what went unsaid, namely that it was the KGB not the Mossad that was running the Pollard case, leaves the reader in limbo, if not astounded.[219]

Another example concerned the charge that an "Anglo-Soviet conspiracy" was part of the assassination of Indira Gandhi, and the implication that Salman Rushdie and *The New Republic (TNR)* magazine, whose publisher "was Michael

---

218. Investigative Leads, April 1989, p. 6. *IL* says "sources close to Swedish law enforcement" were working on the hypothesis that Emma was a Soviet agent while the "lover of Swedish PM Oleg Palme," and that the Soviets killed Palme and blamed it on the CIA.
219. *IL*, December 1988, p. 6.

Straight," were involved. *IL* noted that *TNR* had published an anti Gandhi article by Salman Rushdie; it doesn't say when. Next, *IL* said, Straight "later admitted he had been recruited... by Anthony Blunt" at Cambridge "to be part of a Soviet espionage network with Philby, Burgess and Maclean." Straight was once publisher of *The New Republic* (his family started it) but not since the late 1950s. Similarly he had been recruited by Blunt, but in the mid 1930s which he admitted in 1963, as *IL* notes. How this ties into an Anglo-Soviet conspiracy of any kind is unclear.[220] Be careful.

IL was available only by subscription. Those wishing more information should write P.O. Box 17390, Washington, D.C. 20041-0390. The phone number given by IL, 703-771-1570, has been disconnected.

INTERSERVICE JOURNAL (IJ)

The Interservice Journal of Military & Police Science and the Intelligence Profession, was intended to serve as kind of a *Reader's Digest* of mutually interesting articles, although some original material was included. Each issue contained a few book reviews, but they did little to enhance desirability. Editor William Cassidy was a one man show and was not able to generate sufficient interest to keep the quarterly journal going after three issues (January, April, and August 1982). Its format was 7 x 10 inches, gray cover, black printing. Issues ran from 64 to 100 pages. It was published by Interservice Publishing Company, Inc., San Francisco, California 94101.

LE MERCENAIRE
Intelligence Newsletter For Professionals

There is little of substance to be gained by reading the 150 odd issues of this obscure copyrighted monthly newsletter which ended publication in 1989. It is mentioned here only because it might conceivably be found in a citation thus raising

---

220. *IL*, April 1989, p. 4.

the question of credibility. Issues are four single spaced pages long, the first three summarizing national security related world events involving the Soviet military, Cuba, terrorist activities and the like. The final page contains publication data, short comments on new books and "classified ads," like the one for a confidential message service with an 800 number and nothing more. No one connected with *Le Mercenaire* is identified. The editorial "we" proclaims an apolitical approach, but the contents suggests a definite slant to the right. Annual subscriptions cost $15.00, and the publication address was P.O. Box 507, Fredericktown, MO 63645. My request for information was returned with a hand printed unsigned note stating publication had ceased due to a death in the family.

PRAVDA INTERNATIONAL (PI)

Pravda International, the monthly English language news magazine, collapsed in late 1989-early 1990 after its third year apparently due to lack of funds.[221] It managed to publish a number of interesting articles on various aspects of intelligence and related matters in the early glasnost period in the Soviet Union. The September 1988 issue had an interview with Viktor Chebrikov, just before he left the post of KGB Chairman, in which he made a series of surprising glasnostian statements on the need for a KGB more responsible to the public.

The November 1988 issue had a story about George Blake, one of the most important of the British intelligence officers who spied for, and defected to, the KGB. Blake oozes happiness and hinted he was writing a book, since published.[222] A three part series on a former Soviet illegal, Gordon Lonsdale (Konon Trofimovich Molody), began in January 1989 (vol 3, #1). They are interesting both for what they say about the case (although Lonsdale was never knighted by the Queen as claimed), the pictures, and the reasons for writing the article in the first place. The author, Valery Agranovsky, apparently received a request to which he dared not say no. Whatever the reality, the result is an unusual glimpse of how the KGB views its retired

---

221. A call to the present occupants of the *PI* offices gave that as the probable reason for its demise.
222. George Blake, *No Other Choice* (London: Jonathan Cape, 1990).

foreign agents.[223] Other typical topics of interest include an article by Roy Medvedev on Stalin's crimes, and two by Khrushchev's son on how his father was deposed which have now appeared in book form.

PI was a source of intelligence in itself about the Soviet Union as it struggles in the era of glasnost and perestroika. The United States was not left out of the criticism as indicated by the article on "Disinformation technology, a Byte at the Big Apple," a story about how the U.S. controls the world computer market.[224] The real paradox is that one cannot accept what is written, without question, for two reasons. The first is the lack of sources like any Western news magazine. The second is the demonstrated Soviet ability to print what it wants its readers to read. In the end, the burden falls on the reader once again.

Just how official *PI* was is hard to say, but its demise could be interpreted either way. It was published in London, though no editor was listed and most of the photos were supplied by TASS. Moreover, the editor made clear that complimentary copies were sent "to the CPSU Politburo and Secretariat, and to a regularly updated list of managers of Soviet trade associations and cooperatives," among others.

Issues contain about 40 pages in the British 8 x 12" inch format. Pictures inside are in black and white, the cover is in four colors. Subscriptions cost $30.00 (11 issues, one is a double). Back issues may possibly be obtained by writing to the former publisher of *Pravda International* at Pioneer House, 44-48 Clerkenwell Road, London EC1M 5PX, U.K., or phoning 011-44-1-490-1969.

---

223. The February issue, *Pravda International*, vol 3, #2, contains the second part of the Lonsdale series, "The Lonsdale Memorandum," pp. 26-29; the final part appears in vol 3, #3, pp. 14-17. In neither case is the article listed in the table of contents, but it is there and the researcher shouldn't give up. A picture on page 27, #2, shows the trap door in the Kroger house in Ruislip, near London, where some of Lonsdale's espionage equipment was stored. The current owners of the cottage are willing to have visitors; those interested should contact the author of the *RGIP*.
224. Kevin Cahill, "A Byte At The Big Apple," *Pravda International*, vol 3, #4, pp. 33-34.

SPYWATCH

Described as a *"Digest of Intelligence Community News"*, **SPYWATCH** was a 20 page monthly published by Paul M. Rosa, J.D., in Washington D.C. in 1985 and part of 1986. It presented "recent news items on espionage cases, the intelligence services, intelligence methods, and related legislative and political developments."

There are two types of reports in **SPYWATCH**. The first contains short news items that begin with a location, date, and a short headline; e.g., "Washington. 12/12/85. CIA COUNSEL GETS NOD FOR FEDERAL JUDGESHIP." This is followed by a short summary of the story. The second kind of item is a more detailed exposition of specific espionage cases; e.g., three single spaced pages on "The Pollard Affair."[225] Coverage is worldwide in scope and its reporting generally apolitical and accurate; however, no sources are provided, nor is authorship indicated. There is nothing here that could not be obtained from the newspapers, nor is there any indication of a copyright.

Issues are xeroxed on 8 1/2 x 11" paper, about 20 pages. Subscriptions were $250.00/year. The exact date that publication ceased is unknown as is the reason for its demise. Issues from 2 volumes exist. It is not available in the Library of Congress.

---

225. Both of the examples are quoted from *SPYWATCH*, vol. 2, No. 1, Jan 1, 1986, pp. 1 & 10-13 respectively.

PERIODICALS
THAT OCCASIONALLY
CONTAIN INTELLIGENCE ARTICLES

Unless otherwise indicated, the 45 periodicals in this section have at least occasional articles and book reviews on intelligence. Some like, *Aviation Week and Space Technology* frequently contain articles of direct interest. In others, like *Foreign Affairs*, the appearance of articles and book reviews on intelligence is less frequent. Some of the journals, like the British *Defense Analysis*, have devoted special issues to the subject, but may not do so again for quite awhile. Finally, there are some cryptologic journals included which have great interest to intelligence in principle, but seldom carry articles on the subject itself.

This list is not comprehensive and should not be used as a basis for concluding a thorough search has been done if only these have been examined. There is no substitute for browsing through the journals in the library; unexpected finds occur from time to time. As a start, however, those most concerned with your specialty in intelligence are worth monitoring.

The popular US weekly and monthly news magazines have been omitted because they are well known sources of intelligence news and are readily available. Some monthly news magazines have been included because they are not well known, but should be considered in a library search.

THE AMERICAN SPECTATOR has occasional articles of intelligence interest and regularly reviews books on intelligence. The October 1991 issue has an example of each. Jeffrey Gedmin of The American Enterprise Institute writes about "The Stasi Files," while NYU professor Ronald Radosh reviews *The Cambridge Spies: The Untold Story of Maclean, Philby and Burgess in America* by Verne Newton.

THE ARMY QUARTERLY AND DEFENCE JOURNAL (*AQ/DJ*) is a British publication that includes occasional articles on intelligence like the one by Lieutenant Colonel R.W.R. Ramsey, on "German Espionage in South America

1939-45." Subscription information may be obtained by writing *AQ/DJ*, 1 West Street, Tavistock, Devon PL19 8DS, UK.

AVIATION WEEK & SPACE TECHNOLOGY. This is the place to start for those concerned with past, present and future space related intelligence collection systems. Not even *AW&ST* knows for sure how good their track record is, but the consensus among the informed gives them high marks. Subscriptions are $64.00 per year from McGraw-Hill Publishers, 1221 Avenue of the Americas, NY, NY 10020.

THE CANADIAN INTELLIGENCE SERVICE (TCIS) is a 4 page newsletter in 6 1/2 x 9 1/4" format that has little to do with intelligence in the sense the term is used in the *RGIP*. *TCIS* "is a monthly report published by Canadian Intelligence Publications, a private firm engaged in research and education in the defence of freedom and Christian values." It is politically anti-communist and comments frequently on books and events related to this theme. Subscriptions are $20.00 (airmail) US and Canada; elsewhere $30.00. For further information write *TCIS*, Flesherton, Ontario, NOC 1EO, Canada.

CONFLICT INTERNATIONAL, formerly the bimonthly *Terror Update*, is a monthly newsletter (as of May 1991) that seeks to "examine the methods, tactics and motives of various international terrorist factions... to provide a platform for professionals to disseminate news and views about worldwide low intensity conflict... and to provide security management with information to assist in... threat and risk assessments internationally." Currently in volume 6, there have been only a few items directly on intelligence matters, though it does contain more on low intensity conflict issues than it did previously. Like *SIR* (see page 117), each issue contains a summary of terrorist incidents called World Review, but with surprisingly little overlap. This may be because the scope of interest is broader in *Conflict International* which includes "urban violence" not directly related to terrorism. An annual chronology of Terrorism is available for $100.00. Annual subscriptions to *Conflict International* may be obtained by sending $240.00, or your VISA/MC number, to Intel Publishing Limited, Multicom House, 2 Springvilla Park, Edgware, Middlesex HA8 7EB, England, UK. For questions and other details contact Editor Ian Geldard at that address.

CONFLICT QUARTERLY, Journal of the Centre for Conflict Studies, University of New Brunswick, Fredericton, New Brunswick, Canada E3B 5A3. Four issues/year; $18.00 in Canadian currency/check), Canada & U.S.; Overseas, £9.00.

THE CURRENT DIGEST OF THE SOVIET PRESS has been published weekly since it began in 1949, presenting "a selection of the contents of the Soviet press," translated in whole or in part without analysis or comment on content. The selection is not as great as FBIS, nor is there a total overlap. It is a very worthwhile source and is available through *NEXIS* and *DIALOG*. Subscription rates, which include four indexes, are available on request from, *THE CURRENT DIGEST OF THE SOVIET PRESS*, 1480 West Lane Ave., Columbus, Ohio 43221 (tel: 614-292-4234).

CRYPTOSYSTEMS JOURNAL. "A unique international journal devoted to implementation of cryptographic systems on IBM PCs and [compatibles] for the purpose of general scientific, mathematical, engineering, and computer science education research." One unique aspect of this periodical is that it comes with floppy disks which allow the reader to explore cryptographic mysteries on one's PC. For more information write: Tony Patti, 9755 Oatley Lane, Burke VA 22015; or phone, 703-451-6664.

DEFENSE ANALYSIS is concerned primarily with national security problems. But the special June 1987 issue, edited by Dr. Kenneth G. Robertson, University of Reading, UK, contained 11 papers by academics and former intelligence officers, all on some aspect of intelligence. For further details, including subscription rates which are not published, write: Brassey's Defence Publishers Ltd., 24 Gray's Inn Road, London, WC1X 8HR, UK; or 8000 Westpark Drive, 4th floor, McLean VA 22102, USA.

THE ECONOMIST has occasional intelligence-related articles with emphasis on economic espionage, a practice likely to continue in the current era. The 15 March 1980 issue has a fine piece by M.R.D. Foot on British "Inteligence Services." It is also a good source of intelligence book reviews; many of these have also been written by Professor Foot although not always signed. *The Economist* is available on newstands and in libraries in most major cities. Subscriptions for 51 weeks in the US are $110.00 and can be obtained from *The Economist*,

P.O. Box 58524, Boulder CO. 80322-8524. A quarterly index is
available.

ENCOUNTER, like its peers, *QUADRANT* and *SURVEY*,
ENCOUNTER is a post World War Two magazine originally
sponsored by the Congress of Cultural Freedom and secretly
funded by the CIA until the late 1960s. Subsequent support has
been obtained from independent institutions.[226]
ENCOUNTER is a liberal anti-communist magazine of wide
ranging scope. It frequently contains articles directly and
indirectly related to intelligence. An example of the former is
Robert Cecil's contribution in the April 1989 issue. In the later
category Leszek Kolakowski's piece on "The Power Of
Information," is especially good. Annual subscriptions are
£13.50 in the U.K., $29.25 for the USA and Canada, and £14.25
elsewhere. For further details write, *ENCOUNTER*, 44 Great
Windmill Street, London W1E 6UZ, England.

The *FAR EASTERN ECONOMIC REVIEW* is a well
respected weekly that has done features on various intelligence services operating in the region, including the KGB, and
mentions espionage from time to time. It is also worth
monitoring for reviews on intelligence related books. It is
published in Hong Kong. Subscriptions in the USA are $135.00
per year and may be obtained from Datamovers Inc., 36 W. 36th
Street, New York, NY 10018-8073,

FOREIGN AFFAIRS, published 5 times annually by the
Council on Foreign Relations. About once a year there is an
article on some aspect of intelligence. Recent examples include
Ray S. Cline's, "The Cuban Missile Crisis," (Fall 1989), "Intelligence and Glasnost," by George A. Carver, Jr. (Summer 1990)
and Stansfield Turner's "Intelligence for a New World Order"
(Fall 1991). For submissions write *Foreign Affairs*, Inc., 58 East
68th Street, New York, NY 10021. The subscriptions address is,
Foreign Affairs, P. O. Box 53678, Boulder CO 80322-3678. Rates
are $32.00/year US; $39.00 foreign (surface).

FOREIGN POLICY is published quarterly by the Carnegie
Endowment for International Peace. Its articles on intelligence
often analyze the role of intelligence as a factor in world affairs.

226.Peter Coleman, *The Liberal Conspiracy: The Congress For Cultural
    Freedom and the Struggle for the Mind of Postwar Europe* (NY: The
    Free Press, 1989).

Michael Krepon's "Spying From Space," which looks at the impact of satellites on the world power relationships, is a good example. Subscriptions cost $23.00 per year (add $5.00 surface, $20.00 for airmail) and may be obtained from P.O. Box 984, Farmingdale, NY 11737.

HARVARD JOURNAL OF LAW & PUBLIC POLICY, published triannually by The Harvard Society for Law & Public Policy, Inc., Harvard Law School, Cambridge, MA 02138. Vol. 12, No. 2, is devoted to "Intelligence Oversight, National Security, and Democracy." It contains 13 papers by academics, lawyers, Senator Cohen (R. ME), and former intelligence officials. Subscriptions are $30.00 US; foreign: $32.50 per year. Special introductory rates for students and others. For further details write the Society.

THE HISTORICAL JOURNAL has, over the years, published some excellent papers on the history of intelligence. These include an exchange of views on the Zinoviev Letter by Christopher Andrew and E. H. Carr (V22, #1, 1979), David French's "Spy Fever in Britain" (V21, #2, 1978) and Paul S. Fritz's "The Anti-Jacobite Intelligence System of The English Ministers" (V16, #2, 1973).

HOUSTON JOURNAL OF INTERNATIONAL LAW, University of Houston Law Center, Houston, TX 77204-6370. The Fall 1988 issue (vol 11, #1) of this biannual journal contained 18 papers from a symposium on the topic: "Legal And Policy Issues in the Iran-Contra Affair: Intelligence Oversight in a Democracy." Participants included former and current members of government and academia. Annual subscriptions are available for $18.00 USA, $20.00 foreign.

INTELLIGENCE: A Monthly Multidisciplinary Journal is just what it says, but intelligence in the sense used in the *RGIP* is not one of the disciplines. The kind of intelligence discussed is typified by the article "In Vivo Brain Size and Intelligence." *INTELLIGENCE* is published quarterly by Ablex Publishing Corporation, 335 Chestnut Street, Norwood, NJ 07648, $35.00 annually.

INTELLIGENCE SURVEY. This newsletter is included mainly to alert readers that despite its name, it has little to do with intelligence in the sense the term has been applied herein. Its primary concerns are political and economic from the very conservative point of view. All of the issues examined focus on these topics and neither the intelligence services nor their functions are mentioned in the issues available for review. Those wishing further information should write to The Australian League of Rights, 145 Russell Street, Melbourne, Victoria 3000, Australia.

INTERNATIONAL AFFAIRS: A Monthly Journal of World Politics, published by the All Union Znaniye Society, Progress Publishers (English edition). The June 1989 issue has an article by Oleg Kalugin (before his fall), on "Intelligence and Foreign Policy." Subscription information is available from the Editorial Office, 14 Gorokhovsky Pereulok, Moscow K-16.

INTERNATIONAL COUNTERTERRORISM & Security (IC/S) is heavy on assassination, personal protection, the international drug problem, terrorist groups, surveillance techniques and "frontline counterterrorism." There is a column on Security which considers such problems as hijacking and safeguards against terrorism. One of the regular columns called Intelbriefs, summarizes recent terrorist activities around the world. Another column called Tech Report looks at security related hardware. Book reviews are also a regular feature and these include titles directly on intelligence as well as counterinsurgency and counterterrorism. *IC/S* is one of the few magazines to review *Who Will Win?: A Key to the Puzzle of Revolutionary War*, by Douglas Blaufarb and George K. Tanham (NY: Crane Russak, 1989). *IC/S* uses an 8 1/2 x 11" format with four color cover and is published bimonthly by Counterterrorism & Security, Inc., PO Box 10265, Arlington VA 22210. Subscriptions are $15.00 per year. Form more information write the address just given or call 202 429-6621.

INTERNATIONAL SECURITY is sponsored by the Center for Science and International Affairs (CSIA), at Harvard University and published by the MIT Press. It concentrates on national security issues which often bear on intelligence matters. Robert Jervis's article, "Intelligence and Foreign Policy: A Review Essay," is a good example. Subscriptions are $23.00 per year (plus $9.00 for overseas). Write *IS*, 55 Hayward St., Cambridge, MA 02138.

INTERNATIONAL STUDIES QUARTERLY (ISQ). *ISQ* is the journal of the International Studies Association. Content is predominantly on international relations, but the occasional articles on intelligence are worthwhile. A good example is the September 1989 issue which contains a spirited exchange in the form of Richard Betts's review article of Ariel Levite's book, *Intelligence and Strategic Surprises* and Levite's reply. An individual annual non-member subscription in North America is $70.00, $95 elsewhere (postage included). ISA membership also includes a subscription for somewhat less, but amounts vary with income. For details write, ISA, University of South Carolina, Columbia SC 29208.

JOURNAL OF CONTEMPORARY HISTORY, published by SAGE Publications, 275 South Beverly Drive, Beverly Hills, CA 90212, USA; 28 Banner Street, London EC1Y 8QE. Occasional intelligence related articles are worth the search time. Send manuscripts to 4 Devonshire Street, London W1N 2BH. Subscriptions and further information use other addresses.

JOURNAL OF CRYPTOLOGY: The Journal of the International Association for Cryptologic Research. This is a highly specialized mathematical refereed journal dedicated to cryptology research as opposed to practical applications. This is one discipline where the public sector research often parallels the government programs. Contributions are encouraged. Subscriptions are $87.00 per year for three issues. For further information write: Springer-Verlag New York Inc., 44 Hartz Way, Secaucus, NJ 07096-2491.

JOURNAL FOR SOVIET MILITARY STUDIES is edited by Colonel David Glantz, USA, one of America's premier experts in this area. It has occasional articles on intelligence, a subject about which Col. Glantz has written extensively. It is also worthwhile for its book reviews like the one by Nigel West on *KGB: The Inside Story of its Foreign Operations from Lenin to Gorbachev* (NY: HarperCollins, 1991), 776 pp., pb) by Christopher Andrew and Oleg Gordievsky. Subscriptions may be obtained by writing Frank Cass, c/o Allen Press, Inc., Subscription Services, PO Box 1897, Lawrence, KS, USA or calling 913-843-1235 (FAX: 913-843-1274).

LIES OF OUR TIMES - A Magazine To Correct The Record "is a magazine of media criticism," but it does not live up to the claims of its subtitle. It does provide the radical left viewpoint of its writers like Noam Chomsky, Alexander Cockburn, and Ellen Ray and William Schaap. The content echoes the same anti-USA government political line as *CAIB*, e.g., "Minefields of Disinformation." Curious title, but it is a field in which the authors have great experience. Most articles are not on intelligence but enough are to make its perusal worthwhile for students of disinformation. *LIES OF OUR TIMES* is published monthly, except August, by Sheridan Press, Inc., 145 West 4th Street, New York, 10012. Subscriptions cost $24.00 per year. Subscribers names are given to "like minded publications" unless notified not to do so.

MACLEAN'S is a Canadian news and events weekly (since 1905) that monitors "Canada's Spycatchers" and the various Canadian intelligence organizations like the Communications Security Establishment (CSE), the Canadian Security Intelligence Service (CSIS), and their oversight bodies. "The Looking Glass Trade" is a recent example (July 24, 1989). Subscriptions may be obtained from *Maclean's*, P.O. Box 1600, Postal Station A, Toronto, Ontario M5W 2D8. Rates are $52.00 in Canada, $67.00 in USA, $107.00 elsewhere. It is also accessible from *NEXIS* (see page 241)

MIDDLE EAST BUSINESS INTELLIGENCE might just as well be called *Middle East Business "Information."* It is not a source of intelligence in the sense the term is applied in the *RGIP* and is included here to make that point. For more information about the magazine write International Executive Reports, Ltd., 717 D Street, N.W., Suite 300, Washington D.C. 20004-6900.

MILITARY REVIEW is a monthly publication of the US Army Command and Staff College. The occasional article on intelligence is worthwhile and probably reflects the level of attention on the subject in the courses. There are also reviews of intelligence related books worth the scholars attention. The July 1991 issue examines Bob Woodward's The Commanders as a putative work of history. For subscription information write USACGSC, Fort Leavenworth, KA 66027-6910 or call 913-684-5130.

THE NEW STATESMAN & SOCIETY is a politically left weekly magazine that occasionally attacks the Western intelligence agencies. The 10 February 1989 issue tries to link the CIA with the blowing up of PA flight 103. A post Soviet coup article provides a balanced assessment of the problems facing the "new" KGB. It also frequently has worthwhile reviews of intelligence books. Subscriptions are £48.00 in the UK, $106.00 (airmail), USA. Elsewhere, £73. Write, Foundation House, Perseverance Works, 38 Kingsland Rd., London E2 8DQ.

NEW TIMES, English edition, is still being published in Moscow. The September 3-9 1991 issue carried an article about the KGB's role in the August coup by former KGB Lt. Col. Alexander Kichikhin. Lt. Col. Kichikhin "earned" early retirement in 1990 by demonstrating against the KGB outside the Rossiya Hotel (near Red Square). Subscription instructions are provided in each issue and give a Moscow address. In practice the results using this route are not good. A more reliable method is to use Viktor Kamkin Books, Rockville, MD. For information on how to do this call Kamkin Books, 301-881-5973.

OPEN MAGAZINE Pamphlet Series, "founded during wartime..., is an emergency broadcast effort to help understand and act on the present crises in the world's political and natural environments.... The Series advances whatever responses are necessary to defend the earth's natural environment and facilitate international peace." Pamphlet #2 is a "Wartime Interview" of John Stockwell. Number 5, by Craig Hulet, is on "The U.S. Secret Agenda in the Gulf War." In number 9 Howard Zim writes on the subject: "How Mr. Bush Got HIs War: Deceptions, Double-Standards & Disinformation." For details about subscriptions write *OPEN MAGAZINE* Pamphlet Series, P.O. Box 2726, Westfield, NJ 07091, or call 908-789-9608.

ORBIS: A Journal of World Affairs, is a quarterly sponsored by the Foreign Policy Research Institute. It has contained a number of articles on intelligence related matters over the years. The special report by Polish defector Ryszard Kuklinski with the introduction by Richard Pipes and comments by Zbigniew Brzezinski (Winter 1988) is an excellent example. Subscriptions cost $25.00 for individuals, institutions $50.00; overseas add $5.00. Write *ORBIS*, 3508 Market Street, Suite 350, Philadelphia, PA 19104.

PARAMETERS, U.S. Army War College Quarterly, published by the Department of the Army. Intelligence techniques and practices are usually examined in the context of strategic military issues. The June 1989 article by Robert D. Glasser on "Signals Intelligence and Nuclear Preemption," is an example.

Subscriptions available from the Superintendent of Documents, US GPO, Washington, D.C. 20402; rates $7.00 USA, $8.50 foreign. Preferred length of manuscripts, 4000 words.

THE POLITICAL QUARTERLY (TPQ). Like the American *Political Science Quarterly*, the *TPQ* is largely concerned with domestic political issues, but has from time to time some fascinating exchanges of view on matters intelligence. Professor Donald Watt's article on the Peter Wright-spycatcher case (Vol 59, #2, 1988) and its critique by Professor Laurence Lustgarten (Vol 60, #2, 1989) meet the latter criterion. Another example, by James J. Wirtz, "Intelligence To Please: The Order Of Battle Controversy during the Vietnam War," appears in the Summer 1991 issue. Manuscripts are encouraged, for details write Audrey Coppard, Ed. Asst., Birkbeck College, 10 Gower Street, London WC1E 7HX. Annual subscriptions in the UK are £36.50, USA $68.00, elsewhere £39.50. For more information write, Basil Blackwell Ltd, 108 Cowley Road, Oxford OX4 1JF.

POLITICAL SCIENCE QUARTERLY (PSQ). The *PSQ* "is a nonpartisan journal devoted to the study of contemporary and historical aspects of government, politics, and public affairs" published continuously since 1886. The occasional articles on intelligence are of high quality and make the journal worth monitoring. The Fall 1984 paper by Lucien S. Vandenbroucke, "Anatomy of a Failure: The Decision to Land at the Bay of Pigs," is a good example. Subscriptions cost $25.00 per year and may be obtained from the Academy of Political Science, 475 Riverside Drive, Suite 1274, NY, NY 10115-0012.

PRIVACY JOURNAL, "an independent monthly on privacy in a computer age," is concerned with "reporting on legislation, legal trends, new technology, and public attitudes affecting the confidentiality of information and the individual's right to privacy." Items are about a 100 words to a single spaced 8 1/2 x 11" page in length and occasionally impinge on intelligence related matters; e.g., NSA attempts to control private data encryption, wiretapping, and FBI use of databases in the investigation of "intelligence breaches." Publisher and journalist Robert Ellis Smith started the Journal in 1974 and has been described by Bill Moyers as the "Paul Revere of information security." With an annual subscription ($26.00) the subscriber receives a 100 page book describing 600 confidentiality laws which is updated yearly. Write: *PRIVACY JOURNAL*, P.O. Box 15300, Washington D.C. 20003, telephone 202-547-2865.

PROBLEMS OF COMMUNISM is a bimonthly magazine published by the United States Information Agency (USIA) to provide analysis on contemporary affairs in "the Soviet Union, China, and comparable states and political movements." Despite being a government publication is has a solid reputation. For subscription information write the Superintendent of Documents, U.S. GPO, Washington, D.C. 20402, USA.

PROLOGUE: Quarterly of the National Archives is an informative publication whose broad charter often includes articles on intelligence. Some are first person essays like the contribution by William E. Colby, A Participant's Commentary on Vietnam (Spring 1991). Others are scholarly contributions with two unusual features. First they are often well illustrated because the broad scope of materials available in the Archives. Second, they are based mainly on the documents in the archives which are cited to provide easy access for those who follow. Examples in this category include Lawrence H. McDonald's The Office of Strategic Services: America's First National Intelligence Agency, and Charles A. Shaughnessy's Vietnam Records in the National Archives, (both Spring, 1991). Subscriptions are available for $12.00 (USA), $15.00 elsewhere, from NEPS, Cashier, National Archives, Washington, DC 20408.

QUADRANT is an Australian monthly conceived in 1955 in the Russian Tea Room" in New York and initially (but no longer) funded secretly by the CIA. It is now edited by Peter Coleman and Robert Manne. More like *ENCOUNTER*, or the *ATLANTIC*, than the scholarly *SURVEY*, *QUADRANT* contains interesting reviews on intelligence books like the one on Anthony Cave Brown's, *The Secret Servant*[227] in the October 1988 issue. Typical intelligence related articles include the series on Communist journalist and KGB agent Wilfred Burchett and the award winning pieces on the Petrov case, both by Robert Manne. Minimum pay for articles is $80.00, $40.00 for reviews. Subscriptions may be obtained from

---

227. Published in the USA as *"C": The Secret Life of Sir Stewart Menzies, Spymaster to Winston Churchill* (NY: Macmillan, 1987).

QUADRANT, Box 344, Clarence Street Post Office, Sydney, Australia 2000; $40.00 (AUS) individuals.

RUSI Journal. This quarterly is published by the Royal United Services Institute for Defence Studies. Articles and book reviews relating to intelligence appear in most issues. The Summer 1989 edition contains an article by John Bruce Lockhart on "Sir William Wiseman Bart, Agent of Influence." Subscriptions (£27.00) come with membership which is open to all. For details write, The Royal United Services Institute for Defence Studies, Whitehall, London SW1A 2ET, UK.

SLAVIC REVIEW: American Quarterly of Soviet and East European Studies, published by the American Association for the Advancement of Slavic Studies. Available with membership in AAASS. Occasional articles on contemporary and historical intelligence related issues. Membership rates vary with income. For details write: AAASS, 128 Encina Commons, Stanford University, Stanford CA 94305.

SOLDIER OF FORTUNE: The Journal of Professional Adventurers, is a monthly publication heavy on paramilitary subjects with occasional intelligence related articles mostly on military topics. Typical examples are "RECCE Commandos," (February 1990), "Navy SEALs in Libya," (February 1988), and "AIRBORNE RECCON: *SOF* Looks at 82nd's Scout Course," (May 1988). From time to time there are also features on espionage weapons like "CIA's Deer Gun," (January 1983), and history such as Joseph C. Goulden's "CIA's Korean Capers" (May 1983), a story about Hans Tofte. *SOF* often takes controversial positions as it did in a fact filled article about the looney dissembler on MIA issues, "Scott Barnes, My Favorite Flake," by Alan Dawson (Spring 1983). There are frequent book reviews of intelligence interest, often by authors with firsthand experience. *Soldier of Fortune* is available at many newsstands and by subscription ($26.00/year) from *SOF Magazine*, P.O. Box 348, Mt. Morris, IL 61054-9984. Contributions encouraged, instructions in each issues, payment after acceptance.

STRATEGIC REVIEW is a quarterly publication of the United States Strategic Institute, Washington, D.C. Papers from active members of the government are "especially invited." Intelligence articles are infrequent but many issues have good reviews of intelligence books. For example, the Summer 1989 volume contains a review by Jeffrey Wallin, of

Comparing Foreign Intelligence: The US, the USSR, the U.K., and the Third World, edited by Roy Godson. The Winter 1990 issue has a review by Joseph A. Mendenhall of William Colby's, *Lost Victory*. Both are thought provoking and will benefit the academic who must assess their value for classroom use or his own research, and to the reader who lacks experience. Subscription and publication information is provided on request from the Institute's Publishing Office, 265 Winter Street, Waltham, MA 02154.

SURVEY "magazine," as the British call it, is an excellent scholarly journal, published quarterly by Survey Ltd. in association with the Institute For European Defence & Strategic Studies. The emphasis is on the Soviet Union and it has published some major papers on the KGB. Submissions are encouraged and should be sent to Ilford House, 133 Oxford Street, London W1R 1TO. Subscriptions, $39.00 USA, £9.00 UK, elsewhere £20.00 and may be obtained by writing SURVEY, 44 Great Windmill Street., London W1V 7PA.

SURVIVAL is the journal of the International Institute for Strategic Studies (IISS) in London. Its papers are themselves unclassified intelligence estimates of high quality. Specific articles on intelligence subjects are rare but ones like Richard Shultz's "Low Intensity Conflict," specifically involve intelligence and make *SURVIVAL* worth monitoring. Subscriptions are available for £21.00 ($38.00) from Pergamon-Brassey's, Maxwell House, Fairview Park, Elmsford, NY 10523 for the USA and elsewhere from Brassey's, Headington Hill Hall, Oxford OX3 0BW, UK. For information on the IISS, write: IISS, 23 Travistock Street, London WC2E 7NQ.

THE WASHINGTON QUARTERLY, The Center for Strategic and International Studies, 1800 K Street, N.W., Suite 400, Washington, D.C. 20006. Subscription address, *TWQ,* MIT Press Journals, 55 Hayward Street, Cambridge, MA 02142; rates: individuals $25.00/yr, institutions $53.00/yr, outside USA add $9.00 surface postage, $17.00 airmail.

THE WORLD & I is a monthly publication of The Washington Times Corporation, 2850 New York Avenue, N.E., Washington, D.C. 20002. Publishes occasional articles and book reviews on intelligence. Annual subscription rates: $90.00 USA, Western Europe $150.00, Canada and Mexico $120.00; all others $195.00. Each issue is about 700 pages. *THE WORLD &* *I* pays for articles and book reviews.

WORLD POLITICS, sponsored by the Center for International Studies, Princeton University. Published by Princeton University Press, 3175 Princeton Pike, Lawrenceville, NJ 08648. Subscriptions rates: individual USA, $18 per year, foreign $22.50, plus $3.75 for postage.

PERIODIC BIBLIOGRAPHIES
OF INTELLIGENCE LITERATURE

The four bibliographies included in this section vary in periodicity and purpose, but each one has potential value for the scholar, student or reader of intelligence.

The Bibliography Of Intelligence Literature, edited by Walter Pforzheimer for the Defense Intelligence College, is focused on the needs of the military and the spectrum of reading appropriate to their careers. But it also contains titles and comments not found elsewhere which will be of interest to intelligence officers generally.

Likewise, the *Criminal Intelligence And Security Intelligence: A Selective Bibliography*, compiled by Canadians Stuart Farson and Catherine Matthews, is oriented for Canadian intelligence officers and scholars but has value to those below the border and across the Atlantic.

The third offering, *Terrorism, Assassination, Espionage And Propaganda: A Master Bibliography*, is the product of Laird Wilcox in Kansas and is the only periodic bibliography known to cover these subjects.

The Bowen Digital Bibliography (BDB) is my shorthand for a Bibliography of over 8000 books and articles on intelligence. Nothing comes close to answering quickly so many bibliographic questions about intelligence and related topics, in several languages. And it is still growing.

Future students and general readers will become accustomed to databases like those above, but they may never appreciate just how much time they save and the number of books that will turn up which would have been overlooked in the days when library bibliographies had to be selective because there was no *BDB*.

None of these bibliographies contain all the books on intelligence and related matters. Even the Library of Congress is deficient in this regard. Nevertheless, if one starts with those

described here they will provide information leading to nearly
all the titles published.

BIBLIOGRAPHY OF
INTELLIGENCE LITERATURE
(Defense Intelligence College)

The *DIC Bib*, as it is called, is described on its title page as "A Critical and Annotated Bibliography of Open-Source Literature." It was conceived and first edited in 1972 by Lt. Col. John Guenther, USMC, while he served at the Defense Intelligence College (DIC). Succeeding editions bear the imprimatur of Dr. John Dziak (2nd, 1973; 3rd 1975, & 4th, 1976); Mr. Arthur A. Zuehlke, Jr. (5th, 1978 & 6th, 1979) and Walter Pforzheimer (7th, 1983 & 8th, 1985). Dr. Pforzheimer is currently preparing a 9th edition due for publication in late 1992.

Technically, the *DIC Bib* is one of two periodic annotated intelligence bibliographies the other being the Laird Wilcox *"Master Bibliography"* (page 217). But in terms of annotation the latter barely qualifies. Wilcox's comments seldom exceed 15 words. The *DIC Bib* critical annotations average over 100 words and reflect a synthesis of the experience of the several professional editors. And although it has many less entries, about 300 compared to Wilcox's 3000, the *DIC Bib* is focused on professional intelligence books of merit. Wilcox includes many titles dealing with terrorism and assassination that are not directly applicable to intelligence.

The selection of books in the *DIC Bib* covers a balanced mix of military and civilian organizations and operations from the West and East. It includes authors who take issue with intelligence generally and with specific operations, as well as those who are supportive of the profession. The editor provides some guidance for judging the value of the various books. Books "considered particularly valuable for the serious student and the intelligence professional" are designated by an asterisk. In terms of the time period, the focus is on the 20th century, although the contributions of the ancients are not forgotten.[228]

---

228. Aside from periodicity and selectivity, the main difference between the *DIC Bib* and George Constantinides's annotated bibliography (see fn #30) is that the latter makes analytical comparisons with other

Another singular contribution from the *DIC Bib* is the inclusion of entries for defector testimony to Congress, citations of Senate and House Intelligence Committee publications, and reports of investigations of Western intelligence services.

Entries are organized alphabetically by author which is not a problem with this many titles. In addition to the annotation, each entry includes the basic bibliographic data plus an indication as to whether the book contains notes, a bibliography, and whether there is a paperback edition. There are cross references to other volumes in the bibliography.

The principal drawback of the current edition is that it does not include a selection from the several hundred books published since 1985. Still, the *DIC Bib* is a valuable starting point for the interested reader and scholar, especially when used in combination with the other bibliographies mentioned.

The *DIC Bib* is paper bound, 8 1/2 x 11", with a blue, black and white cover (otherwise black and white) and 90 pages long. It may be obtained free of charge from the Defense Intelligence College, Washington, D.C. 20301-6111.

---

books.

CRIMINAL INTELLIGENCE
AND SECURITY INTELLIGENCE
A SELECTIVE BIBLIOGRAPHY

The first edition of this new bibliography appeared in late 1990. It is intended to meet the new requirements for study in these areas generated by the relatively recent separation of Canadian agencies with counterintelligence and security functions, from those with arrest powers. The former now rest with the Canadian Security and Intelligence Service (CSIS), the latter with the RCMP.

The *Bibliography* was compiled by Canadians Stuart Farson and Catherine Matthews, both then with the Centre of Criminology, University of Toronto. It was prepared "with a view to helping scholars who want to draw distinctions between security and criminal intelligence work."[229] Future editions will be bilingual in French and have annotated entries.

Although the focus is on English language material and matters Canadian during the last 20 years, it also contains some books and articles from the USA, New Zealand, Britain and Australia. Topics include "domestic intelligence, political policing, surveillance techniques, undercover operations, the role of informants and agent provocateurs" and the legal aspects of conspiracy.

The bibliography is presented in two sections. The first contains books, articles and papers. Many of the entries are relevant to the general intelligence profession. While some American articles are included, there are many published in Canadian sources that will be new to American readers and scholars.

The second section lists government publications, both Canadian and American. The latter selections do not appear in any other bibliography in the *RGIP* because this is the most

---

229.Catherine Matthews is the Head Librarian of the Centre of Criminology, University of Toronto. Stuart Farson is the Secretary/Treasurer of the Canadian Association for Security and Intelligence Studies (CASIS).

recent of those published. An Appendix lists the sources from which many of the entries were drawn.

The format is 8 1/2 x 11," printed, with a total of 77 pages in a blue paper cover. Copies of the *bibliography* (ISBN 0-91958-466-7) may be obtained by sending an order (no funds) to the Publications Office, Centre of Criminology, University of Toronto, Room 8001, 130 St. George Street, Toronto, Ontario, Canada M5S 1A1. Requesters will be billed separately for the $5.00C per copy charge and appropriate mailing costs.

TERRORISM, ASSASSINATION, ESPIONAGE AND PROPAGANDA
A MASTER BIBLIOGRAPHY

Laird Wilcox has published two editions (1988 & 1989) of his "concise but comprehensive bibliography," another is scheduled for 1992. This bibliography now includes more than 3000 book titles, many on assassination and terrorism. It is the only periodic bibliography with that number of "annotated" entries, many of which are intelligence books. The annotations, however, are very brief and do not always convey the full scope of the content. Furthermore, a sizeable number of books on intelligence have not been included and Marjorie Cline's *Scholar's Guide to Intelligence Literature*, Myron Smith's *The Secret Wars: A Guide To Sources in English*, or, best of all, the *DBD*, the digital version of the Russell Bowen bibliography should also be consulted (see page 219).[230]

Titles in the Wilcox bibliography are organized alphabetically by author but are not separated by major topic. The books from 1986-1989 begin after those printed earlier. Thus the reader must examine each grouping of entries unless the author or date is known.

Most but not all entries are annotated, in the latter cases apparently because Wilcox relies on the secondary title. Where annotations occur they seldom exceed 15 words and then are not always informative or correct. For example, Sandor Rado's, *Code Name DORA* has no secondary title or comments. The notation for Ernest May's, *Knowing One's Enemies: Intelligence Assessment Before The Two World Wars*, says only that

---

230. Marjorie Cline (ed.), *Scholar's Guide to Intelligence Literature: Bibliography of the Russell J. Bowen Collection in the Joseph Mark Lauinger Library, Georgetown University* (Washington, D.C., National Intelligence Study Center, 1983). This bibliography is listed by subject and indexed by author, and contains about 5000 entries. There are about 5000 more titles in the collection currently being cataloged. Myron J. Smith's, *The Secret Wars: A Guide To Sources in English* (Santa Barbara, CA: ABC-Clio Press, 1980), 3 vols, contains about 10,000 total entries listed by category and indexed by author. Cline and Smith are not annotated.

it is an "account of success and failures, etc." Agar's **Baltic Response**, was published in 1963, not 1983; and Philip Agee was a CIA officer not an agent, and he left the CIA in 1968 not 1969. And then there is the note after Jane Foster's memoir, *An Un-American Lady*, which says she was a "woman attacked by Senator McCarthy, etc," though that never happened; she was an indicted Soviet spy and stayed out of the country to avoid prosecution. Others in her network, the Soble Ring, went to jail.

A number of useful inserts are presented after the main entries. These include a list of selected Journals, a description of the Wilcox Collection at the University of Kansas, a directory of publishers with addresses, some data on terrorist incidents, a list of FBI field divisions with addresses and phone numbers, and instructions on how to make a request under the Freedom of Information Act.

The bibliography is spiral bound in 8 1/2 x 11" format, with entries in two columns per page. The pages are not numbered and the book entries occupy about 85 of the approximately 100 pages. Copies are $20.00 and may be obtained from Editorial Research Service, PO Box 2047, Olathe, KS 66061.

BOWEN DIGITAL BIBLIOGRAPHY (BDB)

The official title of this "periodical" is *"The Digital Bibliography of the Russell J. Bowen Collection of Works on Intelligence, Security, and Covert Activities."* Its more than 8,000 entries make the *BDB* the largest known digital database of books and articles on or related to intelligence, in many languages, in the world. About 6500 of the *BDB* entries are books in English; about 2000 are books in other languages (Russian 1000, France 600, the balance in German, Spanish and miscellaneous tongues), and approximately 500 are articles from journals and newspapers in English. The *BDB* is a subset of the 11,000 items in the Bowen collection on intelligence now resident in the Georgetown University Lauinger Library. All 11,000 items and will eventually be included in the *BDB*.

The books in the *BDB* were originally acquired by former Army officer, M.I.T. graduate, scientist and CIA analyst, Colonel Russell Bowen. That the definition of intelligence is context dependent becomes very clear when one examines the breadth and scope of the *BDB* titles. In addition to the expected categories of military intelligence, espionage, covert action, analysis, security and counterintelligence, one finds the related topics of psychological warfare, propaganda, cryptology, deception, guerrilla warfare, resistance movements, congressional and parliamentary actions, legal requirements and cases, tech-transfer, science, aerial and space reconnaissance, and memoirs; to name a few.

There are two reasons for this comprehensiveness; the ubiquitous nature of intelligence itself, and Colonel Bowen's own interests. The collection was begun after World War II when Col. Bowen began a search for an explanation as to why it had started. He soon identified intelligence in all its ramifications as a major contributor to the answer. Before long he was enmeshed in the excitement of collecting intelligence books, acquiring more new and out-of-print titles every year.

Looking back, Col. Bowen (now retired) says it gradually became evident that there were relatively few really good books from any period, in any language, that addressed the essence of the subject and this remained so until the mid 1970s. Then, partly from the attention generated by Vietnam and Watergate, a distinct shift in quantity and quality of intelligence books is evident. "Most good books on intelligence," he says, "have been written in the last 10 - 15 years." This reality has had a noticeable impact on the configuration of the *BDB*.

What began as a simple log of basic bibliographic data necessary to account for the books in his collection, gradually became a reservoir of information about authors, publishers, dates, editions, a description of contents, and eventually an extensive keyword section. As the books covered more complex topics in a more scholarly fashion, the entries grew from a few lines to several pages, single spaced, all typed by Bowen on his portable typewriter. The descriptions available for many of the books are crafted so as to highlight the topics that should be covered in a good review.

By 1980, when the first 3800 books of the collection were placed in Lauinger Library at Georgetown University, it was clear some form of written guide to the collection was required. The initial step toward this end was completed in 1983 with publication of *The Scholar's Guide To Intelligence Literature*, edited by Majorie Cline.[231] *The Scholar's Guide*, catalogues the first 5000 entries of the collection under various categories, minus keywords and annotation.

By 1988, when the collection had more than doubled in size and exceeded 10,000 items, the same accountability problem existed but this time the decision was made to create a digital version which could be conveniently updated as new volumes are added. This task was undertaken by the National Intelligence Book Center which markets the current product.

The software program chosen for the *BDB*, a variation of *FOLIO VIEWS*, is extremely fast and easy to use. All a user needs to get started is a PC (a 286, 386 or 486 IBM or compatible) and a hard disk with space to add 6 megabytes of data. Once the *BDB* is loaded onto a hard disk (it cannot be used with floppies), a user can instruct the PC in ordinary language to find specific titles, authors, participants, keywords, dates, publishers, or some combination of these options. In less than a second the number of entries meeting the conditions

---

231.Cline, op. cit.

specified is presented on the monitor. One can then examine each entry identified and select those worth a closer look. A bibliographic search that would take hours to complete manually can be done in seconds with the *BDB*.

"But," one may reason, "most modern libraries today have their indexes on computers, why not just use them?" The answer, of course, is that you can do just that. But having done so, will you have identified the pertinent books on intelligence? There are two good reasons to suppose that you will have missed many. First, libraries are selective, they don't buy all books published in any category and don't keep all they buy. Second, for the most part, even the largest libraries only record in the index, the approved Library of Congress [subject] Headings (LCH) and they frequently do not identify the intelligence links in books, especially ones before 1960.

For example, if one is doing a study of military intelligence, the book, Slatin Pasha, is likely to be missed for two reasons. First, few libraries have it. Second, for those that do, the LCHs do not identify it as having anything to do with intelligence. In fact, it is a biography of a former Austrian Lieutenant, who was also an honorary British major-general and a lieutenant general in the Egyptian army, who eventually became Assistant Director of Egyptian Military Intelligence.

Likewise, the LCH subjects listed for Robert Boucard's, *The Secret Services of Europe*, do not include secret service, espionage, or any related subjects, nor do they indicate that the book has several chapters on women spies. Thus a subject search of the card or digital catalog, on any of these topics, does not turn up this volume. Similarly, H.V.F. Winstone's *Leachman: O.C. Desert: The Life of Lt. Colonel Gerard Leachman, D.S.O.*, and the biographies of Joseph Fouché, Napoleonic era spymaster, do not indicate the intelligence links on the library card. Fortunately the LCH's in many of the recent and more well known books, like Allen Dulles's *Craft Of Intelligence* (1963) and Cord Meyer's *Facing Reality*, do indicate either intelligence or espionage as a subject category. But over half the entries in the collection are dated before 1960.

Other recent intelligence books, like *Tale of the Scorpion*, by Australian Harvey Barnett, who served in both the Australian security and intelligence services (ASIO and ASIS) are likely to be missed because it won't be acquired by many libraries. With the *BDB* one can learn of the existence and often the content of such a book, whether or not the library has it, and can then arrange to borrow a copy if necessary.

Despite the obvious power and flexibility of the *BDB*, there are some trade-offs in its current state of development. First, while over 4200 of the 8000 entries now in the database also have keywords, and over 2000 of these have detailed descriptive annotations (theme summaries, persons and place names, code words, operations, etc.), the balance (about 3800) have only the basic bibliographic data (author's name, title, sub-title, and the publishing data). This will limit the speed of general category *BDB* searches. But, since these 3800 titles are in *the Scholar's Guide* where they are categorized, a comprehensive search of the 8000 entries can be accomplished by using both forms of the bibliography.

Second, more than 3000 titles remain to be added. Of these about 1500 are in English, 800 are in Russian, 500 in French and two hundred in other languages. The Special Collections staff at Georgetown University are carding these titles so the *BDB* will eventually include all 11,000 volumes. Those added each year will be available to subscribers in the form of updates.

The third factor to consider is that the *BDB* (like *NAMEBASE*) is a protected "read-only" database. This means a user cannot change (add to or delete) what is there when it is purchased. Consequently, updates are necessary to keep it current; hence the descriptor, "periodical" above. Furthermore, the results of a search cannot, with one exception, be printed. The exception is, that at any given time, the data appearing on the screen of the monitor can be printed to a paper printer, if one is available. If not, manual extraction is required (as in libraries), but at least one doesn't have to go through hundreds of index cards and bibliographies at the end of books; that has all been done for you.

One application of the *BDB* yet to be mentioned is its value to collectors of intelligence books. Whether one is building a general or specialized collection, the *BDB* will serve as the baseline reference.

The *BDB* is furnished on floppy disks from which it must be transferred to a hard disk for use. It is available from the National Intelligence Book Center, Suite 607, 1700 K Street NW,

Washington, D.C. 20006, tel 202 785-4334. The purchase price is $400.00; this includes the database search program and instructions for use.

DIGITAL INTELLIGENCE-RELATED PERIODICALS (DIRPs) and DATABASES

The 4 entries in this category provide subscribers with two specialized intelligence databases, one bare bones database program (you fill in the details) and a digital bulletin board. The latter provides two intelligence-related newsletters and a forum for communicating with others similarly inclined who want to exchange information, solve problems, and discuss the profession. Whether researcher, reader, scholar or neophyte, the general methods and techniques involved in using these periodicals are identical to those used in research organizations, intelligence agencies, universities and industry.

The two databases, *CIABASE* and *NAMEBASE* are similar in design and operations. The former concentrates on events, the latter on names. As with most databases size constraints makes them selective, but other factors account for the tilt to the political left. Nevertheless, they are simple to operate and will often provide answers not found elsewhere because many of the periodicals from which they extract or index data are not readily available, or just plain obscure.

The database program, *SpyBase*, comes from Australia and has been tested in the area of criminal intelligence investigation and analysis.

The Military Roundtable & Bulletin Board in the *GEnie* database (see page 245) has, despite its title, the only bulletin board with a section devoted to espionage and related issues. One can learn something, meet others, and besides using bulletin boards is fun.

The two newsletters obtainable in electronic or digital form are, *For Your Eyes Only (FYEO)* [page 149] and *Counter-Terrorism Security Intelligence (CT-SI)* [page 117]. Both are available through a database service called *NEWSNET* (see page 246). For convenience both versions (paper & digital) of each one are described at the page numbers indicated and will not be further discussed here.

CIABASE
A computer database on the CIA

The publicity brochure provided by *CIABASE* states that the information in this 4 megabyte annotated database was "gleaned from 200+ sources of various political ideologies — congressional reports, newspapers, magazines and over 170 books." The result is that "*CIABASE* offers a vital, easy-to-use historical resource for policy makers, academicians, journalists and students."

As an example of what *CIABASE* seeks to accomplish, the brochure notes that

> *Former government historian Warren Cohen resigned because the CIA distorted information making the official record a 'fraud.' CIABASE helps defeat this practice by providing detailed information enabling the writing of accurate history (emphasis added).*

One should notice that there is no claim for providing accurate detailed information, perhaps because most of the sources are secondary.

An example of why the point on accuracy is important occurs when analyzing the quote above about Mr. Warren Cohen. Searching *CIABASE* for entries on Warren Cohen one finds that he is a professor at Michigan State and the former "Chairman of [a] Department of State advisory committee of outside scholars," not a government historian. Furthermore, *CIABASE* does not quote him saying the "CIA distorted information," the word "distorted" is not used. The entry suggests Mr. Cohen wrote that the CIA refused to release details of operations more than 30 years old and therefore contributed to "falsifying U.S. history." Cohen is not quoted as saying the "official record is a fraud." *CIABASE* does say that the "American record of role in Iran in 53 is useless, a farce, a fraud." The clipped syntax is typical and unexplained.

Whether these or any other assertions are correct, incorrect, or distorted, cannot be determined until the sources cited are checked, and *CIABASE* explicitly leaves this validation task to the user. The disclaimer presented on the first screen of the database reads: "Checking cited sources for accuracy and content is *strongly advised*." (emphasis added). Consequently, a more appropriate description of *CIABASE* is that it can be a useful first step to the "writing of accurate history." It can provide a quick first-cut response to the question, has something been published on a given topic? Of course, failure to get a hit does not mean nothing has been published, only that other databases must be used. Presumably this problem will occur less and less over time as more data are added.

Each of the 100 or so categories in *CIABASE* contains short excerpts from articles, books, etc. Sometimes quotes are included, most often not. Entries varying in length from two or three lines to most of a page. While there is some selectivity in what to enter, there appears to be little, if any, attempt to analyze the data itself. The number of entries in each category varies. Counterintelligence (which includes counterespionage), for example, has about 35 entries for the period 1940-1991, small for such a wide and active field. On the other hand, a search for entries on defectors, for which there is no specific category, yields another 35 or so. Searches by name and event within categories and time periods may also be made. Clearly, the search options are not arranged so that one topic is adequate and a multiple topic search strategy is recommended.

Typical categories include, "assassinations, book review, covert action, deception, FBI (almost all negative), KGB, deaths, forgery ("in CIA ops" not KGB), funding, history, intel failure, leaks, mind control, NSC, oversight, propaganda, sex, terrorism, torture, white paper (Agee), and youth."

When the CIA, which is not a category, is mentioned, it is usually in a negative sense. This projects the impression that the author, Ralph McGehee (a former CIA officer), either does not like or understand that organization, or perhaps both. This assessment gains credence when one searches the "intel success" category and finds most of the entries concern failures. In short, additional sources should be consulted if objectivity and accuracy are a concern.

Like most databases, a search using *CIABASE* varies in length depending on the complexity. Technically, it does, as claimed, provide "rapid access to specific data, scanning *in minutes* (emphasis added) the entire database." Most of the time however the first "hits" come up in seconds and the remainder are scrolled on the monitor as found. Depending on the topic and the computer used, some searches will take several minutes. Results can be sent to the printer or a disk file for use in a word processor. The *CIABASE* program disk contains two files, "SUBJECTS" and "BOOKS," that the user may copy to a word processor and print to obtain a listing of the sources and subjects categories under which data have been entered. These files are not readable in *CIABASE*.

Those acquainted with *NAMEBASE* (see page 230) will notice a similarity in *CIABASE* design, not surprising when it is learned that Daniel Brandt wrote the software for both programs. There is some source overlap (e.g., both cite *CAIB*) between the two. But the major differences are the greater number of sources and names cited by *NAMEBASE* (with only a few annotations to date), while *CIABASE* has fewer sources, a somewhat narrower focus, and most, though not all, citations are annotated. Those that are not are given as sources of additional data.

There are only three and one-half pages of instructions, single spaced. They are simple and with the examples, easy to grasp. *CIABASE* works with any IBM compatible PC (DOS 2.1 or higher), requires a hard disk with about 4.50 MB of storage, and is supplied on 5.25 or 3.5 inch disks.

Users may acquire a copy from a friend without paying a fee to *CIABASE*, but to get updates ($49.00) and any technical support, they must register (send $25.00) with *CIABASE* headquarters. A new copy costs $99.00. Those wishing to purchase, register, get an update or more information, should write to *CIABASE*, P.O. Box 5022, Herndon, VA 22070.

MILITARY ROUNDTABLE
& BULLETIN BOARD (MR&BB)
("GENIE" DATA BASE SYSTEM)

Technically, the *MR&BB* is a forum for the discussion and exchange of information on a variety of military-related subjects. It is periodic only in the sense that it can be read at regular (or irregular) intervals. New information is often added by the users and the system operator.

Some entries, like book reviews and military history, often concern intelligence. But one specific category is devoted to espionage, security issues, technology transfer and terrorism.

Participation in the *MR&BB* requires access to two things; a personal computer (with communications software & modem), and a subscription to the *GEnie* (General Electric Network Information Exchange). Once you have the former, you can acquire access to *"GEnie"* by calling (voice phone) 1-800-638-9636 and following the instructions. Signing on to *GEnie* gets you a user ID# and a password and this is all done over the phone using the PC. There is a one-time initial fee of $29.00. From then on costs depend on when you call *GEnie* and how long you stay connected. For more details on *GEnie* see page 245.

Once you have you user ID number and password, you may log-on, whenever you wish. Step by step instructions are provided. But to go quickly to the ESPIONAGE category, enter M155 at the first prompt, hit your "return" key, and wait a few seconds until the Military Roundtable heading appears on your monitor. A list of "Libraries" will then be presented and your cursor will stop at another prompt. You then enter the number opposite the topic of your choice, which is "1" for the "Military Bulletin Board," and hit "return". More choices will appear, you enter 3, hit return, and when you get the next list of choices, enter a 5. This gets you to the espionage BB. From then on you have three options. You may just read what is there, ask (type in) questions which will be answered later by other users, or you can answer questions placed on the BB by others.

Recent topics include comments on the Cambridge spies, the TOP HAT case, 78 messages on intelligence agencies, a discussion on defector Victor Suvorov and his works, and the changes going on in the East European intelligence services. Then there was a notice from Senator Moynihan's office which announced that the Information Security Oversight Office of the General Services Administration, reported that 6,796,501 secrets were created in 1989. No mention was made of how they identified a secret or how they counted them.

Every BB has a system operator (SYSOP) and the SYSOP for the *MR&BB* is Frank Dooling. He monitors the board twice a day and is available to answer questions via the electronic mail system. He also controls the "real-time conferences," another way to communicate, on topics of interest, with amateurs and experts.

Using a BB can be fun, informative and not expensive if you log-on in the low priority time period, 1800-0600 HRS ($6.00/hour, pro-rated). The range of contacts is large and one can often get data and find sources that are not otherwise available. If you prefer having your information on paper, write for details to *GEnie*, 401 N. Washington Street, Rockville, Maryland 20850. Otherwise call the number above.

NAMEBASE

(formerly called *SpyBASE*)[232]

In the beginning, the central idea behind *NAMEBASE* was the preservation of data from the numerous arcane political publications which made their debut in the 1960s and 1970s, many of which no longer exist. The data collection phase began in 1974 and was concerned with, inter alia, the activities of political groups and their contacts with American intelligence agencies. Initially, names of individuals and organizations appearing in these publications, together with the source, were extracted and recorded on paper, or hardcopy as some prefer to call it.

Input to the digital database began in 1982 and the first issue of *NAMEBASE* (then called *SpyBASE*) was published in 1985 (using 4, 5 1/4" floppy disks). Subscribers (mostly journalists, news organizations, researchers, and scholars) could then query *NAMEBASE* on their PC to find the publication in which the person's name or the organizational name had appeared; modest, but a start. Since then, data from additional publications have been added, including some of those in this guide, bringing the total to over 300 books, and several hundred periodicals.

For example, *NAMEBASE* now contains name and page entries from Peter Wright's *SPYCATCHER*, David Wise's *The Spy Who Got Away*, Tom Powers's *The Man Who Kept The Secrets*, Edward Jay Epstein's *Deception*, N. Yakovlev's *Washington Silhouettes* (Moscow: Progress Press, 1985), and *WIDOWS* by William Corson and S. & J. Trento, John Prados's *Keepers of The Keys* and Tom Mangold's *Cold Warrior: James Jesus Angleton The CIA's Master Spy Hunter*. The kinds of questions *NAMEBASE* answers include, "Where can I read about James Angleton?" In this case the user is provided with over 100 citations of books and articles with dates and pages

---

232. The *SpyBASE* mentioned here should not be confused with the *SpyBase* listed on page 235. The former no longer exists and it now called *NAMEBASE*. *SpyBASE* is a recent contribution from Australia and is quite different from its American ancestor.

numbers. *NAMEBASE* does not yet record or summarize the content of material in the citations, although in some cases country of origin and some foreign service are indicated. An annotation feature has recently been added to *NAMEBASE* but only a few entries have been annotated to date. Thus the entry for the Association of Former Intelligence Officers (AFIO) has a paragraph explaining the organization and another discussing the policy for entering data about AFIO members. By 1993 all entries should contain annotations.

NAMEBASE tends to stay away from popular sources but does extract data from a few newspapers and magazines in this category which are likely to have items of interest. These include *The New York Times*, *The Washington Times* and *The Washington Post*. Selected items also come from the popular news magazines like *Time*, but no attempt is made to duplicate the indexing services of any publication. Stories are indexed by author, subject name, or agency, date and page number. The range of topics from *the New York Times* runs from Philip Agee to *the Dartmouth Review*, with Dino Brugioni, the Free Europe Committee, James Geer, Walter Pforzheimer and Samuel Huntington each having citations.

In addition to the sources mentioned above, the current version of *NAMEBASE* also includes material from 25 reports and directories (e.g., the AFIO membership directory), government and private, many of which are not indexed elsewhere. Entries are selective; for example, from *Who's Who In America* names with Radio Free Europe or Radio Liberty in their biography are included as are those with NSC in their personal data.

In short, since 1962, *NAMEBASE* has acquired more than 53,000 names of groups and individuals. Most of these have multiple citations, that is to say, most names appear in more than one source cited. Thus *NAMEBASE* has more than 107,000 entries on intelligence related people and subjects from books and periodicals often neglected by other databases.

What will *NAMEBASE* do for you? In its current configuration, it provides fast answers to several questions about people, countries, and publications having something to do with intelligence. For example, if your are concerned about Soviet GRU officer Oleg Penkovsky who was an agent of the British and Americans, 37 references will be displayed in about

2 seconds after entering the name (somewhat slower for 286 PCs faster for certain 386 & 486 PCs). Each reference or "hit" gives the name, date, issue and page number(s) of the publications where he is mentioned in the database. If your interest is in names linked to a certain country, say Somalia, you may task the database and it will list them according to the publication, date, and pages. Search strategies allow partial names and combinations of countries within time periods. Starting last year, *NAMEBASE* began annotating entries with descriptions of content. When this modification is completed in 1992, its value will be greatly enhanced. *CIABASE* (see page 225) has annotations now but it covers somewhat different sources and not nearly as many as *NAMEBASE*.

For selected periodicals, even defunct ones like *CounterSpy* (see page 183), *NAMEBASE* will list most of the names mentioned in each issue and give the pages on which they appeared; in this case, these data are not available in any other digital database. Likewise with current magazine and newsletters, if you want all the names indexed by *NAMEBASE* in say *CAIB* or *FILS*, it will list them for a particular issue or all issues where hits occur, indicating issue number, date and pages. The same approach can be taken to find the names entered from books like Steven Emerson's *Secret Warriors*, Nigel West's, *The Circus*, Felix Rodriguez's, *Shadow Warrior*, or F. Sergeyev's, *Chile: CIA Big Business*, to name a few already in *NAMEBASE*.

Some words of caution are necessary. Since not all entries are cross referenced, you should search more than one category to find all listings of a given name. For example, if one searches for Nigel West under the name category of *NAMEBASE*, the result will be a list of all publications in which his name appears, but his book *The Circus* will not be listed since his name does not appear in the book per se. That is the way the database is setup. On the other hand, when one also searches under West in the source category, his name appears again with the title of the book used as a source for the database, in this case just The Circus. A "name search" for David Wise gives similar results. But a "source search" for Wise lists several of his books because they were used as sources. In other words, use more than one category in your searches and remember that *NAMEBASE* is not a bibliography of all works published by a given name.

There are also two database content limitations worth
noting. First, not all the names which appear in a periodical or
book used as a source for the database have been included in
NAMEBASE. And for those names which do appear after a
search, not all the instances the name is mentioned are
included. Rather only those names and instances that
NAMEBASE deems pertinent are entered. For example, a name
may be cited at the point where it is first mentioned in a book.
If the name also occurs frequently throughout the book, there
may or may not be any indication of this fact in *NAMEBASE*.
Thus the user is cautioned to consider *NAMEBASE* a starting
point.

The second limitation worth mentioning is that not all the
intelligence related materials in a given source are included in
the database. For example, although *FILS* (see page 46) is a
source for *NAMEBASE*, neither all the issues nor all the articles
in an issue, nor all the names in each article, are included.

Clearly, there are additional books that if added to the
database would increase its user value. The reasons for any
omissions are mainly limitations of time and resources
according to Daniel Brandt, *NAMEBASE* originator, editor,
and sole data in-putter (all 107,000 entries and still going). For
those sources cited, however, Brandt maintains the original
documents and extracts or copies are available to subscribers
for a small reproduction and handling fee. *NAMEBASE* is
continually growing and it remains a good place to start. A list
of publications used as sources for the database, which also
indicates how many citations came from each source, is
available in the database.

The change of name from *SpyBASE* to *NAMEBASE* resulted
from the realization that some users, at least, expected to find
the names of spies in the database. This may in fact happen,
but not all names entered are spies. As *Foreign Affairs*
magazine said, while the database is a "helpful and easily
accessible resource," the name is "gratuitously lurid and quite
misleading."

Finally, there is one other *NAMEBASE* attribute of which
subscribers should be aware: it is a read-only database; the user
cannot add to or change what is found there. It is possible,
however, to print the results of any search to a printer or
computer disk. Should one be interested in creating his/her

own database using the *NAMEBASE* model, Brandt provides the needed digital tools, with instructions, in what he calls MiniBASE; cost $29.00, which is a bargain. For a more costly less flexible alternative see the new *SpyBase* page 235.

As text databases go *NAMEBASE* is inexpensive and fast. All one needs is access to an Apple or IBM compatible PC (with dual floppy drives or a hard disk) and $49.00 which you send to the publisher. This brings you, by return mail, several floppy disks (5 1/4 or 3 1/2") and simple instructions. It is not copy protected so copies may be given legally to friends. But only those users registered with the publisher, Public Information Research, Inc., will get update notices. *NAMEBASE* is updated about 2 times per year. If you have a "borrowed" or bootlegged copy, you may register it for $10.00 and get the updates for $24.00 each whenever they are announced. Although *NAMEBASE* is easy to use, there is a help file with detailed instructions for each operation.

For registration, purchase or further information write, Public Information Research, P.O. Box 5199, Arlington, VA 22205, or call (703) 241-5437.

SpyBase

An Indexing System for Law Enforcement
Intelligence Operations and Other Research Projects

"*SpyBase* is a program for law enforcement operations. It fulfils the analyst's need to organize large amounts of raw information for decision making purposes." This statement, quoted from the *SpyBase* user's manual (p. 7) should be interpreted carefully.

It does not, like *NAMEBASE* and *CIABASE* (see pages 230 and 225) come with any data already entered. It is merely a receptacle into which one can place data for later use. Consequently, this software, as purchased, has nothing to do with spies. And if it ever does, it will only be because the user entered the spy data.

Consider next the statement that it "fulfils the analyst's need to organize large amounts of raw information for decision making purposes" (emphasis added). This is only true if one needs to index a large number of hardcopy files, reports or books, etc., by number and subject, and even then the subject descriptions are limited to about ten words, depending on word size. The large amounts of "raw information" normally used by an analyst will remain in the hardcopy files or in another database, they can't be entered in *SpyBase*, the entry size limitations prevent this.

Finally, the decisions one can make from *SpyBase* data concern the file identification and location, and the secretary or administrative assistant, not the analyst, is likely to be making them.

What then, can *SpyBase* do for you? Not much if what you need is a place to record information about events or people, which can be quickly retrieved, categorized and easily augmented. If you have a large number of paper files that need a number or short subject index, it could do the job. But there are others that will do it better while providing unlimited space for annotations and as much descriptive data as is practical. *FOLIO VIEWS, AskSam, Q&A,* and even *NOTEBOOK* (which is slow but versatile) are four examples.[233] It is true these programs, which cost between $125.00 -$400.00, are several times more expensive than *SpyBase* ($43.00). But for most intelligence-related research or scholarly applications, the capability provided by the more expensive options makes them worth every penny.

SpyBase author, Henry W. Prunckun, Jr., (originally from Massachusetts), has apparently used it successfully in his work in the Australian criminal justice system. He also suggests it would be good for indexing books, but it will not accommodate a standard bibliographic citation which requires far more entry space than *SpyBase* makes available.

In short, *SpyBase* gives you a limited keyword based, quick search, fixed field software program for $43.00 including postage to the USA. A *SpyBase* Source Code License (disk) may be obtained for $202.00, credit cards accepted. For more information write Slezak Associates, 57 Davenport Terrace, Wayville, South Australia, 5034.

---

233. For details about any of these text database programs contact a good software store.

GENERAL INFORMATION SERVICES & DATABASES

With Intelligence Related Utility

The 5 database services discussed below are potential sources of information on various aspects of the intelligence profession and related topics. They are used by intelligence analysts, historians, students, scholars and the general reader. The amount of time one can save doing a bibliographic search using one or more of these data bases is measured in days; unfortunately the cost is measured in dollars and can be very high. For this reason and for limitations of space, several, but not all, very good ones have been included. Depending on one's requirements the choice of database may vary.

If one tends to prefer using a single database for all requirements (scholarly, electronic mail, fax, game playing, bulletin boards, buying by computer etc), try *COMPUSERVE*. For most of these qualities plus the only bulletin board specifically related to intelligence, and extraordinary access to the foreign English press, explore *GEnie*. If the need is for professional information (on any subject, let alone intelligence), or access to the on-line books in print, one might start with *DIALOG*.

When the requirement is for the highest likelihood for complete text articles in the world of commerce and science, plus access to some foreign press and electronic mail, and a powerful array of databases, *NEXIS* is a good starting point, but it is clearly oriented toward corporate customers as opposed to low budget scholars or writers.

In each case the subscriber must have a PC with a communications modem and software. There is also some preparation to do. Although any of these databases can be explored randomly, one had better have a Platinum credit card if that is the approach taken. There are more efficient ways and each digital periodical named here has training available (some require it) to help subscribers get going efficiently.

As a rule, none of the news or information related databases contain all issues (since volume 1, number 1) of the periodicals they can search. Some begin in the 1960s, most later and the date of first entry is clearly marked. This is true even for periodicals like The Washington Times which began publication in the mid 1980s, but was not picked up by *NEXIS* until 1989. Now it is also available on *COMPUSERVE*.

Aside from the value of having encyclopedic databases at your fingertips, the use of these systems as an alternate source of the periodicals one wishes to read has begun. In fact, two of the publications described herein are also available through NewsNet for reading or recording on your PC. But no matter what the advantages in space or what computer boffins say, they'll never replace books (hard copy), in my library.

DIALOG

This digital information database describes itself as the "World's Largest Online Knowledgebank." It is comprised of over 350 databases, with "more than 150 million items of information," that is big! Besides including all major areas of inquiry and electronic mail service, *DIALOG* is the only database that provides access to books in print; it even has a database on other available databases.

DIALOG is constructed to allow the user to find the information needed even when neither the exact titles nor authors are known. For example, when asked by *DIALOG* what your subject interest is, just reply "espionage" (or whatever) and a number of sources that mention that topic will be listed. The more "hits" the greater the cost, so if your interested in a particular time period, include that in your request.

If you wish to monitor one source regularly, say *The Washington Post* for stories on East European intelligence services since 1989, or *Aviation Week and Space Technology*, or *Reuters* news service, that can be done too and the results will be stored in your own file for reading as your time allows. (*COMPUSERVE* offers a similar option.)

Each subscriber receives written (real paper) procedures (with frequent updates) and software for using *DIALOG*. The software will do the dialing, structure the search (with your help), present the results to the monitor or have them sent to you in the mail. But, beware: a self-teaching approach can be expensive. Perhaps the best way to start is to take the one day *DIALOG* System Seminar given frequently at various locations throughout the USA, (cost about $200.00), or by trying the less costly starter packages which include video tapes. Either option comes with $100.00 worth of free connect time so that your training is productive.

There are, of course, some drawbacks. The periodicals in *DIALOG* do not start with volume one, issue one. Most go back to the mid 1980s, some earlier. The start date varies with each publication. It will be a while before students and researchers will be able to pursue their craft without relying on microfilm or delving into musty archives. In the same vein, *DIALOG* does not have as many full text articles as *NEXIS*, though this appears to be changing.

Remember *DIALOG* may be accessed through *COMPUSERVE*, but this adds to the cost compared to dealing with *DIALOG* directly. Since content is updated frequently and user costs vary greatly depending on application and experience, your best bet for more information is to call *DIALOG* Marketing, 1-800-334-2564.

NEXIS

NEXIS, like its semantic parent *LEXIS* (a legal database), is a trademark. While *LEXIS* is derived from the Latin for law, *NEXIS* was coined for the occasion of naming a news-information related database. It has become that and more — an electronic library.

Mead Data Central, *NEXIS's* owner, says it is "the world's largest full-text on-line information service," with 60 million full text articles available. When compared with *DIALOG's* claim to be "World's largest Online Knowledgebank," there would appear to be few differences, but there are some. The omission of "full-text" by *DIALOG* is significant in some specialties, although in the general information categories both have this capability. Aside from differences in periodicals included (like *the Washington Times*), the principal distinction is one of outlook or interests. *NEXIS* is heavily weighted in the direction of business and commerce perspective and the corporate over the individual user. But since it includes entries others do not, one should be aware of its capabilities.

In addition to the standard news periodicals, many of the entries included in this Reader's Guide are found in *NEXIS*. A subscriber then has prompt access for example, to *The New York Times* [from June 1980], *Aviation Week & Space Technology*, [from January 1975], *Foreign Affairs* [from 1981], *TASS* [from January 1987], *Current Digest of the Soviet Press*, [from June 1983], *Maclean's* [from January 1985], *The [London] Times and the Sunday Times* [from January 1990], *the Washington Post* [from January 1977], *the Washington Times* [from July 1989], plus the wire services and major news weeklies, to list just a few. Unfortunately, none of the intelligence specific periodicals are included. The most current entries are about 72 hours old for U.S. newspapers, about one to two weeks for foreign newspapers.

There are some topics *NEXIS* has chosen not to include. For example, *Books In Print* (US and UK), *Book Review Index*, and Books and Monographs (for these try *DIALOG*). Nor does it have customer participation round tables or bulletin boards like *COMPUSERVE* or *GEnie*. It is strictly a very large information database.

NEXIS also has an impressive training program for both introductory and more advanced students. Session topics vary somewhat depending on the geographic area. The session format is either class or seminar. Customer support is excellent.

In addition to a minimum monthly charge, user costs are based on time connected to the database (connect time), the number of searches, and the size of the database searched. As with any of the major databases, it can be expensive to use for the individual scholar, researcher, author, etc., but it may give you access you otherwise would not have had in a reasonable time, unless you happen to live near the Library of Congress. It is not accessible through *COMPUSERVE*.

COMPUSERVE

Although not a database itself, *COMPUSERVE* provides access to many databases including *DIALOG* and *NewsNet* (see pages 239 and 246) but not *GEnie* or *NEXIS*. It also has electronic mail, fax (send only), bulletin board and forum facilities in the United States and Europe, the latter an option not available with most other information services.

Some of the options which have an intelligence-related utility are:

(1) I-QUEST, COMPUSERVE's compartment for accessing over 800 publications and databases (bibliographic and full text);

(2) the NEWSPAPER LIBRARY which contains full text articles from 42 newspapers from around the country (two day lag);

(3) the MAGAZINE DATABASE PLUS that provides full text coverage of over 90 publications (news, sports, science, finance etc);

(4) the EXECUTIVE NEWS SERVICE which provides an electronic clipping service from AP, UPI and other news wires. The user merely identifies the topics of interest and *COMPUSERVE* does the clipping and places the articles in your personal file to be read at your convenience; and

(5) the JOURNAL GRAPHICS TRANSCRIPTS service that provides (by mail) transcripts of TV shows within 24 hours of broadcast for $10.00 each. Some of the shows regularly available are ABC's NIGHTLINE, This Week with David Brinkley, 60 Minutes, Larry King Live (frequently interviews intelligence personalities, e.g., William Colby), 48 Hours, CBS Reports, Evans & Novak, Crossfire, Science & Technology, and Bill Moyers: World of Ideas. One of Moyers's shows, "The Secret Government ... The Constitution in Crisis," is largely an attack on the CIA, and provides insights into the popular distortions regarding modern intelligence. Call (212) 732-8552 for details.

COMPUSERVE has an information management software program ($24.95) with windows and menus intended to make it easier and less costly to access those features of the system you wish to use. In practice, it is just the opposite; its use is more efficient without the program, if you already have communications software. If not, you will want to consider buying a commercial package; they all work with *COMPUSERVE*, but the *COMPUSERVE* package only works with *COMPUSERVE*. The idea behind the *COMPUSERVE* software is good, but it is terribly slow. They will no doubt overcome these problems, but until they do, be careful.

Several other things should be kept in mind when considering *COMPUSERVE*. Potential members must purchase a membership kit from *CompuServe* telephone sales or a local computer software store. It costs about $39.00, provides an instruction book, user codewords and generally gets one started. There is also a monthly membership support fee of $1.50. All other charges are based on use, such as the connect fees, which are comparatively reasonable; $6.00 for 300 baud (I find this rate good for most low volume uses) and $12.00 for 1200 baud anytime of the day. After these fees, when the subscriber starts using the databases mentioned above, additional fees come into play. They are clearly identified before use and vary for each database.

Overall, *COMPUSERVE* is an extremely powerful single source of information. Since it has access to *DIALOG* and *NewsNet* most sources can be explored with one membership fee, though additional charges will result when using the other database services. For further details about joining *CompuServe*, call 1-800-848-8199, or write, *CompuServe*, 5000 Arlington Centre Blvd, Columbus OH 43220.

GEnie

GEnie has an excellent electronic mail service, is easy to use and reasonable in price. There are two *GEnie* features of particular interest here. The first is the *Military Roundtable* which is discussed on page 228. The other is called NewsGrid and will be described here.

The NewsGrid option is unique to *GEnie* in that besides coverage from three USA news services, it carries items from wire services in France, West Germany, Spain, Japan, China. It also allows you to create your own clipping file for items in your area of interest, which you can read and print when time allows. Another feature of the service is the option to monitor the wires live as the news comes in. In any case, this service provides the quickest information on worldwide stories available to our computer.

Joining *GEnie* is easy and can be done over the phone using your PC and modem by calling 800-638-8369. The User Manual comes later in the mail, but it isn't necessary to wait for it to begin, the instructions from the monitor are clear and easy to follow. For information on how to become a subscriber, or for answers to questions, write GE Information Services, 401 N. Washington Street, Rockville, MD 20850, or call 800-638-9636.

NEWSNET

NEWSNET is a business oriented network that provides 24 hour on-line access to over 420 newsletters (full text) and the major news wire services from around the world. It has no electronic mail, fax service, or access to major databases. It is designed to present current news quickly on specific subjects. The wire services include AP, Jiji Press Ticker service (Japan) Xinhua English Language New Service of China, Reuters, and UPI.

Two of the newsletters in this Guide appear regularly on *NEWSNET*; *For Your Eyes Only (FYEO)* [page 149] and *Counter-Terrorism Security Intelligence (CT-SI)* [page 117]. Several others of interest are unique to *NEWSNET*; these include, *East Asian Business Intelligence*, *Middle East Business Intelligence*, *Political Risk Services* (70 countries), the *C³I Report* (Command, Control, Communications & Intelligence) and the SDI Intelligence Report. The system is set up so that one may use key words to find articles of interest or an electronic clipping folder (called NewsFlash) can be set up to do the work and then the subscriber may read as time allows.

NEWSNET has introductory subscriptions of one month ($30.00), six months ($75.00) and twelve months ($120.00). In addition to the subscription rate, there are two other basic costs, the Connect Rate and the Read Rate. The Connect Rate varies, depending on the speed of data acquisition (baud rate), from $60.00 to $90.00 per hour (pro-rated). The Read Rates are in addition to the Connect Rates and they vary with the publication, averaging about $80.00 per hour. Clearly the strategy to employ is to record the data to your disk, leave *NEWSNET*, and read it off-line. For those wishing further information, contact *NEWSNET* by calling 1-800-345-1301 in the continental USA and 1-215-527-8030 outside the USA. A representative will help you work out search strategies and learn the basic procedures.

TITLE INDEX